The Curiosities Of Food

Or The Dainties And Delicacies Of Different Nations Obtained From The Animal Kingdom

by

Peter Lund Simmonds

Double 9
BOOKS

The Curiosities Of Food
Or The Dainties And Delicacies Of Different Nations Obtained From The Animal Kingdom
by Peter Lund Simmonds

ISBN: 978-93-61156-60-1

Published by

DOUBLE 9 BOOKS
2/13-B, Ansari Road
Daryaganj, New Delhi – 110002
info@double9books.com
www.double9books.com
Tel. 011-40042856

ABOUT THE AUTHOR

Peter Lund Simmonds, a prolific 19th-century writer and editor, authored the noteworthy work "The Curiosities of Food: Or, The Dainties and Delicacies of Different Nations Obtained from the Animal Kingdom." Simmonds became an English author, agriculturalist, and advocate for technological advancements in agriculture in the course of the Victorian era. In his masterful book, "The Curiosities of Food," Simmonds explores the fascinating and diverse global of culinary delights from diverse cultures. The subtitle, "Or The Dainties And Delicacies Of Different Nations Obtained From The Animal Kingdom," guidelines at the focal point at the animal nation as a source of diverse and uncommon ingredients. Simmonds in all likelihood takes readers on a gastronomic journey, detailing specific and curious culinary practices, elements, and dishes from around the globe. The book may delve into the ancient, cultural, and medical factors of meals, offering insights into the ways specific societies have harnessed the bounty of the animal country for sustenance and satisfaction. Simmonds, recognized for his know-how in agricultural and culinary topics, may additionally have infused the book with a blend of clinical inquiry and an appreciation for the wealthy tapestry of world food traditions.

CONTENTS

PREFACE

The sustentation of the body, and the repairing of its waste by an adequate supply of wholesome and nutritious daily food, is a subject of general importance, and necessarily occupies a large share of attention. But all nations have not the advantages of skilful cattle-breeders, slaughter-houses, well-supplied meat and poultry markets, and butchers' shops graced with all the tempting joints of beef, mutton, and pork, which gladden the eyes of an Englishman, and keep up his stamina for labour. The traveller, the settler, and the savage, must be content to put up with what they can most readily obtain, and to avail themselves of many an unusual article of food, which would be rejected under more favourable circumstances, and with a greater choice for selection.

The subject of Food, in a physiological point of view, has been often discussed. Popular and learned treatises on all the art and mysteries of Cookery have been sold by thousands. We have had pleasant details furnished us too on the Food and the Commissariat of London.—But with respect to the animal substances, eaten by other people in foreign countries, we have known little—except from mere scraps of information.

The basis of the present volume is a lecture on the Curiosities of Food, which I delivered at several of the metropolitan literary institutions. Having been favourably received,—from the novelty of the subject, and the singularity of the specimens from my private museum by which it was illustrated,—I have been led to believe that it might prove generally interesting in a more amplified shape.

In order, however, to bring the details within a convenient compass, I have limited myself to a description of the Curiosities of Animal Food; but should the work be well received, I may follow it up hereafter by a companion volume, on the Curiosities of Vegetable Food.

In the arrangement of the materials for this work, one of two modes of description was open to me, either to dress up the details in characteristic pictures of the food-customs and viands in use in different quarters, and by different people; or to group the whole scientifically under natural history divisions. As the subject is curious and striking enough in its simplicity without the aid of fiction or embellishment, I have preferred adopting the latter arrangement, and have followed it as closely as the miscellaneous character of the selections and quotations would permit.

Many of the articles of food named are so outrageously repulsive, and the consideration of the subject, in a collected form, is altogether so new, that I have preferred citing authorities in all instances, so as to relieve myself from the charge of exaggeration, or the imputation of untenable assertions. For this reason, and from the varied and very extended nature of the field of enquiry, I can claim no merit for original writing in this work. I have merely desired to present the public with a readable volume; and I think its perusal will show that in this, as in other cases, truth is often stranger than fiction.

After a perusal of these pages, it can scarcely be said that, 'there is nothing new under the sun,' for many of the articles of food which I have described as being served up in different parts of the world, will be certainly new to many. Probably, some of the hints thrown out will make the fortune of any restaurateur in the city or at the west-end, who chooses to dish up one or more of the reputed delicacies, under a proper disguise, and with a high-sounding name.

P.L.S.

8, Winchester Street, Pimlico,
  December 1858.

THE CURIOSITIES OF FOOD

What is the prevailing food of the people? Is it chiefly animal or vegetable, and whence is it derived in the two kingdoms? Do they trust to what the bounty of Nature provides, or have they the means of modifying or controlling production, whether in the cultivation of vegetables, or the rearing of animals? Describe their modes of cooking, and state the kinds of condiments they employ. Have they in use any kind of fermented liquor? What number of meals do they make, and what is their capacity for temporary or sustained exertion?

These are some of the enquiries to which a traveller is directed to pay attention, if he wishes to furnish and diffuse useful information.

I do not intend to go over this wide field of investigation in the systematic and scientific manner shadowed forth by these enquiries, but merely desire to assist the reader to pass a leisure hour, although he may probably glean some useful information at the same time.

I propose bringing under notice some of the Animal food in which people in various countries indulge, not that I wish persons to test these meats, or to live upon them, unless they please. I do not deal in them, and have no interest in their collection or sale, but I merely desire to introduce them to notice that the reader may ascertain the opinions entertained of them, think over them, and know how much better an Englishman is fed than any one else in the world. So that, despite our habit of grumbling, there is at least this undeniable fact before us, that the middle classes are in very easy circumstances; and that English workmen earn good wages, or they could not consume the quantity of animal food they do at the present prices.

According to Vauban, Bossuet, and La Grange, the richest and most comfortable nation is that which eats the most meat. At the present prices of this article here, it certainly must be so, for a poor nation could not indulge in the luxury.

Beef and mutton, and mutton and beef, no matter what their price, John Bull will not dispense with; and although they are 40 or 50 per cent. dearer now than they were ten years ago, and although we import animals largely from abroad, and our cattle-breeders do their best to meet the demand, cattle and sheep will not increase and multiply fast enough to bring down the price for the consumer.

A writer in *Household Words* thus alludes to our national weakness.— 'Next to the Habeas Corpus and the Freedom of the Press, there are few things that the English people have a greater respect for and a livelier faith in than beef. They bear, year after year, with the same interminable, unvarying series of woodcuts of fat oxen in the columns of the illustrated newspapers; they are never tired of crowding to the Smithfield Club cattle-show; and I am inclined to think that it is their honest reverence for beef that has induced them to support so long the obstruction and endangerment of the thoroughfares of the metropolis by oxen driven to slaughter. Beef is a great connecting link and bond of better feeling between the great classes of the commonwealth. Do not Dukes hob and nob with top-booted farmers over the respective merits of short-horns and Alderneys? Does not the noble Marquis of Argentfork give an ox to be roasted whole on the village green when his son, the noble Viscount Silvercoral, comes of age? Beef makes boys into men. Beef nerves our navvies. The bowmen who won Cressy and Agincourt were beef-fed, and had there been more and better beef in the Crimea a year or two ago, our soldiers would have borne up better under the horrors of a Chersonesean winter. We feast on beef at the great Christian festival. A baron of beef at the same time is enthroned in St. George's Hall, in Windsor's ancient castle, and is borne in by lacqueys in scarlet and gold. Charles the Second knighted a loin of beef, and I have a shrewd suspicion that the famous Sir Bevis of Southampton was but an ardent admirer and doughty knight-errant in the cause of beef. And who does not know the tradition that even as the first words of the new-born Gargantua were 'A boyre, à boyre,' signifying that he desired a draught of Burgundy wine—so the first intelligible sounds that the infant Guy of Warwick ever spake were 'Beef, beef!' When the weary pilgrim reaches the beloved shores of England after a long absence, what first does he remark—after the incivility of the custom-house officers—but the great tankard of stout and the noble round of cold beef in the coffee-room of the hotel? He does not cry 'Io Bacche! Evöe Bacche!' because beef is not Bacchus. He does not fall down and kiss his native soil, because the hotel carpet is somewhat dusty, and the action would be, besides, egregious; but he looks at the beef, and his eyes filling with tears, a corresponding humidity takes place in his mouth; he kisses the beef; he is so fond of it that he could eat it all up; and he does ordinarily devour so much of it to his breakfast, that the thoughtful waiter gazes at him, and murmurs to his napkin, 'This man is either a cannibal or a pilgrim grey who has not seen Albion for many years.'

It has been well observed, that there are few things in which the public have so great and general an interest, and concerning which they possess so little real knowledge, as of the provision trade and the wholesale traffic in animals live and dead, in their own and other countries. When, where, and how raised, and what processes meat passes through before it reaches their tables, are questions which, though highly important, are very seldom asked by the consumers—all that they usually trouble themselves with is, the current retail price, and the nature of the supply.

Few of us think as we sit down to our rump steak or pork chop, our sirloin or leg of mutton, of the awful havoc of quadrupeds necessary to furnish the daily meals of the millions. I will not weary the reader with statistics, although I have a long array of figures before me, bearing upon the slaughter of animals for food in different countries. It will be sufficient to generalize.

If the hecatomb of animals we have each consumed in the years we have lived, were marshalled in array before us, we should stand aghast at the possibility of our ever having devoured the quantity of animal food, and sacrificed for our daily meals the goodly number of well-fed quadrupeds of the ovine, bovine, and porcine races, or the fish, fowl, reptiles, and insects, which would be thus re-embodied.

The average quantity of animal food of all kinds consumed in France is stated on good authority—that of M. Payen—to be as low as one-sixth of a pound per diem to each person. Even in the cities and large towns, especially Paris, the amount of food upon which a Frenchman lives is astonishingly small. An Englishman or an American would starve upon such fare.

In proportion to its population, New York consumes as nearly as possible the same quantity of meat as London, about half-a-pound a day to each person; more beef, however, is consumed there and less mutton, and the latter fact may be accounted for by the comparative inferiority of quality.

It is curious to notice the various parts of animals that are eaten, or selected as choice morsels by different persons or classes. Sheep's head, pig's head, calf's head and brains, ox head, the heads of ducks and geese, ox tongue, reindeer tongue, walrus tongue, crane's tongue, &c. Fowls and ducks' tongues are esteemed an exquisite Chinese dainty. The pettitoes of the sucking pig, or the mature feet and hocks of the elder hog, sheep's trotters, calf's feet, cow heel, bear's paws, elephant's feet, the feet of ducks and geese, and their giblets; ox tail, pig's tail, sheep's tail, kangaroo tail, beaver's tail. And the entrails again are not despised, whether it be bullock's heart or sheep's heart, liver and lights, lamb's fry or pig's fry, tripe and chitterlings, goose liver and gizzard, the cleaned gut for our sausages, the fish maws, cod liver, and so on. The moufle, or loose covering of the nose, of the great moose deer or elk is considered by New Brunswick epicures a great dainty. The hump of the buffalo, the trunk of the elephant, are other delicacies. Deer's sinews, and the muscle of the ox, the buffalo, and the wild hog, jerked or dried in the sun, and then termed, 'dendeng,' is a delicacy of the Chinese, imported at a high price from Siam and the eastern islands.

The eggs of different animals, again, form choice articles of food, whether they be those of the ordinary domestic poultry, the eggs of sea fowl, of the plover, and of game birds, of the ostrich and emu, of the tortoises and other reptilia, as alligator's eggs, snake's eggs, and those of the iguana, or the eggs of insects, and of fishes.

Amid all the multiplicity of special dainties, appreciated by different peoples, the prejudices of the stomach are, perhaps, more unconquerable than any other that tyrannize over the human mind. It is almost impossible to get people to adventure, or experimentalize upon a *new* kind of food. There is a great want of courage and enterprise on this head among Englishmen. John Bull is resolved to eat, drink, and do only what he has been accustomed to. He wants none of your foreign kickshaws, frogs, and snails in fricassées, or sea slug, or bird's nest soup, or horse flesh steak. It is true he has gradually adventured upon, and now appreciates, a few select foreign delicacies. Real lively turtle and caviar, reindeer tongue, an imitation Indian curry, and such like, have become luxuries; and, probably, under the mysterious manipulations of Gunter, Soyer, and other distinguished *chefs de cuisine*, some other foreign delicacies have found, or may yet find, their way upon English tables.

They will probably displace ere long the four standard Scotch dishes, a haggis, a sheep's head, tripe, and black puddings, or the common dishes of the Devonshire peasant and Cornish fisherman, parsley and squab pies, in which fish, apples, onions, and pork are incongruously blended.

Queen Elizabeth and her ladies breakfasted on meat, bread, and strong ale. Our modern ladies take tea or coffee, and thin slices of toast or bread. The Esquimaux drink train oil, and the Cossacks koumis, an ardent spirit made from mares' milk. The inhabitants of France and Germany eat much more largely than we do of vegetable diet; and drink, at all times of the day, their acid wines. In Devonshire and Herefordshire, cyder is the common beverage, and in the Highlands of Scotland, oatmeal porridge is, in a great measure, the food, and whiskey the drink of the inhabitants. The Irish peasant lives, or used to do, chiefly on potatoes, and most of the Hindoos of the maritime provinces on rice.

Yet all this variety, and much more, is digested, yields nutriment, and promotes growth; affording undeniable evidence that man is really omnivorous, that he can be supported by great varieties of food.

A recent writer speaking of human diet says, 'it is a remarkable circumstance, that man alone is provided with a case of instruments adapted to the mastication of all substances,—teeth to cut, and pierce, and champ, and grind; a gastric solvent too, capable of contending with any thing and every thing, raw substances and cooked, ripe and rotten,—nothing comes amiss to him.'

If animals could speak, as Æsop and other fabulists make them seem to do, they would declare man to be the most voracious animal in existence. There is scarcely any living thing that flies in the air, swims in the sea, or moves on the land, that is not made to minister to his appetite in some region or other.

Other creatures are, generally, restricted to one sort of provender at most. They are carnivorous or graminivorous, piscivorous, or something ivorous; but man is the universal eater. He pounces with the tiger upon the kid, with the hawk upon the dove, with the cormorant upon the herring, and with the small bird upon the insect and grub. He goes halves with the bee in the honey cell, but turns upon his partner and cheats him out of his share of the produce. He grubs up the root with the sow, devours the fruit with the earwig, and demolishes the leaves with the caterpillar; for all these several parts of different vegetables furnish him with food.

Life itself will not hinder his appetite, nor decay nauseate his palate; for he will as soon devour a lively young oyster as demolish the fungous produce of a humid field. This propensity is, indeed, easily abused. Viands of such incongruous nature and heterogeneous substance, are sometimes collected, as to make an outrageous amalgamation, so that an alderman at a city feast might make one shudder; but this is too curious an investigation, it is the abuse of abundance too, and we know that abuse is the origin of all evil. The fact should lead us to another point of appreciation of goodness and beneficence. The adaptation of external nature to man has often been insisted on; the adaptation of man to all circumstances, states, and conditions, is carrying out the idea. The inferior animals are tied down, even by the narrowness of their animal necessities, to a small range of existence; but man can seldom be placed in any circumstance in which his universal appetite cannot be appeased. From the naked savage snatching a berry from the thorn, to the well-clad, highly civilized denizen of the court, surrounded by every comfort, every luxury; from the tired traveller, who opens his wallet and produces his oaten cake beside the welling lymph which is to slake his thirst, to the pursy justice, 'in fair round belly with capon lined,' who spreads the damask napkin on his knees, tucks his toes under the table, and revels in calapash and calapee,—what an infinite diversity of circumstances!

Man, with all his natural and artificial necessities, all his social and domestic dependencies,—more dependent, indeed, upon his fellows than the fowls of the air, from the grand exuberance of nature, and his remarkable adaptation to it in the point alluded to, finds subsistence under circumstances in which other animals might starve.

Perhaps we might properly urge the advice of a recent writer.—'Make use of every material possible for food, remembering that there are chemical affinities and properties by which nutriment may be extracted from almost every organic substance, the greatest art being in proper cooking. Make soup of every kind of flesh, fish, and leguminosæ.—Every thing adds to its strength and flavour.'

Man eats to satisfy his hunger, and to supply warmth to the body; but the lover of good things, who finds a pleasure in eating, may also be told that there is a beautiful structure of nerve work spread out on the tongue, which carries upwards to the brain messages from the nice things in the mouth.

Moderation in food is, however, one of the great essentials to health. Sydney Smith, in a letter to Lord Murray, tells him that, having ascertained the weight of food that he could live upon, so as to preserve health and strength, and what he had lived upon, he found that between ten and seventy years of age, he had eaten and drunk forty-four one-horse wagon loads of meat and drink more than would have preserved him in life and health, and that the value of this mass of nourishment was about £7,000.

Sir John Ross tells us that an Esquimaux will eat twenty pounds of flesh and oil daily. But the most marvellous account of gormandizing powers is that published by Captain Cochrane, who in his *Narrative of a Pedestrian Journey through Russia and Siberian Tartary*, says, that the Russian Admiral, Saritcheff, was told that one of the Yakuti consumed in twenty-four hours, 'the hind quarter of a large ox, twenty pounds of fat, and a proportionate quantity of melted butter for his drink.' The Admiral, to test the truth of the statement, gave him 'a thick porridge of rice, boiled down with three pounds of butter, weighing together twenty-eight pounds; and although the glutton had already breakfasted, yet did he sit down to it with great eagerness, and consumed the whole without stirring from the spot; and, except that his stomach betrayed more than ordinary fulness, he showed no sign of inconvenience or injury!' The traveller I have just quoted also states, that he has repeatedly seen a Yakut, or Tongouse, devour forty pounds of meat a day; and he adds, 'I have seen three of these gluttons consume a reindeer at one meal.'

It has been well remarked by Dr. Dieffenbach, in the *Transactions of the Ethnological Society*, that the labours of modern chemistry have thrown a new and most interesting light on the food of the various races of men, or inhabitants of parts of the globe which are widely different from each other in their geographical and climatological relations. The substances which serve as food, or the quantity which is taken, appear to the superficial observer often of a most extraordinary nature, because they are apparently so heterogeneous from what we are accustomed to; so that travellers relating such facts, do not withhold their astonishment or reprobation.

But it has been demonstrated, that the general use of certain articles, for instance, tea and coffee, betel-nut, tobacco, and wine, depends upon the presence in those substances of elements which are often identical, and which are necessary to the maintenance of the animal economy, more or less, according to the presence or absence of other elements in the food, the different occupation, mode of living, and so on. These points have been well illustrated and explained in the *Chemistry of Common Life*, of the late Professor Johnston. The fact of the Esquimaux consuming large quantities of train oil and blubber ceases to be astonishing, when we reflect that these highly carbonized substances serve to furnish fuel for his increased respiration.

In one word, it is necessary in the present state of chemical and physiological science, to collect analyses of all the substances which are consumed by a particular race, either as food or drink, or by an habitual custom, as so called matters of luxury, or as medicine. The ethnologist has the great merit of working here hand in hand with chemists and physiologists, and fills up in this manner a most important chapter in the natural history of man; as it shows how instinct and necessity have led him to adopt different customs, and to make use of different articles of consumption in different climates.

Among the ordinary domestic animals, there is little of novelty in the food they supply to man. But I may notice in passing, before proceeding to an investigation of unusual or extraordinary articles of consumption, a few things that may not be generally known.

Jerked beef, or *tasajo*, as it is termed in Cuba, is imported to the extent of 200 to 350 thousand quintals a year into that island, for feeding the slaves on the plantations.

That imported from Buenos Ayres and Monte Video is preferred for consumption on the sugar estates, to that which is received from Rio Grande, Venezuela, Campeachy, and the United States, it being more substantial, coming in larger and thicker pieces, better cured and salted, and also of handsomer appearance. The class imported from Venezuela and Campeachy, comes in thin pieces called *rebenque*, which is not generally liked, and only bought in small parcels, for consumption in the city of Havana. The beef which is cured in the River Plate, from December to May, or in summer, is preferred in Cuba, by reason of its being more nutritive than that which is cured in the other or winter months; the colour is yellowish, and it keeps a longer time.

In South America, the jerked beef is called *charqui*, and when salted, and smoked or dried in the sun, *sesina*. The commerce is very large in this species of provision.

The mode of preparing it in Chili is as follows:—When the horned cattle are sufficiently fat, or rather at the killing season, which is about the months of February and March, from 500 to 1000, according to the size of the farm, are slaughtered. The whole of the fat is separated from the meat and melted, forming a kind of lard, called *grasa*, which is employed for domestic purposes. The tallow is also kept separate, and the meat is jerked. This process is performed by cutting the fleshy substance into slices of about a quarter-of-an-inch thick, leaving out all the bones. The natives are so dexterous at this work that they will cut the whole of a leg, or any other large part of a bullock, into one uniformly thin piece.

The meat thus cut is either dipped into a very strong solution of salt and water, or rubbed over with a small quantity of fine salt. Whichever mode is adopted, the whole of the jerked meat is put on the hide, and rolled up for ten or twelve hours, or until the following morning. It is then hung on lines or poles to dry in the sun, which being accomplished, it is made into bundles, lashed with thongs of fresh hide, forming a kind of network, and is ready for market. In this operation it loses about one-third of its original weight. The dried meat, or *charqui*, finds immediate sale at Lima, Arica, Guayaquil, Panama, and other places. About 6000 quintals of *charqui*, with a proportionate quantity of tallow and fat (*grasa*) are shipped from Talcahuana to Lima alone. Besides the large quantity consumed in Chili, it furnishes a great part of the food of the slaves in Brazil, the negroes in some of the West India Islands, and seamen, being the general substitute for salt beef and pork. The *grasa* and tallow are also readily sold throughout South America, and are of more value than the meat.

The slaughtering season is as much a time of diversion for the inhabitants of that country as a sheep shearing is in England. The females too are all busied cutting up the fat, frying it for *grasa*, and selecting some of the finer meat for presents and home consumption. The tongue is the only part of the head that is eaten, the remainder being left to rot.[1] Dried meat enters largely into consumption in several other countries.

In the Cape Colony dried meat is called *biltonge*. In the East, especially in Siam, the dried sinews of animals are considered a great delicacy; and dried elephant's flesh we shall find is stored up for food, under the name of *pastoormah*. Beef is preserved in Asia Minor with garlic and pepper, and dried in the sun for winter food. It is prepared in Wallachia and Moldavia, and largely shipped from Varna in the Black Sea. Besides providing all Anatolia, Aleppo, and Damascus, 6000 cwt. or more is yearly sent from Kaissariah to Constantinople. Hung beef from Germany is well known at our tables.

Portable and concentrated animal food is of great consequence to explorers and travellers, and therefore it may be well to allude here to the article *pemmican*, which is so much used by arctic travellers and the Hudson's Bay Company's traders. This is meat of any kind dried and pounded, and saturated with fat. There is as much nourishment in one pound of pemmican as in four pounds of ordinary meat. It may be eaten as it is, or partially cooked, and has a pleasant taste. Sometimes it is mixed with a sufficient quantity of Indian meal and water to cause it to adhere, and then fried or stewed.

The North American Indians dry their venison by exposing thin slices to the heat of the sun, on a stage, under which a small fire is kept, more for the purpose of driving away the flies than for promoting exsiccation; and then they pound it between two stones on a bison hide. In this process the pounded meat is contaminated by a greater or smaller admixture of hair and other impurities.

The fat, which is generally the suet of the bison, is added by the traders, who purchase it separately from the natives, and they complete the process by sewing up the pemmican in a bag of undressed hide, with the hairy side outwards. Each of these bags weighs 90 lbs., and obtains from the Canadian voyageurs the designation of 'un taureau.' A superior pemmican is produced by mixing finely powdered meat, sifted from impurities, with marrow fat, and the dried fruit of the Amilanchier.

Sir John Richardson having been employed by government to prepare pemmican on a large scale, at the Victualling Yard, Gosport, for the use of the different arctic expeditions, it will be interesting to describe the process he adopted, as given in his *Arctic Searching Expedition, or a Journal of a Boat Voyage, &c.—*

'The round or buttock of beef of the best quality having been cut into thin steaks, from which the fat and membraneous parts were pared away, was dried in a malt kiln, over an oak fire, until its moisture was entirely dissipated, and the fibre of the meat became friable. It was then ground in a malt mill, when it resembled finely grated meat. Being next mixed with nearly an equal weight of melted beef suet or lard, the preparation of plain pemmican was complete; but to render it more agreeable to the unaccustomed palate, a proportion of the best Zante currants was added to part of it, and part of it was sweetened with sugar. Both these kinds were much approved of in the sequel by the consumers, but more especially that to which the sugar had been added. After the ingredients were well incorporated by stirring, they were transferred to tin canisters, capable of containing 85 lbs. each; and having been firmly rammed down and allowed to contract further by cooling, the air was completely expelled and excluded by filling the canister to the brim with melted lard, through a small hole left in the end, which was then covered with a piece of tin and soldered up.

'As the meat in drying loses more than three-fourths of its original weight, the quantity required was considerable, being 35,651 lbs. (reduced by drying to about 8000 lbs.); and the sudden abstraction of more than one thousand rounds of beef, from Leadenhall Market, occasioned speculation among the dealers, and a rise in the price of a penny per pound, with an equally sudden fall when the extra demand was found to be very temporary.'

We import about 13 or 14 tons of gelatine a year from France, besides what is made at home, and the greater part of what passes under this name is, I believe, used for food. The Americans, some years ago, tried to pass off upon us isinglass made from fish bones, but it would not go down.

Gelatine of all kinds has usually been considered wholesome and nourishing; and while few object to cow-heel or calf's foot jelly, very many are possibly unaware of the sources of much of the gelatine vended in shapes so beautifully transparent, but which is made from bones and hide clippings, and parchment shavings. It is said that a pair of lady's gloves have ere now made a ragout; and there is a hiatus in the parchment specifications at the Patent Office, caused by an unlucky boy, who changed them away for tarts, in order that they might be converted into jellies.

The dust of the ivory turner in working up elephants' tusks forms an excellent material for jellies, and is commonly sold for this purpose, at about 6*d.* per lb.

M. Payen has recently been at pains to disprove the vulgar notion that bones make good soup. The celebrated *Gelatine Commission*, some years ago, declared, as the results of many experiments, that gelatine was not nutritious; and this result has been repeated in almost every text-book of physiology as conclusive, and is adopted by M. Payen, who tests it in another series of experiments. He boiled in one pot a portion of beef completely divested of bone, and in another the bone taken from the beef, with only a little salt. After five hours' slow boiling, the liquid from the beef was perfectly limpid, and of a light amber colour, leaving that aroma and delicate taste known to belong to good beef tea. The liquid from the bones was whitish-gray, troubled and opaque, having a very slight odour, and a not agreeable taste. Nothing could be more opposed than the two soups thus produced. In another experiment, he repeated this process with the addition of some vegetables, and even some drops of caramel. The beef-soup here maintained its delicious aroma, agreeably combined with that of the vegetables; its limpidity was the same, but its colour of course stronger. The bone-soup had a dominant odour of vegetables, but its troubled and opaque aspect made it very unappetising. From these experiments M. Payen concludes that the prejudice in favour of the addition of bones to the soup is a prejudice, and that, in fact, bones are not at all nutritious.

Liebig also, in his *Letters on Chemistry*, pp. 424 and 425, says:—'It has now been proved by the most convincing experiments, that gelatine, which by itself is tasteless, and when eaten excites nausea, possesses no nutritive value; that even when accompanied by the savoury constituents of flesh, it is not capable of supporting the vital process, and when added to the usual diet as a substitute for plastic matter, does not increase, but on the contrary diminishes the nutritive value of the food, which it renders insufficient in quantity and inferior in quality; and that its use is hurtful rather than beneficial, because it does not, like the non-nitrogenous substances provided by nature for respiration, disappear in the body without leaving a residue, but overloads with nitrogenous products, the presence of which disturbs and impedes the organic processes.' And he further observes, that 'the only difference between this and joiner's glue is its greater price.' Jellies no doubt were considered most nutritious during the Peninsular war, but we have learned many things since then, of which our poor soldiers ought to have the benefit.

Portable soup is prepared in a very simple manner. The meat is boiled, and the scum taken off as it rises, until the soup possesses the requisite flavour. 'It is then suffered to cool, in order that the fat may be separated. In the next place it is mixed with the whites of five or six eggs, and slightly boiled—this operation serves to clarify the liquid, by the removal of opaque particles, which unite with the white of egg, at the time it becomes solid by the heat, and are consequently removed along with it. The liquor is then to be strained through flannel, and evaporated on the water bath, to the consistence of a very thick paste, after which it is spread rather thin upon a smooth stone, then cut into cakes, and lastly dried in a stove, until it becomes brittle. These cakes may be kept four or five years, if defended from moisture. When intended to be used, nothing more is required to be done than to dissolve a sufficient quantity in boiling water.'[2]

For some years past there have been imported into the Continent rather large quantities of dried meat from the southern countries of America, where it is known under the name of *assayo*. It gives a soup nearly similar to that of fresh meat. Another sort of food which is prepared in Texas, the *meat-biscuit*, is generally used in the American navy; but, although greatly appreciated at the Great Exhibition of London, it has not yet entered into general use in Europe. It is made of boiled beef free from grease, the liquor of which is evaporated to the consistency of syrup, and this is mixed with wheaten flour in sufficient proportion to form a solid paste. This paste is then spread out by a rolling pin, is pierced with a number of little holes, is cut into the ordinary dimensions of sea biscuits, and then baked and properly dried. The biscuit is eaten dry, or may be broken, boiled in twenty or thirty times its weight in water, for from twenty-five to thirty minutes, and then seasoned with salt or other things.

The following is the process of manufacturing this biscuit:—

There are four wooden caldrons or tubs for boiling the meat and evaporating the liquid or broth—the two for boiling the meat, holding 2,300 gallons, will each boil 7,000 lbs. of meat in twelve to sixteen hours. The other two, for evaporating, will contain some 1,400 gallons each. All the tubs are heated or boiled by steam passing through long coiled iron pipes, supplied at pleasure, either from the escape steam from the engine, or direct from the boiler.

When the meat is so far boiled or macerated, that the liquid or broth contains the entire nutriment, the meaty, or solid portions are separated by a simple process of filtering, so that the broth goes into the evaporator pure and free from fibrous matter. It is then evaporated to a degree of consistency resembling the golden or Stewart's sugar house syrup, its uniform density being determined by a liquid or syrup gauge. Two pounds of this syrup or extract contains the nutriment of some eleven pounds of meat (including its usual proportion of bone) as first put into the caldron. This is then mixed with the best and finest flour, kneaded and made into biscuit by means of machines. The biscuit is baked upon pans in an oven so constructed as to produce an uniform firmness. The proportion is as two pounds of extract are to three pounds of flour, but by baking, the five pounds of dough is reduced to four pounds of biscuit, and this will make what the inventor claims—the nutriment of over five pounds of meat in one pound of bread, which contains, besides, over ten ounces of flour.

The biscuit resembles in appearance a light coloured sugar-cake. It is packed in air-tight casks or tin canisters of different sizes, part of the biscuit being pulverized by grinding in a mill for the purpose, and then packed with the whole biscuit.

In discussing the extension of our resources of animal food, it is strange to notice that while we eat the blood of pigs and fowls, we throw aside as waste the blood of oxen, sheep, goats, calves, &c. Now blood contains all the principles out of which the tissues are formed, and must, one would therefore imagine, be eminently nutritious. Why prejudice has excluded these, while admitting the blood of pigs, is an anomaly which I cannot understand.

In France, where there are not, as in America, large quantities of animals which are killed simply for the sake of their hides, it would be impossible to prepare or supply at a low price either the assayo or the meat biscuit; but the idea of using the blood of animals killed, which blood is at present wasted without profit, or, at best, is used as manure, might have occurred to some one. M. Brocchieri has conceived this idea. In treating the blood of our slaughter-houses by means which he has invented, and uniting to flour of the best quality, the albumen and fibrine which he extracts from it—he makes bread and biscuits which are easily preserved, and which may be employed to make very nutritious soups.

At the Great Exhibition, in 1851, he produced *bon-bons* made of the blood of the ox, cow, sheep, and hog; biscuits and patties of the blood of the bull, and delicacies made of calves' blood. I have specimens of these preserved in my private museum, although I have not ventured to taste them.

Generally speaking in England, we do not do much with the blood of animals, at least, in the shape of food—unless it be in those strings of black-puddings, with tempting little bits of fat stuck in them, which stare us in the face in some shops.

But M. Brocchieri has attempted to utilize the nutritious principles of the blood of animals killed for food, by reducing it to a concentrated and dried state, for preservation during long periods. The first step is to prepare a liquid, considered innocuous and antiseptic by the inventor, by which various bloods are kept fluid and apparently fresh. Samples of these were shown, and the series of specimens illustrated the solid parts forming the crassamentum or clot, in a dried and semi-crystalline state. These solid constituents, including the gelatine, albumen, and fibrine are next produced, combined with small proportions of flour, in the form of light, dry masses, like loaves, cakes, or biscuits. These are inodorous, almost flavourless, and may be made the bases of highly nutritious soups. They are very uniform in composition, containing half the nitrogen of dried blood, or forty-four per cent. of dry flesh, the equivalent of double the nutritive value of ordinary butcher's meat. Both the bull's and calf's blood gave 6·6 per cent. of nitrogen, equal to forty-three per cent. of flesh-forming principles. Combined with sugar, the cakes have been made into *bon-bons*.

The evidence, as to the value of the process, in preserving the samples in an undecomposed state, is now satisfactorily arrived at. It was stated in 1851, that the preparations had been advantageously employed in long voyages. The samples I have in my collection have now been kept seven years, and have not shown any tendency to decay. Thus proving that the first attempt has been successful, in rendering available for food, and portable in form, the otherwise wasted blood of cattle.

This notice of blood recalls to my recollection a laughable story told in a French work, of the life of an unfortunate pig.

'A French curé, exiled to a deserted part of our forests—and who, the whole year, except on a few rare occasions, lived only on fruit and vegetables—hit upon a most admirable expedient for providing an animal repast to set before the curés of the neighbourhood, when one or the other, two or three times during the year, ventured into those dreadful solitudes, with a view of assuring himself with his own eyes that his unfortunate colleague had not yet died of hunger. The curé in question possessed a pig, his whole fortune: and you will see the manner in which he used it. Immediately the bell announced a visitor, and that his cook had shown his clerical friend into the parlour, the master of the house, drawing himself up majestically, said to his housekeeper: 'Brigitte, let there be a good dinner for myself and my friend.' Brigitte, although she knew there were only stale crusts and dried peas in her larder, seemed in no degree embarrassed by this order; she summoned to her assistance 'Toby the Carrot,' so called because his head was as red as that of a native of West Galloway, and leaving the house together, they both went in search of the pig. This, after a short skirmish, was caught by Brigitte and her carroty assistant; and, notwithstanding his cries, his grunts, his gestures of despair, and supplication, the inhuman cook, seizing his head, opened a large vein in his throat, and relieved him of two pounds of blood; this, with the addition of garlic, shalots, mint, wild thyme, and parsley, was converted into a most savoury and delicious black-pudding for the curé and his friend, and being served to their reverences smoking hot on the summit of a pyramid of yellow cabbage, figured admirably as a small Vesuvius and a centre dish. The surgical operation over, Brigitte, whose qualifications as a seamstress were superior, darned up the hole in the neck of the unfortunate animal: and as he was then turned loose until a fresh supply of black-puddings should be required for a similar occasion, this wretched pig was never happy. How could he be so? Like Damocles of Syracuse, he lived in a state of perpetual fever; terror seized him directly he heard the curé's bell, and seeing in imagination the uplifted knife already about to glide into his bosom, he invariably took to his heels before Brigitte was half-way to the door to answer it. If, as usual, the peal announced a diner-out, Brigitte and Gold-button were soon on his track, calling him by the most tender epithets, and promising that he should have something nice for his supper—skim-milk, &c.,—but the pig with his painful experience was not such a fool as to believe them. Hidden behind an old cask, some fagots, or lying in a deep ditch, he remained silent as the grave, and kept himself close as long as possible. Discovered, however, he was sure to be at last, when he would rush into the garden, and, running up and down like a mad creature, upset everything in his way. For several minutes it was a regular steeplechase—across the beds, now over the turnips, then through the gooseberry-bushes—in short, he was here, there, and everywhere; but, in spite of all his various stratagems to escape the fatal incision, the poor pig always finished by being seized, tied, thrown on the ground, and bled: the vein was then once more cleverly sewn up, and the inhuman operators quietly retired from the scene to make the curé's far-famed black-pudding. Half-dead upon the spot where he was phlebotomized, the wretched animal was left to reflect under the shade of a tree on the cruelty of man, on their barbarous appetites; cursing with all his heart the poverty of Morvinian curates, their conceited hospitality, of which he was the victim, and their brutal affection for pig's blood.'

Sir George Simpson, speaking of some of the northern tribes of Indians in America, says, the flexibility of their stomachs is surprising. At one time they will gorge themselves with food, and are then prepared to go without any for several days, if necessary.

Enter their tents; sit there if you can for a whole day, and not for an instant will you find the fire unoccupied by persons of all ages cooking. When not hunting or travelling, they are in fact always eating. Now it is a little roast, a partridge or rabbit perhaps; now a tit-bit, broiled under the ashes; anon a portly kettle, well filled with venison, swings over the fire; then comes a choice dish of curdled blood, followed by the sinews and marrow-bones of deer's legs, singed on the embers. And so the grand business of life goes unceasingly round, interrupted only by sleep.

Dining within the arctic circle, when such a thing as dinner is to be had, is a much more serious matter than when one undergoes that pleasing ceremony at a first-rate eating house, hotel, or club.

In arctic banquets, the cheerful glass is often frozen to the lip, or the too ardent reveller splinters a tooth in attempting to gnaw through a lump of soup. We, in these temperate climes, have never had the pleasure of *eating* ship's rum, or *chewing* brandy and water. It is not only necessary to 'first catch your fish,' but also essential to *thaw* it; and there is no chance of the fish being limber, although it is not unusual for heat to bring them to life after they have been frozen stiff a couple of days. In the arctic circle even the very musquitoes, which, by the way, are frightfully large and numerous, become torpid with the intense cold, and are frozen into hard masses, which the heat of the sun, or fire, may restore to animation.

Dr. Sutherland, in his voyage in Baffin's Bay, says—'It was necessary to be very careful with our drinking cups. Tin never suited, for it always adhered to the lips, and took a portion of the skin along with it. A dog attempting to lick a little fat from an iron shovel stuck fast to it, and dragged it by means of his tongue, until by a sudden effort, he got clear, leaving several inches of the skin and adjacent tissue on the cold metal. One of the seamen, endeavouring to change the size of the eye of the splice in his tack-rope, put the marling spike, after the true sailor fashion, into his mouth; the result was that he lost a great portion of his lips and tongue.'

We hear frequent jokes of the partiality of the Russians for tallow candles, and, like all inhabitants of the polar regions, the Esquimaux are very fond of fat, the physiology of their craving for fat is now known to everybody. My esteemed friend, the late Mr. Hooper, one of the officers of H.M.S. *Plover*, in his account of his residence on the shores of Arctic America, states, that 'one of the ladies who visited them was presented, as a jest, with a small tallow candle, called a purser's dip. It was, notwithstanding, a very pleasant joke to the damsel, who deliberately munched it up with evident relish, and finally, drew the wick between her set teeth to clean off any remaining morsels of fat.'

He gives also in detail, the history of a Tuski repast of the most sumptuous nature, to which he and his companions were invited, and I must find room for some portion of it.

'First was brought in, on a huge wooden tray, a number of small fish, uncooked, but intensely frozen. At these all the natives set to work, and we essayed, somewhat ruefully it must be confessed, to follow their example; but, being all unused to such gastronomic process, found ourselves, as might be expected, rather at a loss how to commence. From this dilemma, however, our host speedily extricated us, by practical demonstration of the correct mode of action; and, under his certainly very able tuition, we shortly became more expert. But, alas! a new difficulty was soon presented; our native companions, we presume, either made a hasty bolt of each morsel, or had, perhaps, a relish for the flavour of the viands now under consideration. Not so ourselves—it was sadly repugnant to our palates; for, aided by the newly-acquired knowledge that the fish were in the same condition as when taken from the water, uncleaned and unembowelled, we speedily discovered that we could neither bolt nor retain the fragments, which, by the primitive aid of teeth and nails, we had rashly detached for our piscatorial share. It was to no purpose that our host pressed us to 'fall to;' we could not manage the consumption of this favourite preparation (or rather lack thereof), and succeeded with difficulty in evading his earnest solicitations. The next course was a mess of green stuff, looking as if carefully chopped up, and this was also hard frozen. To it was added a lump of blubber, which the lady presiding, who did all the carving, dexterously cut into slices with a knife like a cheesemonger's, and apportioned out at different quarters of the huge tray before mentioned, which was used throughout the meal, together with a modicum of the grass-like stuff, to the company; the only distinction in favour of the strangers and guests of high degree being, that their slices were cut much thinner than for the rest. We tasted this compound, and ... we didn't like it: at this no one will wonder—the blubber speaks for itself; and the other stuff, which really was not very unpalatable, we discovered in after-times to be the unruminated food of reindeer which had been slaughtered—at least, so we were told: but I am not quite clear on this point. Our dislike to the dish had no offensive effect upon our host, who only seemed to be astonished at our strange want of taste, and, with the rest of the guests, soon cleared the board; the managing dame putting the finishing stroke by a rapid sweep of her not too scrupulously clean fingers over the dish, by way of clearing off the fragments to prepare for the reception of the next delicacy. After this interesting operation she conveyed her digits to her mouth, and, engulfing them for a brief period, withdrew them, quite in apple pie order once more. The board was now again replenished, this time with viands less repellent to our unnurtured tastes. Boiled seal and walrus flesh appeared, and our hospitable friends were greatly relieved when they beheld us assist in the consumption of these items, which, being utterly devoid of flavour, were distasteful only from their extreme toughness and mode of presentation; but we did not, of course, desire to appear too singular or squeamish. Next came a portion of whale's flesh, or rather whale's skin. This was perfectly ebony in hue, and we discovered some apprehensions respecting its fitness as an article of food; but our fears were groundless. It was cut and re-cut crosswise into diminutive cubes; venturing upon one of which we were agreeably surprised to find it possessing a cocoa-nut flavour, like which it also cut, 'very short;' indeed, so much astonished were we on this occasion, that we had consumed a very considerable number of these cubes, and with great relish too, before we recovered from our wonder. The dish was ever afterwards a favourite with me. On its disappearance, a very limited quantity of boiled reindeer meat, fresh and fat, was served up, to which we did ample justice; then came portions of the gum of the whale, in which the ends of the bone lay still embedded; and I do not hesitate to declare that this was perfectly delicious, its flavour being, as nearly as I can find a parallel, like that of cream cheese. This, which the Tuski call their sugar, was the wind-up to the repast and ourselves, and we were fain to admit that, after the rather unpleasant auspices with which our feast commenced, the finale was by no means to be contemned.'

A merchant at a banquet to which he was invited with several respectable Greenlanders, counted the following dishes:—Dried herrings; dried seal's flesh; the same boiled; half-raw, or putrid seal's flesh, called Mikiak; boiled auks; part of a whale's tail in a half-putrid state, which was considered as a principal dish; dried salmon; dried reindeer venison; preserves of crow-berries mixed with the chyle from the maw of the reindeer; and lastly, the same enriched with train oil.

Dr. Kane, enumerating arctic delicacies, says, 'Our journeys have taught us the wisdom of the Esquimaux appetite, and there are few among us who do not relish a slice of raw blubber or a chunk of frozen walrus-beef. The liver of a walrus (awuktanuk), eaten with little slices of his fat—of a verity it is a delicious morsel. Fire would ruin the curt, pithy expression of vitality which belongs to its uncooked juices. Charles Lamb's roast pig was nothing to awuktanuk. I wonder that raw beef is not eaten at home. Deprived of extraneous fibre, it is neither indigestible nor difficult to masticate. With acids and condiments, it makes a salad which an educated palate cannot help relishing; and as a powerful and condensed heat-making and antiscorbutic food, it has no rival. I make this last broad assertion after carefully testing its truth. The natives of South Greenland prepare themselves for a long journey in the cold by a course of frozen seal. At Upernavik they do the same with the narwhal, which is thought more heat-making than the seal; while the bear, to use their own expression, is 'stronger travel than all.' In Smith's Sound, where the use of raw meat seems almost inevitable from the modes of living of the people, walrus holds the first rank. Certainly this pachyderm, whose finely-condensed tissue and delicately-permeating fat— (oh! call it not blubber)—assimilate it to the ox, is beyond all others, and is the very best fuel a man can swallow. It became our constant companion whenever we could get it; and a frozen liver upon our sledge was valued far above the same weight of pemmican.'

Mr. Augustus Petermann, in a paper upon Animal Life in the Arctic Regions, read before the Royal Geographical Society, thus enumerates the food resources:—

'Though several classes of the animal creation, as for example, the reptiles, are entirely wanting in this region, those of the mammals, birds, and fishes, at least, bear comparison both as to number and size with those of the Tropics: the lion, the elephant, the hippopotamus, and others not being more notable in the latter respect than the polar bear, the musk ox, the walrus, and, above all, the whale. Besides these, there are the moose, the reindeer, the wolf, the polar hare, the seal, and various smaller quadrupeds. The birds consist chiefly of an immense number of aquatic birds. Of fishes, the salmon, salmon trout, and herring, are the principal, the latter especially crowding in such myriads as to surpass everything of that kind found in tropical regions.

'Nearly all these animals furnish wholesome food for men. They are, with few exceptions, distributed over the entire regions: their number, however, or the relative intensity of the individuals, is very different in different parts. Thus, on the American side, we find the animals decreasing in number from east to west. On the shores of Davis' Straits, in Baffin's Bay, Lancaster Sound, Regent Inlet, &c., much less in number are met with than in Boothia Felix, and Parry groups. The abundance of animal life in Melville Island and Victoria Channel, is probably not surpassed in any other part on the American side. Proceeding westward to the Russian possessions, we find considerable numbers of animals all round and within the sea of Kamtschatka, as also to the north of Behring's Straits. The yearly produce of the Russian Fur Company, in America, is immense, and formerly it was much greater. Pribylon, when he discovered the small islands named after him, collected, within two years, 2,000 skins of sea otters, 40,000 sea bears, (ursine seals,) 6,000 dark sea foxes, and 1,000 walrus-teeth. Lütke, in his *Voyage Round the World*, mentions that, in the year 1803, 800,000 skins of the ursine seal alone were accumulated in Unataski, one of the depôts of the Russian Fur Company, 700,000 of which were thrown into the sea, partly because they were badly prepared, and partly to keep up the prices. But in no other part of the arctic zoological region is animal life so abundant as in the northern parts of Siberia, especially between the Rivers Kolyma and Lena.

'The first animals that make their appearance after the dreary winter, are large flights of swans, geese, ducks, and snipes; these are killed by old and young. Fish also begin to be taken in nets and baskets placed under the ice.

'In June, however, when the river opens, the fish pour in in immense numbers. At the beginning of this century, several thousand geese were sometimes killed in one day at the mouth of the River Kolyma. About twenty years later, when Admiral Wrangel visited those regions, the numbers had somewhat decreased, and it was then called a good season when 1,000 geese, 5,000 ducks, and 200 swans were killed at that place. The reindeer chase forms the next occupation for the inhabitants. About the same time, the shoals of herrings begin to ascend the rivers, and the multitudes of these fish are often such that, in three or four days, 40,000 may be taken with a single net.

'On the banks of the River Indejiska the number of swans and geese resorting there in the moulting season, is said to be much greater even than on the River Kolyma.'

The choicest dish of the Greenlanders is the flesh of the reindeer. But as those animals have now become extremely scarce, and several of them are soon consumed by a hunting party, they are indebted to the sea for their permanent sustenance, seals, fish, and sea-fowl. Hares and partridges are in no great estimation as delicacies. The head and fins of the seal are preserved under the grass in summer, and in winter a whole seal is frequently buried in the snow. The flesh, half frozen, half putrid, in which state the Greenlanders term it mikiak, is eaten with the keenest appetite. The ribs are dried in the air and laid up in store. The remaining parts of the seal, as well as birds and small fishes, are eaten, well boiled or stewed with a small quantity of sea-water. On the capture of a seal, the wound is immediately stopped up to preserve the blood, which is rolled into balls like forcemeat.

The intestines of small animals are eaten without any further preparation than that of pressing out the contents between the fingers.

They set a great value on what they find in the reindeer's maw, making it into a dish which they call Nerukak (the eatable), and send presents of it to their friends. The entrails of the rypeu, mixed with fresh train oil and berries, compose another mess which they consider as a consummate delicacy. Their preserves for winter are composed of fresh, rotten and half-hatched eggs, crake berries, and angelica, thrown together into a sack of seal skin, filled up with train oil. They likewise suck out the fat from the skins of sea-fowls; and, in dressing seal skins, they scrape off the grease which could not well be separated in the skinning, to make a kind of pancake.

In the second voyage of Sir John Ross to the arctic regions, it is related of the steward, that he purchased a sledge of the Esquimaux, and on examining it, it was found to be made of salmon, with skins sewed over them; but the cross pieces were the leg bones of the reindeer. It was not an erroneous conjecture of some of the crew, that when these poor creatures are driven to extremity for food, they turn to and make a dainty meal of their sledges, as, with the exception of the reindeer bones, the whole of them is eatable. When we refer to the description which the late Sir John Franklin gives of the different articles of food by which he and his party were maintained, the component parts of the sledge of an Esquimaux would, under circumstances of extreme want, be considered a real dainty.

There cannot be any comparison between a meal of *tripe de roche* and the stinking marrow of a reindeer bone, and a piece of dried salmon, which by its exposure to the frost has been kept from putridity; indeed, the epicures amongst the Esquimaux do not hesitate to declare, that the flavor of the salmon is rather enhanced by its long keeping, on the same principle we suppose that the flavour of game of this country rises in the estimation of the epicure in proportion as the bird or animal approaches to putridity. At all events, it must be a novel and curious exhibition, to observe a party of Esquimaux cutting up a sledge, and carving out pieces of salmon, according to their respective tastes, and seasoning them with some of the oil extracted from the blubber of the whale. The latter condiment is to the Esquimaux what Burgess' anchovy is to the citizen of London; and instances are not rare, in which an Esquimaux has been known to devour four pounds of seal flesh, or of salmon, well soaked in whale oil, at one meal, with about half-a-gallon of water as the beverage.

Much of the animal food comes frozen to the markets of St. Petersburg. The sledges which bring it are used as stalls to sell it. The matting is thrown aside, and the poultry and frozen carcases are arranged so as to attract buyers. Whole sledge loads of snow-white hares find their way to the market. The little animals are usually frozen in a running position, with their ears pointed, and their legs stretched out before and behind, and when placed on the ground, look at a first glance as if they were in the act of escaping from the hunter.

Bear's flesh is also sometimes offered for sale in the market, and here and there may be seen a frozen reindeer lying in the snow, by the side of a booth, its hairy snout stretched forth upon the ground, its knees doubled up under its body, and its antlers rising majestically into the air. It looks as if on our approaching it, it would spring up and dash away once more in search of its native forests.

The mighty elk is likewise no rare guest in this market, where it patiently presents its antlers as a perch for the pigeons that are fluttering about, till, little by little, the axe and the saw have left no fragment of the stately animal, but every part of the carcase has gone its way into the kitchens of the wealthy.

The geese are cut up, and the heads, necks, legs, and carcases sold separately by the dozen, or half dozen, strung upon small cords. Those who cannot afford to dine on the breast of a goose, purchase a string of frozen heads, or a few dozen of webbed feet, to boil down into soup. The frozen oxen, calves, and goats, stand around in rows. Sucking pigs are a favourite delicacy with the Russians. Hundreds of these, in their frozen state, are seen ranged about the sledges, mingled with large frozen hogs.

The bones and meat being all rendered equally hard by the frost, the animals are sawn up into a number of slices, of an inch or two in thickness, and by this operation a quantity of animal sawdust is scattered on the snow, and afterwards gathered up by poor children, who haunt the market for that purpose. Fish, which is offered for sale, is sawn and sold in the same frozen condition.[3]

'If one is to judge from the *restaurants* at Moscow,' writes a correspondent of the *Times*, 'there is no better place in the world to come to in order to try the temper. The best of them is dear and bad beyond comparison, and the only things good are the wine and the bread. It must be admitted that the latter is excellent, light, sweet, white, and wholesome, and our London bakers would do well if they came to Moscow for an apprenticeship in the art of making bread. It is very hard to have to pay 1*l.* for cabbage soup, *filet du cheval*, a bit of bad fish, one stewed pear, and a bottle of light French wine; but it is harder still to wait for twenty minutes between every dish, while leaden-eyed waiters are staring at you with a mixture of contempt and compassion because of your ignorance of the Russian tongue. Tired, cross, and dyspeptic, the stranger seeks a Russian dining room where the arts of French cookery have never been employed to render bad meat still worse. There, amid the odours of tobacco—for a Russian not being able to smoke in the streets makes up for it *chez lui*—you resign yourself to an unknown bill of fare and the caprices of your bearded attendant. It is fair to say of the said waiter, that he is clad in a milk-white and scrupulously clean robe, which descends in easy folds from his neck to his heels, so that he looks like a very high priest of the deity of gastronomy, and that you need not be as uneasy about his fingers and hands as you have good cause to be at the Russo-French *restaurants*. First you will be presented with a huge bowl of cabbage soup, a kind of *pot-au-feu*, which must be eaten, however, with several odd adjuncts, such as cakes stuffed with chopped vegetables, a dish of guelots, chopped fat, fried brown and crisp, and lastly a large ewer full of sour milk. Then comes a *vol-au-vent* of fowl and toad-stools. Next, if you are alive, porosenok, or a boiled sucking pig, with tart sauce; then a very nasty little fish, much prized in Moscow, and called sterlet; a fid of roast beef and a dish of birds about the size of pigeons, called guillemots; a compote of fruit closes the meal. I have forgotten to say how it begins. Before dinner a tray is laid out with caviare, raw salt herrings, raw ham and sardines, bottles of brandy, vodka, anisette, and doppel kümmel, a sweet spirit with a flavour of mint. It is *de rigueur* to eat some of this, and as the caviare is generally good, it is the best part of the dinner.'

The Governor of Cape Coast Castle, in his official report to the Colonial Office, in 1856, speaking of the food and cooking in the interior, remarks:— 'An officer of government, who has been about two years here, says, that he reckons he has eaten, during that time, 700 fowls, it being difficult at out-stations to cater in anything else but fowls.

'In cooking, the natives seem to have almost a homeopathic prepossession for trituration. They pound and grind by hand labour, between stones, their maize, and bake it; so with their yams, and, I believe, cassada; they pound also their plantains and make soup of them.

'Fish with a strong flavour and snails are favorites. The latter grow to a large, I had almost said formidable, size. I have in my possession the shell of one which I found buried about a foot in the ground, within a few yards of Government house, and which measures in length about five inches, and in circumference, in the widest part, about seven inches. A collection of these snails was once sent to me as a compliment, but I need hardly say, that I cannot speak of their taste from experience, though I do not know why I should not as well as I can of land crabs, which, when properly cooked, are, I think, general favorites with us. On the subject of cooking, I may observe, that the country cooked dishes (if of materials of a nature, and in a state, admitted in the category of our edibles) brought to table in the black native-made earthen pots in which they are cooked on the fire, are almost without exception favorites with the Europeans.'

The African Bushmen, who have few or no cattle, live upon what they can get. Hunger compels them to eat every thing, roots, bulbs, wild garlic, the core of aloes, the gum of acacias, berries, the larvæ of ants, lizards, locusts, and grasshoppers—all are devoured by these poor wanderers of the desert. Nothing comes amiss to them.

The principal diet of the Kaffir is milk, which he eats rather than drinks in a sour and curdled state. One good meal a day, taken in the evening, consisting of the curdled milk and a little millet, is almost all that he requires, and with this he is strong, vigorous, and robust, proving that large quantities of animal food are by no means necessary for the sustenance of the human frame.

Singularly enough a Kaffir, like a Jew, will never touch pork. To him it is unclean, though why he thinks so I suspect he cannot tell. Fish is likewise abstained from by him, as it is said to have been by the Egyptian priesthood. Yet with these antipathies he will eat the flesh of an ox, cooked or raw, when he can obtain it, not excepting portions of the animal from which one would imagine he would turn away with disgust.

To such tribes as the Shangalla negroes, occupying the wild tracts bordering on Abyssinia, roots are their daily food, and locusts and lizards their luxuries.

The Indians of Brazil do not reject any kind of food, and devour it almost without being cooked; rats and other small vermin, snakes, and alligators, are all accepted.

The aborigines of Australia live chiefly on the native animals they can procure—the kangaroo, the wallaby, bandicoot, kangaroo rat, opossum, and wombat; every bird and bird's egg that can be procured; and in the case of tribes near the sea, cray-fish, and shell-fish, form the staple article of their diet.

Under the influence of Christianity, the fish, flesh, or fowl, which the Pacific Islanders previously regarded as incarnations of their gods, are now eaten without suspicion or alarm. One, for instance, saw his god in the eel, another in the shark, another in the turtle, another in the dog, another in the owl, another in the lizard; and so on throughout all the fish of the sea, and birds, and four-footed beasts, and creeping things. In some of the shell-fish, even, gods were supposed to be present. A man would eat freely of what was regarded as the incarnation of the god of another man, but the incarnation of his own particular god he would consider it death to injure or to eat. The god was supposed to avenge the insult by taking up his abode in that person's body, and causing to generate diseases.

The Sonthal, or lowlander of Bengal, being unfettered by caste, eats without scruple his cow or buffalo beef, his kids, poultry, pork, or pigeons, and is not over particular as to whether the animals have been slain, have died a natural death, or have been torn by wild animals. When the more substantial good things of life, such as meat and poultry are scarce, he does not refuse to eat snakes, ants, frogs, and field rats.

In Eastern Tibet regular meals are not in vogue; the members of a family do not assemble to dine together, but 'eat when they're hungry, drink when they're dry.' 'We remember,' says a writer in *Blackwood*, 'to have heard a graphic description of the Tibetan *cuisine*, from a humorous *shikaree*, or native Nimrod of our Himalayan provinces. The Bhoteea folk (he said) have a detestable way of eating. They take a large cooking pot full of water, and put in it meat, bread, rice, and what not, and set it on the fire, where it is always a-simmering. When hungry, they go and fish out a cupful of whatever comes uppermost, perhaps, six or seven times a day. Strangers are served in the same way. If a man gets hold of a bone, he picks it, wipes his hands on his dress, and chucks it back into the pot. So with all crumbs and scraps, back they go into the pot, and thus the never-ending still-beginning mess stews on.'

If we visit Burmah, we find there a rather indiscriminate use of all that can satiate the appetite, without much regard to selection. Immense quantities of pressed fish are prepared, called *gnapee*, which constitutes a main article of their diet. In some cases the fish is washed and pounded, and this description generally consists of prawns. In the coarser sorts the pieces of fish are entire, half putrid, half pickled. They are all fetid and offensive to Europeans.

A kind of red ant is eaten fried, or with their dried fish, and a worm, which in the lower provinces of Burmah is found in the heart of a shrub, is considered such a delicacy, that every month a great quantity is sent to the capital to be served up at the table of the emperor. It is eaten either fried or roasted.

According to Sir John Bowring, the Chinese have no prejudices whatever as regards food; they eat anything and everything from which they can derive nutrition. Dogs, especially puppies, are habitually sold as food. In the butchers' shops large dogs skinned and hanging with their viscera, may be seen by the side of pigs and goats. Even to the flesh of monkeys and snakes they have no objection.

The sea slug is an aristocratic and costly delicacy, which is never wanting, any more than the edible birds-nests, at a feast where honour is intended to be done to the guests. These birds-nests are worth twice their weight in silver. They are glutinous compositions formed by a kind of swallow, in vast clusters, found in Java, Sumatra, and the rocky islets of the Indian Archipelago. Dried sharks' fins and fish maws are also highly prized.

But while the rich fare sumptuously, the mass of the poor subsist on the veriest garbage. The heads of fowls, their entrails and fat, with every scrap of digestible animal matter, earth-worms, sea reptiles of all kinds, mice, and other vermin are greedily devoured. Lots of black frogs, in half dozens, tied together, are exposed for sale in shallow troughs of water. The hind-quarters of a horse will be seen hung up in a butcher's shop, with the recommendation of a whole leg attached.

Unhatched ducks and chickens are a favorite dish. Nor do the early stages of putrefaction create any disgust. Rotten eggs are by no means condemned to perdition. Fish is the more acceptable when it has a strong fragrance and flavour to give more gusto to the rice, which forms the two meals of the population, morning and evening. In the shops, fat pork chops will be found dried and varnished to the colour of mahogany, suspended with dry pickled ducks' gizzards, and strings of sausages cured by exposure to the sun.

In Hong Kong, rice with salt fish and fat pork is the principal article of Chinese diet; and for drink, tea and hot samshew, a spirit distilled from rice, and very unpalatable to Europeans.

Nearly all the beasts of the forest are eaten by the Dyaks of Borneo; even monkeys, alligators (if small), snakes, and other reptiles are esteemed. Like the French, they regard frogs as a delicate dish, and bestow considerable pains in procuring them.

The Greenlanders, although they do not usually eat their meat raw, have a superstitious custom, on every capture, of cutting out a piece of the raw flesh and drinking the warm blood. And the woman who skins the seal, gives a couple of pieces of the fat to each of the female spectators.

An European writer states, that he frequently followed the example of the Greenlanders in the chase, and assuaged his hunger by eating a piece of raw reindeer's flesh; nor did he find it very hard of digestion, but it satisfied his appetite much less than cooked meat. The inhabitants of the high table-lands of Abyssinia, are also accustomed to eat raw flesh—the climate being as cold as that of the northern parts of Scotland. My friend, Mr. C. Johnston, in his travels in that country, thus puts in a plea for the practice by the Abyssinians.

In a country but poorly wooded, the chief supply of fuel being the dung of cattle, an instinctive feeling, dependent upon the pleasures of a state of warmth, has taught the Abyssinians that the flesh of animals eaten raw, is a source of great physical enjoyment, by the cordial and warming effects upon the system produced by its digestion, and to which I am convinced bon vivants more civilized than the Abyssinians would resort, if placed in their situation.

Travellers who have witnessed their *brunde* feasts, can attest the intoxicating effects of this kind of food, and they must have been astonished at the immense quantities that can be eaten in the raw state, compared to that when the meat is cooked, and at the insensibility which it sometimes produces.

Eating raw meat, which among the Esquimaux is for the most part an absolute necessity, by the Abyssinians is considered a luxury, or in fact, as a kind of dissipation; for eating it in that state is only indulged in by them at festivals, and it is then taken as a means of enjoyment, and is not more barbarous or disgusting than getting tipsy upon strong drinks.[4]

Another writer on 'Life in Abyssinia,' thus describes the native mode of eating meat.—'There is usually a piece of meat to every five or six persons, among whom arises some show of ceremony as to which of them shall first help himself; this being at length decided, the person chosen takes hold of the meat with his left hand, and with his sword or knife cuts a strip a foot or fifteen inches long, from the part which appears the nicest and tenderest. The others then help themselves in like manner. If I should fail in describing the scene which now follows, I must request the aid of the reader's imagination. Let him picture to himself thirty or forty Abyssinians, stripped to their waists, squatting round the low tables, each with his sword, knife, or 'shotel' in his hand, some eating, some helping themselves, and some waiting their turn, but all bearing in their features the expression of that fierce gluttony which one attributes more to the lion or leopard than to the race of Adam. The imagination may be much assisted by the idea of the lumps of raw pink and blue flesh they are gloating over. But I have yet to describe how they eat the strip of meat which I have just made one of the party cut off. A quantity of 'dillikh' or 'aou-a-zé' being laid on his bread, he dips one end of the meat into it, and then, seizing it between his teeth, while he holds the other end in his left hand, he cuts a bit off close to his lips by an upward stroke of his sword, only just avoiding the tip of his nose, and so on till he has finished the whole strip.'

Australian delicacies are somewhat different to our own. The flying-fox (*Pteropus*), an animal of the bat family, which makes sad havoc at night among the fruit trees of the colonists, is in return shot down without mercy. Their flesh is delicate, and they are almost invariably very fat, but owing to the demoniac appearance of their black leathery wings, and to the prejudice which this appearance excites, they are seldom eaten by the settlers. Travellers in the wilderness, however, are frequently indebted for a hearty meal to their success in bringing down these creatures.

The burrowing wombat, or native pig, which feeds chiefly on roots, is not deemed bad food. When divested of its fur and tough skin, its flesh, although red and coarse in appearance, resembles that of a pig in flavour, and is usually cooked by the colonists like fresh pork would be. The flesh of the porcupine ant-eater somewhat resembles that of a young sucking pig, and is highly esteemed.

There are several other small quadrupeds, including a burrowing or prairie-rat, which, at particular seasons, and in certain localities in Australia, constitute the chief animal food of the natives. The flesh of the little short-legged bandicoot is very white and delicate. Cooked like a rabbit, it furnishes the sportsman's table with a splendid dish.

Among quadrupeds, besides the ordinary domestic fed or wild animals commonly eaten as food, we find apes and monkeys, the spider monkey, the marmozet, bats, hedgehogs, bears, racoons, badgers, and dogs; many of the carnivorous animals, as foxes, lions and tigers, the puma, &c., are also eaten. Then again we have the seal and the walrus.

QUADRUMANA

African epicures esteem as one of their greatest delicacies a tender young monkey, highly seasoned and spiced, and baked in a jar set in the earth, with a fire over it, in gipsy fashion. Monkeys are commonly sold with parrots and the paca, in the markets at Rio Janeiro. The Indians, many negroes, and some whites, in Trinidad, eat of the flesh of the great red monkey, and say it is delicious. This, however, seems a semi-cannibal kind of repast—for it is the most vociferous and untameable of the Simian tribe.

Several species of monkey are used as food by the aboriginal inhabitants of the Malayan peninsula. As all kinds of monkeys are very destructive to his rice fields, the Dyak of Borneo is equally their enemy; and as this people esteem their flesh as an article of food, no opportunity of destroying them is lost.

Mr. Hugh Low says, he once saw some Dyaks roasting a monkey, but did not stay to observe whether they did not boil it afterwards, as they generally partially roast these animals to free them from the hair.

Monkeys are eaten in Ceylon by some of the natives, and the Africans on the Gold Coast eat them, according to the report of Governor Connor, in his Dispatch to the Colonial Office, March 2, 1857.—*Reports on Colonial Possessions, transmitted with the Blue Book, for the year 1856.*

In South America monkeys are ordinarily killed as game by the natives, for the sake of their flesh; but the appearance of these animals is so revolting to Europeans, that they can seldom force themselves to partake of such fare.

Mr. Wallace (*Travels on the Amazon*) says, 'having often heard how good monkey was, I had it cut up and fried for breakfast; the meat somewhat resembled rabbit, without any peculiar or unpleasant flavour.' The manner in which these animals are roasted by the natives, as described by Humboldt, further contributes to render their appearance disgusting.

'A little grating or lattice of very hard wood is formed, and raised a foot from the ground. The monkey is skinned, and bent into a sitting posture, the head generally resting on the arms, which are meagre and long; but sometimes these are crossed behind the back. When it is tied on the grating, a very clear fire is kindled below; the monkey, enveloped in smoke and flame, is broiled and blackened at the same time. Roasted monkeys, particularly those that have a round head, display a hideous resemblance to a child; the Europeans, therefore, who are obliged to feed on them, prefer separating the head and hands, and serve only the rest of the animal at their tables. The flesh of monkeys is so dry and lean, that M. Bonpland has preserved, in his collection at Paris, an arm and hand, which had been broiled over the fire at Esmeralda, and no smell arises from them after a number of years.'

Sir Robert Schomburgk, in the Journal of his expedition to the Upper Corentyne, and interior of Guiana, when suffering the pangs of hunger, reports that at last their Indian hunter arrived, with heavy step, carrying on his shoulder a large, black, female spider monkey.

'I glanced,' he observes, 'at Mr. Goodall, whose countenance depicted disappointment and disgust, but which sad necessity, and the large vacuum that two ounces of farinha must have left in his stomach, induced him to get the better of. He watched the preparations as the Indians proceeded step by step, first singeing off the hair from this human-like form, and then placing it in an upright position, with the arms crossed; when, the skin looking white now the hair was off, the sight proved too much for him, and I myself felt something like disgust at the meal before us. The sound of a heavy body falling on the ground drew my attention to a different direction, and to my great joy, I beheld a fine young forest deer, over which young Ammon stood, leaning on his gun with proud satisfaction. This was indeed, a happy turn in our affairs.

'I have tasted the smaller kind of monkeys several times, but have never partaken of one which approached so nearly to the human form as this. The Indians were less scrupulous.'

The ateles, as well indeed as all other American quadrumanes, are esteemed as an article of food by the native Indians; and even Europeans, whom curiosity or necessity has induced to taste it, report their flesh to be white, juicy, and agreeable. Nor is it without being strongly disposed to question the nature of the act, that European sportsmen, unaccustomed to shooting monkeys, witness for the first time the dying struggles of these animals; without uttering a complaint, they silently watch the blood as it flows from the wound, from time to time turning their eyes upon the sportsman with an expression of reproach, which cannot be misinterpreted. Some travellers even go so far as to assert that the companions of the wounded individual will not only assist him to climb beyond the reach of further danger, but will even chew leaves and apply them to the wound, for the purpose of stopping the hemorrhage.

One of the spider monkeys, the marimonda (*Ateles belzebuth*, Desm.), is termed *aru* by the Indians of the Rio Guiana, and is a favourite article of food with the natives of the borders of the Cassiquiare, the higher Orinoco, and other rivers, and its boiled limbs are commonly to be seen in their huts.

The howling monkeys (*Mycetes*), which are of larger size, and fatter than some of the other species, are in great request with the Indians as food. Mr. Gosse states that the flavour of their flesh is like that of kid. The Aturian Indians, as well as those of Esmeralda, eat many kinds of monkeys at certain seasons of the year, and especially the couxio, or jacketed monkey (*Pithecia sagulati*, Traill).

Mr. Grant in his *History of Brazil* states, that apes and monkeys are esteemed good food by the natives.

The negroes and natives of New Granada, according to Bonnycastle, also eat the monkey.

To prepare this dish, the body is scalded in order to remove the hair, and after this operation has been performed, it has the exact appearance of a young dead child, and is so disgusting, that no one, excepting those pressed by hunger, could partake of the repast. It is not at all improbable that many savage nations who have been accused of cannibalism, have been very unjustly charged with it, for, according to Ulloa, the appearance of the monkey of Panama, when ready to be cooked, is precisely that of a human body.

CHEIROPTERA, OR HAND-WINGED ANIMALS

The fox monkey or flying lemur (*Galeopithecus volans*) diffuses a rank disagreeable odour, yet the flesh is eaten by the natives of the islands of the Indian Archipelago.

The Dutch, when in the island of Mauritius are said to have been fond of the flesh of bats, preferring it to the finest game, but I have never heard the opinion corroborated there by others. The Indians of Malabar and other parts of the East Indies, are said to eat the flesh of bats.

The flesh of most bats is eaten in the Eastern Archipelago, and by some esteemed, being compared to that of hare or partridge in flavour. The flesh of the largest and most common, the black-bellied roussette (*Pteropus edulis*, Geoff.), has a musky odour, but is esteemed by the natives. They catch them in bags at the end of a pole.

Fancy a great frightful animal like a weasel, with wings two feet in length, being served up at table. Still they must be palatable, since one species has thus been named by naturalists, 'the eatable' bat. The flesh is stated to be white, delicate, and remarkably tender, and is regarded by the inhabitants of Timor as a dainty. The body is ten inches long, covered with close and shining black hair, and the extended wings are about four feet.

CARNIVORA

Carnivorous animals,—the terrible wild hunters of the forests and deserts,—are themselves preyed upon by man.

The low Arabs do not object to the flesh of the hyena, although the smell of the carcase is so rank and offensive, that even dogs leave it with disgust, yet their own voracious kindred obligingly gobble them up.

Even that pestilential animal the pole-cat, or skunk, falls a prey to the voracity of hungry men. When care is taken not to soil the carcase with any of the strong smelling fluid exuded by the animal, the meat is considered by the natives of North America to be excellent food. They eat foxes in Italy, where they are sold dear, and thought fit for the table of a cardinal. Mr. Kennedy, a recent voyager to the arctic regions, speaks of the delicacy of a fox pie, which was pronounced by competent authorities in his mess to be equal to rabbit; but then he honestly admits, that there were others to whom it suggested uncomfortable reminiscences of dead cats, and who generally preferred the opposite side of the table, when the dish made its appearance. This repugnance is even shared by the brute creation, for although Esquimaux dogs may kill a fox, they will not eat him. This is the more extraordinary, as they are the most voracious and dirty-feeding animals known; nothing they can possibly get at being safe. Buffalo robes, seal skins, their own harness, even boots, shoes, clothes, and dish cloths are sure to be destroyed.

The prairie wolf is eaten by the Indians of North America. The flesh of the sloth is devoured with great avidity by the natives of Demerara; and that of the lion by the Hottentots, while a tribe of Arabs between Tunis and Algeria, according to Blumenbach, live almost entirely upon its flesh.

The natives of the Malay Peninsula eat the flesh of the tiger, believing it to be a sovereign specific for all diseases, besides imparting to him who partakes of it the courage and sagacity of the animal.

Some people have ventured to eat the *cujuacura* or American panther, and say it is very delicate food; and the flesh of the wild cat of Louisiana is said to be good to eat.

The flesh of the cougar or puma (*Felis concolor*), a fierce carnivorous animal, is eaten in Central America, and is said to be agreeable food. The injunction of St. Paul, 'to eat what is set before us, and ask no questions for conscience sake,' would hardly be a safe maxim in Central America, at an entertainment given 'under the greenwood tree' by the 'Ancient Foresters' of Honduras. The sylvan dainties would not be composed of precisely the same materials as a *petit diné* at the *Trois Frères*, or the *Café de Paris*.

Mr. Darwin, in his *Journal of a Naturalist*, tells us that 'once at supper, from something which was said, I was suddenly struck with horror at thinking I was eating one of the favourite dishes of the country, namely, a half formed calf, long before its proper time of birth. It turned out to be puma; the meat is very white, and remarkably like veal in taste. Dr. Shaw was laughed at for stating that the flesh of the lion is in great esteem, having no small affinity with veal, both in colour, taste, and flavour. Such certainly is the case with the puma. The Gauchos differ in their opinion, whether the jaguar is good eating, but are unanimous in saying that cat is excellent.'

Mr. Wallace, when travelling up the Amazon, writes—'Several jaguars were killed, as Mr. C— pays about 8s. each for their skins. One day we had some steaks at the table, and found the meat very white and without any bad taste. It appears evident to me that the common idea of the food of an animal determining the quality of its meat, is quite erroneous. Domestic poultry and pigs are the most unclean animals in their food, yet their flesh is most highly esteemed, while rats and squirrels, which eat only vegetable food, are in general disrepute. Carnivorous fish are not less delicate eating than herbivorous ones, and there appears no reason why some carnivorous animals should not furnish wholesome and palatable food.'

Bears' paws were long reckoned a great delicacy in Germany, for some authors tell us, that after being salted and smoked, they were reserved for the tables of princes. In North America, bears' flesh was formerly considered equal to pork, the meat having a flavour between beef and pork; and the young cubs were accounted the finest eating in the world. Dr. Brooke, in his *Natural History*, adds—'Most of the planters prefer bears' flesh to beef, veal, pork, and mutton. The fat is as white as snow, and extremely sweet and wholesome, for if a man drinks a quart of it at a time, when melted, it will never rise on his stomach! It is of very great use for the frying of fish and other things, and is greatly preferred to butter.'

Tastes have naturally altered since this was written, nearly a century ago, and it would be somewhat difficult to carry on the sport of bear hunting on the extensive scale then practised, when we are told 500 bears were killed in two of the counties in Virginia in one winter.

The Indians seem to have shared largely in the sport and spoils of the chase, for at their subsequent feast, the largest bear was served up as the first course, and they 'roasted him whole, entrails, skin and all, in the same manner as they would barbecue a hog.'

As the paws of the bear were held to be the most delicious morsels about him, so the head was thought to be the worst, and always thrown away; but the tongue and hams are still in repute.

The white bear is eaten by the Esquimaux and the Danes of Greenland; and when young, and cooked after the manner of beef steaks, is by no means to be despised, although rather insipid; the fat, however, ought to be avoided, as unpleasant to the palate.

The flesh of the badger (*Taxus vulgaris*, Desm.) is said to be good eating, and to taste like that of a boar. The omnivorous and thrifty Chinese eat it, as indeed they do that of the flesh of most animals, and consider its hams a very great dainty.

Many nations consider the flesh of the dog excellent. The Greeks ate it; and Hippocrates was convinced that it was a light and wholesome food. The common people of Rome also ate it. The Turks and some of the Asiatic citizens would thank any one who would rid the thoroughfares of the tribes of dogs which infest the streets and courts; and there is a reward given for their slaughter. Fine feasts might be made of them by those who liked them, while the skins would come in for dog-skin gloves. Many of the South Sea islanders fatten dogs for eating, but these live wholly on vegetable food.

The domestic dog of China is uniformly one variety, about the size of a moderate spaniel, of a pale yellow, and occasionally a black colour, with coarse bristly hair on the back, sharp upright ears, and peaked head, not unlike a fox's, with a tail curled over the rump.

In China, the dog is fattened for the table, and the flesh of dogs is as much liked by them as mutton is by us; being exposed for sale by their butchers, and in their cook-shops.

At Canton, the hind quarters of dogs are seen hanging up in the most prominent parts of the shops exposed for sale. They are considered by the Chinese as a most dainty food, and are consumed by both rich and poor.

The breeds common in that country are apparently peculiar to itself, and they are objects of more attention to their owners than elsewhere in Asia. The Celestials, perhaps, having an eye to their tender haunches, which bad treatment would toughen and spoil.[5]

The Africans of Zanzibar hold a stew of puppies, as amongst us in the days of Charles the Second, as a dish fit for a monarch.

The Australian native dog or dingo, in aspect and colour resembling a fox, is hunted down by the colonists owing to its depredations among the flocks. The flesh even of this animal is eaten by the blacks. The aborigines are often driven for subsistence to the most wretched food, as snakes and other reptiles, grubs, lizards, and the larvæ of the white ant. When they do obtain better food, they prepare it with more care than might be expected. In cooking fish, they wrap it in soft bark and place it in hot ashes. By this process an acid from the bark is communicated to the fish, which gives it a most agreeable flavour.

A traveller in the Sandwich Islands, relating his experience, says,— 'Near every place at table was a fine young dog, the flesh of which was declared to be excellent by all who partook of it. To my palate its taste was what I can imagine would result from mingling the flavour of pig and lamb; and I did not hesitate to make my dinner of it, in spite of some qualms at the first mouthful. I must confess, when I reflected that the puppy now trussed up before us, might have been the affectionate and frolicsome companion of some Hawaiian fair—they all have pet pigs or puppies—I felt as if dog-eating were only a low grade of cannibalism. What eat poor Ponto?—

'The poor dog, in life the firmest friend,

The first to welcome, foremost to defend;

Whose honest heart is still his master's own;

Who labours, fights, lives, breathes for him alone.

Unhonoured falls, unnoticed all his worth—

Denied in heaven the soul he held on earth.'

'However, the edible dog is not one of your common curs, but a dainty animal, fed exclusively on vegetables, chiefly taro (a root), in the form of poë (dough), and at the age of two years is considered a dish wherewith to regale royalty. Indeed, the Sandwich Island monarch, I suspect, would be always well satisfied to see it before him, in spite of the assertion of Dr. Kidd, that 'it is worthy of consideration that the flesh of those animals, of whose living services we stand hourly in need, as the *horse* and the *dog*, are so unpalatable, that we are not tempted to eat them unless in cases of dreadful necessity.' The doctor probably never assisted at a native luaü or feast, or associated with the trappers upon the prairies of the Far West.'[6]

Mr. John Dunn, in his *History of the Oregon Territory*, tells a story of a Canadian cook, who, wishing to do honour to a dear and respected friend, whom he had been dining with on board his ship, studied long what he could get good enough to set before him, and at last bethought him of dog, which is, or was, a favourite dish among Canadian voyageurs or boatmen.

At the banquet the old boatswain ate heartily of it, as did the cook. After he had done, the cook enquired how he had enjoyed his dinner. He said it was beautiful. He then asked him whether he knew what he had been dining on? He said he supposed from a goat.

'Yes,' says the cook, 'you have been eating from a goat with von long tail, that don't like grass or heather.'

'How is that?' inquired the boatswain.

'Vy you see,' replied the cook, 'it was my best dog you have dined from.'

The old boatswain stormed and swore; and then ran as fast as possible to the vessel to get a little rum for his stomach. He vowed that he never again wished to dine with a Canadian cook, or eat pet dogs.

Brooke, in his *Natural History of Quadrupeds*, tells us, that 'in the southern coast of Africa, there are dogs that neither bark nor bite like ours, and they are of all kinds of colours. Their flesh is eaten by the negroes, who are very fond of all sorts of dogs' flesh, and will give one of their country cows for a large mastiff. I do not know what part of Africa this refers to.

In old medical works we are told, that the flesh of a fox, either boiled or roasted, was said to be good for consumption; but I do not think it is often prescribed or used for that purpose now.

MARSUPIALIA, OR POUCHED ANIMALS

The kangaroo is *par excellence* the wild game of Australia, and coursing it gives active employment to its pursuers. The flesh of all the several species is good. The fore-quarters, indeed, of the forester, the largest of the family, an animal which frequently weighs 200 lbs., are somewhat inferior, and are usually given to the dogs; but from the hind-quarters some fine steaks may be cut. When cooked in the same manner, they are very little inferior to venison collops.

The brush kangaroo (*Macropus cœruleus*) is a very fleet active animal, sometimes of about 20 lbs. weight, having fur of a silver grey colour, with a white stripe on each side of its face.

The flesh of the larger kangaroo, as well as that of the wallaby, a smaller animal, averaging about 12 or 14 lbs., is often hashed, and with a little seasoning and skill in preparation, it is excellent. The wallaby is commonly stewed for soup.

The best part of the kangaroo is its tail. Talk of ox-tail soup, ye metropolitan gourmands! Commend us to the superb kangaroo-tail soup of Australia, made from the tail weighing some 10 or 12 lbs., if a full-grown forester.

The pademelon, a smaller species of kangaroo, weighs about 9 or 10 lbs., and when cooked like a hare, affords a dish with which the most fastidious gourmand might be satisfied.

The following is the native mode of cooking a kangaroo steak:—It is placed in a scooped out stone, which is readily found in the streams, and pressed down by heavy stones on the top of it; the heat is applied beneath and round the first top stone; at the critical moment the stones are quickly removed, and the steak appears in its most savoury state.

The aborigines of Australia always roast their food; they have no means of boiling, except when they procure the service of an old European saucepan or tin pot. 'It is a very remarkable fact' (remarks Mr. Moore) 'in the history of mankind, that a people should be found now to exist, without any means of heating water, or cooking liquid food; or, in short, without any culinary utensil or device of any sort. The only mode of cooking was to put the food into the fire, or roast it in the embers or hot ashes; small fish or frogs being sometimes first wrapped in a piece of paper-tree bark. Such was their state when Europeans first came among them. They are now extremely fond of soup and tea.'

A native will not eat tainted meat, although he cannot be said to be very nice in his food, according to our ideas. Their meat is cooked almost as soon as killed, and eaten immediately.

The parts of the kangaroo most esteemed for eating are the loins and the tail, which abound in gelatine, and furnish an excellent and nourishing soup; the hind legs are coarse, and usually fall to the share of the dogs. The natives (if they can be said to have a choice) give a preference to the head. The flesh of the full-grown animal may be compared to lean beef, and that of the young to veal; they are destitute of fat, if we except a little being occasionally seen between the muscles and integuments of the tail. The colonial dish, called a *steamer*, consists of the flesh of the animal dressed, with slices of ham. The liver when cooked is crisp and dry, and is considered a substitute for bread; but I cannot coincide in this opinion.

The goto, or long bag of kangaroo skin, about two feet deep, and a foot and a half broad, carried by the native females in Australia, is the common receptacle for every small article which the wife or husband may require or take a fancy to, whatever its nature or condition may be. Fish just caught, or dry bread, frogs, roots, and clay, are all mingled together.

Mr. George Bennett (*Wanderings in New South Wales*) thus speaks of Australian native cookery:—

'After wet weather they track game with much facility; and from the late rains the hunting expeditions had been very successful; game was, therefore, very abundant at the camp, which consisted of opossums, flying squirrels, bandicoots, snakes, &c.

'One of the opossums among the game was a female, which had two large-sized young ones in her pouch; these delicate morsels were at this time broiling, unskinned and undrawn, upon the fire, whilst the old mother was lying yet unflayed in the basket.

'It was amusing to see with what rapidity and expertness the animals were skinned and embowelled by the blacks. The offal was thrown to the dogs; but, as such a waste on the part of the natives does not often take place, we can only presume it is when game, as it was at present, is very abundant. The dogs are usually in poor condition, from getting a very precarious supply of provender. The liver being extracted, and gall-bladder removed, a stick was thrust through the animal, which was either thrown upon the ashes to broil, or placed upon a wooden spit before the fire to roast. Whether the food was removed from the fire cooked, or only half dressed, depended entirely on the state of their appetites. The flesh of the animals at this time preparing for dinner, by our tawny friends, appeared delicate, and was no doubt excellent eating, as the diet of the animals was in most instances vegetable.'

Another traveller in the Bush thus describes the aboriginal practices and food:—'We had scarcely finished the snake, when Tomboor-rowa and little Sydney returned again. They had been more successful this time, having shot two wallabies or brush kangaroos and another carpet-snake of six feet in length. A bundle of rotten branches was instantly gathered and thrown upon the expiring embers of our former fire, and both the wallabies and the snake were thrown into the flame. One of the wallabies had been a female, and as it lay dead on the grass, a young one, four or five inches long, crept out of its pouch. I took up the little creature, and, presenting it to the pouch, it crept in again. Having turned round, however, for a minute or two, Gnunnumbah had taken it up and thrown it alive into the fire; for, when I happened to look towards the fire, I saw it in the flames in the agony of death. In a minute or two the young wallaby being sufficiently done, Gnunnumbah drew it out of the fire with a stick, and eat its hind-quarters without further preparation, throwing the rest of it away.

'It is the etiquette among the black natives for the person who takes the game to conduct the cooking of it. As soon, therefore, as the skins of the wallabies had become stiff and distended from the expansion of the gases in the cavity of their bodies, Tomboor-rowa and Sydney each pulled one of them from the fire, and scraping off the singed hair roughly with the hand, cut up the belly and pulled out the entrails. They then cleaned out the entrails, not very carefully by any means, rubbing them roughly on the grass or on the bushes, and then threw them again upon the fire. When they considered them sufficiently done, the two eat them, a considerable quantity of their original contents remaining to serve as a sort of condiment or sauce. The tails and lower limbs of the two wallabies, when the latter were supposed to be done enough, were twisted off and eaten by the other two natives (from one of whom I got one of the vertebræ of the tail and found it delicious); the rest of the carcases, with the large snake, being packed up in a number of the *Sydney Herald*, to serve as a mess for the whole camp at Brisbane. The black fellows were evidently quite delighted with the excursion; and, on our return to the Settlement, they asked Mr. Wade if he was not going again to-morrow.'

The kangaroo rat, an animal nearly as large as a wild rabbit, is tolerably abundant, and very good eating, when cooked in the same manner. The natives take them by driving a spear into the nest, sometimes transfixing two at once, or by jumping upon the nest, which is formed of leaves and grass upon the ground.

It is less sought for than its larger relatives, except by thorough bushmen, owing to the prejudice excited by the unfortunate name which has been bestowed upon it. Those who have once tried it usually become fond of it; and to the sawyers and splitters these animals yield many a fresh meal, during their sojourn amidst the heavily timbered flats and ranges of Victoria and New South Wales. The animal is not of the rat species, but a perfect kangaroo in miniature.

The flesh of the phalangers is of delicate flavor. The large grey opossum (*Phalangista vulpina*) forms a great resource for food to the natives of Australia, who climb the tallest trees in search of them, and take them from the hollow branches. The flesh is very good, though not much used by the settlers, the carcase being thrown to the dogs, while the sportsman contents himself with the skin.

The common opossum (*Didelphys Virginiana*) is eaten in some of the states and territories of America; it is very much like a large rat, and is classed among the 'vermin' by the Americans. Their flesh is, however, white and well-tasted; but their ugly tail puts one out of conceit with the fare.

The wombat, a bear-like marsupial quadruped of Australia, (the *Phascolomys wombat*,) is eaten in New South Wales and other parts of the Australian Continent. In size it often equals a sheep, some of the largest weighing 140 lbs.; and the flesh is said by some to be not unlike venison, and by others to resemble lean mutton. As it is of such considerable size, attaining the length of three feet, it has been suggested that it might be worth naturalizing here.

RODENTIA

Passing now to the rodents or gnawing animals, we find that the large grey squirrel (*Sciurus cinereus*, Desm.) is very good eating. The flesh of the squirrel is much valued by the Dyaks, and it will, doubtless, hereafter be prized for the table of Europeans.

The marmot (*Arctomys Marmotta*), in its fat state, when it first retires to its winter quarters, is in very good condition, and is then killed and eaten in great numbers, although we may affect to despise it.

The mouse, to the Esquimaux epicures, is a real *bonne bouche*, and if they can catch half-a-dozen at a time, they run a piece of horn or twig through them, in the same manner as the London poulterers prepare larks for the table; and without stopping to skin them, or divest them of their entrails, broil them over the fire; and although some of the mice may have belonged to the aborigines of the race, yet so strong is the mastication of the natives, that the bones of the animal yield to its power as easily as the bones of a rabbit would to a shark.

There is a very large species of rat spoken of as found in the island of Martinique, nearly four times the size of the ordinary rat. It is black on the back, with a white belly, and is called, locally, the piloris or musk rat, as it perfumes the air around. The inhabitants eat them; but then they are obliged, after they are skinned, to expose them a whole night to the air; and they likewise throw away the first water they are boiled in, because it smells so strongly of musk.

The flesh of the musk rat is not bad, except in rutting time, for then it is impossible to deprive it of the musky smell and flavour.

So fat and sleek do the rats become in the West Indies, from feeding on the sugar cane in the cane fields, that some of the negroes find them an object of value, and, with the addition of peppers and similar spiceries, prepare from them a delicate fricassée not to be surpassed by a dish of French frogs.

There is a professional rat-catcher employed on each sugar plantation, and he is paid so much a dozen for the tails he brings in to the overseer. Father Labat tells us that he made his hunters bring the whole rat to him, for if the heads or tails only came, the bodies were eaten by the negroes, which he wished to prevent, as he thought that this food brought on consumption! The health of the negroes was then a matter of moment, considering the money value at which they were estimated and sold. A rat hunt in a cane field affords glorious sport. In cutting down the canes, one small patch is reserved standing, into which all the rats congregate, and the negroes, surrounding the preserve, with their clubs and bill-hooks speedily despatch the rats, and many are soon skinned and cooked.

The negroes in Brazil, too, eat every rat which they can catch; and I do not see why they should not be well-tasted and wholesome meat, seeing that their food is entirely vegetable, and that they are clean, sleek, and plump. The Australian aborigines eat mice and rats whenever they can catch them.

Scinde is so infested with rats, that the price of grain has risen 25 per cent. from the destruction caused to the standing crops by them. The government commissioner has recently issued a proclamation granting head-money on all rats and mice killed in the province. The rate is to be 3d. a dozen, the slayer having the privilege of keeping the body and presenting the tail.

In China, rat soup is considered equal to ox-tail soup, and a dozen fine rats will realize two dollars, or eight or nine shillings.

Besides the attractions of the gold-fields for the Chinese, California is so abundantly supplied with rats, that they can live like Celestial emperors, and pay very little for their board. The rats of California exceed the rats of the older American States, just as nature on that side of the continent exceeds in bountifulness of mineral wealth. The California rats are incredibly large, highly flavoured, and very abundant. The most refined Chinese in California have no hesitation in publicly expressing their opinion of 'them rats.' Their professed cooks, we are told, serve up rats' brains in a much superior style to the Roman dish of nightingales' and peacocks' tongues. The sauce used is garlic, aromatic seeds, and camphor.

Chinese dishes and Chinese cooking have lately been popularly described by the fluent pen of Mr. Wingrove Cooke, the *Times'* correspondent in China, but he has by no means exhausted the subject. Chinese eating saloons have been opened in California and Australia, for the accommodation of the Celestials who now throng the gold-diggings, despite the heavy poll-tax to which they have been subjected.

Mr. Albert Smith, writing home from China, August 22, 1858, his first impressions, says:—

'The filth they eat in the eating houses far surpasses that cooked at that old *trattoria* at Genoa. It consists for the most part of rats, bats, snails, bad eggs, and hideous fish, dried in the most frightful attitudes. Some of the *restaurateurs* carry their cook-shops about with them on long poles, with the kitchen at one end, and the *salle-à-manger* at the other. These are celebrated for a soup made, I should think, from large caterpillars boiled in a thin gravy, with onions.'

The following is an extract from the bill of fare of one of the San Francisco eating houses—

Grimalkin steaks	25	cents.
Bow-wow soup	12	"
Roasted bow-wow	18	"
Bow-wow pie	6	"
Stews ratified	6	"

The latter dish is rather dubious. What is meant by stews *rat*-ified? Can it be another name for rat pie? Give us light, but no pie.

The San Francisco *Whig* furnishes the following description of a Chinese feast in that city:—'We were yesterday invited, with three other gentlemen, to partake of a dinner *à la* Chinese. At three o'clock we were waited upon by our hosts, Keychong, and his partner in Sacramento-street, Peter Anderson, now a naturalized citizen of the United States, and Acou, and escorted to the crack Chinese restaurant in Dupont-street, called Hong-fo-la, where a circular table was set out in fine style:—

'Course No. 1.—Tea, hung-yos (burnt almonds), ton-kens (dry ginger), sung-wos (preserved orange).

'Course No 2.—Won-fo (a dish oblivious to us, and not mentioned in the cookery-book).

'No. 3.—Ton-song (ditto likewise).

'No. 4.—Tap-fau (another *quien sabe*).

'No. 5.—Ko-yo (a conglomerate of fish, flesh, and fowl).

'No. 6.—Suei-chon (a species of fish ball).

'Here a kind of liquor was introduced, served up in small cups, holding about a thimbleful, which politeness required we should empty between every course, first touching cups and salaaming.

'No. 7.—Beche-le-mer (a dried sea-slug, resembling India rubber, worth one dollar per pound).

'No. 8—Moisum. (Have some?)

'No. 9.—Su-Yum (small balls, as bills of lading remark, 'contents unknown').

'No. 10.—Hoisuigo (a kind of dried oyster).

'No. 11.—Songhai (China lobster).

'No. 12.—Chung-so (small ducks in oil).

'No. 13.—Tong-chou (mushrooms, worth three dollars per pound).

'No. 14.—Sum-yoi (birds' nests, worth 60 dollars per pound).

'And some ten or twelve more courses, consisting of stewed acorns, chestnuts, sausages, dried ducks, stuffed oysters, shrimps, periwinkles, and ending with tea—each course being served up with small china bowls and plates, in the handiest and neatest manner; and we have dined in many a crack restaurant, where it would be a decided improvement to copy from our Chinese friends. The most difficult feat for us was the handling of the chop sticks, which mode of carrying to the mouth is a practical illustration of the old proverb, 'many a slip 'twixt the cup and lip.' We came away, after a three hours' sitting, fully convinced that a China dinner is a very costly and elaborate affair, worthy the attention of epicures. From this time, henceforth, we are in the field for China, against any insinuations on the question of diet *à la* rat, which we pronounce a tale of untruth. We beg leave to return thanks to our host, Keychong, for his elegant entertainment, which one conversant with the Chinese bill of fare informs us, must have cost over 100 dollars. *Vive la China!*'

Mr. Cooke, in his graphic letters from China, speaks of the fatness and fertility of the rats of our colony of Hong Kong. He adds: 'When Minutius, the dictator, was swearing Flaminius in as his Master of the Horse, we are told by Plutarch that a rat chanced to squeak, and the superstitious people compelled both officers to resign their posts. Office would be held with great uncertainty in Hong Kong if a similar superstition prevailed. Sir John Bowring has just been swearing in General Ashburnham as member of the Colonial Council, and if the rats were silent, they showed unusual modesty. They have forced themselves, however, into a state paper. Two hundred rats are destroyed every night in the gaol. Each morning the Chinese prisoners see, with tearful eyes and watering mouths, a pile of these delicacies cast out in waste. It is as if Christian prisoners were to see scores of white sucking pigs tossed forth to the dogs by Mahommedan gaolers. At last they could refrain no longer. Daring the punishment of tail-cutting, which follows any infraction of prison discipline, they first attempted to abstract the delicacies. Foiled in this, they took the more manly course. They indited a petition in good Chinese, proving from Confucius that it is sinful to cast away the food of man, and praying that the meat might be handed over to them to cook and eat. This is a fact, and if General Thompson doubts it, I recommend him to move for a copy of the correspondence.'

A new article of traffic is about to be introduced into the China market from India, namely, *salted rats!* The genius with whom the idea originated, it would appear, is sanguine; so much so, that he considers himself 'on the fair road to fortune.' The speculation deserves success, if for nothing else than its originality. I have not, as yet however, observed the price that rules in Whampoa and Hong Kong nor the commodity quoted in any of the merchants' circulars, though it will, doubtless, soon find its place in them as a regular article of import.

A correspondent of the *Calcutta Citizen*, writing from Kurrachee, the chief town of the before mentioned rat infested province of Scinde, declares that he is determined to export 120,000 salted rats to China. The Chinese eat rats, and he thinks they may sell. He says:—'I have to pay one pice a dozen, and the gutting, salting, pressing, and packing in casks, raises the price to six pice a dozen (about three farthings), and if I succeed in obtaining anything like the price that rules in Whampoa and Canton for corn-grown rats, my fortune is made, or rather, I will be on the fair road to it, and will open a fine field of enterprise to Scinde.'

Rats may enter into consumption in other quarters, and among other people, than those named, when we find such an advertisement as the following in a recent daily paper at Sydney:—

'Rats! Rats! Rats!—To-night at 8 o'clock, rattling sport; 200 rats to be entered at G. W. Parker's Family Hotel.'

Query.—What ultimately becomes of these rats, and who are the persons who locate and take their meals at this 'Family Hotel?' Probably they are of the rough lot whose stomachs are remarkably strong.

Some classes of the Malabars are very fond of the bandicoot, or pig rat (*Perameles nasuta*, Geoff. Desm.), which measures about fourteen inches in length from head to tail, the tail being nearly as long as the body. They are much sought after by the coolies, on the coffee estates in Ceylon, who eat them roasted. They also eat the coffee rat (*Golunda Ellioti* of Gray), roasted or fried in oil, which is much smaller, the head and body only measuring about four or five inches. These animals are migratory, and commit great damages on the coffee tree, as many as a thousand having been killed in a day on one estate. The planters offer a reward for the destruction of these rodents, which brings grist to the mill in two ways to the coolies who hunt or entrap them, namely, in money and food.

The fat dormouse (*Myoxus glis*, Desm.) is used for food in Italy, as it was by the ancient Romans, who fattened them for the table in receptacles called Gliraria.

Dr. Rae, in his last arctic exploring expedition, states, that the principal food of his party was geese, partridges, and lemmings (*Arvicola Hudsonia*). These little animals were migrating northward, and were so numerous that their dogs, as they trotted on, killed as many as supported them all, without any other food.

There is another singular little animal, termed by naturalists the vaulting rat, or jerboa. On an Australian species, the *Dipus Mitchelli*, the natives of the country between Lake Torrens and the Great Creek, in Australia seem chiefly to subsist. It is a little larger than a mouse, and the hind legs are similar to those of the kangaroo.

Captain Sturt and his exploring party once witnessed a curious scene. They came to a native who had been eating jerboas, and after they met him they saw him eat one hundred of them. His mode of cooking was quite unique. He placed a quantity, for a few seconds, under the ashes of the fire, and then, with the hair only partially burnt off, took them by the tail, put the body in his mouth, and bit the tail off with his teeth. After he had eaten a dozen bodies, he took the dozen tails, and stuffed them into his mouth.

The flesh of the beaver is looked upon as very delicate food by the North American hunters, but the tail is the choicest dainty, and in great request. It is much prized by the Indians and trappers, especially when it is roasted in the skin, after the hair has been singed off; and in some districts it requires all the influence of the fur-traders to restrain the hunters from sacrificing a considerable quantity of beaver fur every year to secure the enjoyment of this luxury. The Indians of note have generally one or two feasts in a season, wherein a roasted beaver is the prime dish. It resembles pork in its flavour, but it requires a strong stomach to sustain a full meal of it. The flesh is always in high estimation, except when they have fed upon the fleshy root of a large water lily, which imparts a rank taste to it.

The flesh of a young porcupine is said to be excellent eating, and very nutritious. The flavour is something between pork and fowl. To be cooked properly, it should be boiled first, and afterwards roasted. This is necessary to soften the thick, gristly skin, which is the best part of the animal. The flesh of the porcupine is said to be used by the Italians as a stimulant; but, never having tasted it myself, I cannot speak from experience as to the virtue of this kind of food.

The Dutch and the Hottentots are very fond of it; and when skinned and embowelled, the body will sometimes weigh 20 lbs. The flesh is said to eat better when it has been hung in the smoke of a chimney for a couple of days.

The flesh of the crested porcupine (*Hystrix cristata*) is good and very agreeable eating. Some of the Hudson Bay trappers used to depend upon the *Hystrix dorsata* for food at some seasons of the year.

Rabbits, which form so large an article of consumption with us, are not much esteemed as an article of food by the negroes in the West Indies, resembling, in their idea, the cat. Thus, a black who is solicited to buy a rabbit by an itinerant vendor, would indignantly exclaim, 'Rabbit? I should just like to no war you take me for, ma'am? You tink me go buy rabbit? No, ma'am, me no cum to dat yet; for me always did say, an me always will say, dat dem who eat rabbit eat pussy, an dem who eat pussy eat rabbit. Get out wid you, and your rabbit?'

And yet, with all this mighty indignation against rabbits, they do not object, as we have seen, to a less dainty animal in the shape of the rat.

Although the negroes in the West Indies do not care for rabbits, yet their brethren in the American States are by no means averse to them. A field slave one day found a plump rabbit in his trap. He took him out alive, held him under his arm, patted him, and began to speculate on his qualities. 'Oh, how fat. Berry fat. The fattest I eber did see. Let me see how I'll cook him. I'll broil him. No, he is so fat he lose all de grease. I fry him. Ah yes. He so berry fat he fry hisself. Golly, how fat he be. No, I won't fry him—I stew him.' The thought of the savory stew made the negro forget himself, and in spreading out the feast in his imagination, his arms relaxed, when off hopped the rabbit, and squatting at a goodly distance, he eyed his late owner with cool composure. The negro knew there was an end of the stew, and summoning up all his philosophy, he thus addressed the rabbit, at the same time shaking his fist at him, 'You long-eared, white-whiskered rascal, you not so berry fat arter all.'

I need not here touch upon hare soup, jugged hare, or roasted hare, from the flesh of our own rodent; but the Arctic hare (*Lepus glacialis*) differs considerably from the English in the colour and quality of its flesh, being less dry, whiter, and more delicately tasted; it may be dressed in any way. When in good condition it weighs upwards of 10 lbs.

The capybara, or water hog (*Hydrochœrus capybara*), an ugly-looking, tailless rodent, the largest of the family, is hunted for its flesh in South America, and is said to be remarkably good eating. It grows to the size of a hog two years old.

The flesh of the guinea pig (*Cavia cobaya*, Desm.) is eaten in South America, and is said to be not unlike pork. When he is dressed for the table his skin is not taken off as in other animals, but the hair is scalded and scraped off in the same manner as it is in a hog.

The white and tender flesh of the agouti (*Dasyprocta Acuti*, Desm.), when fat and well dressed, is by no means unpalatable food, but very delicate and digestible. It is met with in Brazil, Guiana, and in Trinidad. The manner of dressing them in the West Indies used to be to roast them with a pudding in their bellies. Their skin is white, as well as the flesh.

The flesh of the brown paca (*Cœlogenus subniger*, Desm.), a nearly allied animal, is generally very fat, and also accounted a great delicacy in Brazil.

Another South American rodent, the bizcacha, or viscascha (*Lagostomus trichodactylus*), is eaten for food. It somewhat resembles a rabbit, but has larger gnawing teeth, and a long tail. The flesh, when cooked, is very white and good.

EDENTATA, OR TOOTHLESS ANIMALS

Wallace, in his travels on the Amazon, tells us that the Indians stewed a sloth for their dinner, and as they considered the meat a great delicacy, he tasted it, and found it tender and very palatable.

Among other extraordinary animals for which Australia is proverbial, is the *Echidna hystrix*, or native porcupine, which is eaten by the aborigines, who declare it to be 'cobbong budgeree (very good), and, like pig, very fat.' Europeans who have eaten of them confirm this opinion, and observe that they taste similar to a sucking pig. There appear to be two species of this animal, the spiny echidna and the bristly echidna; the first attains a large size, equalling the ordinary hedgehog. It has the external coating and general appearance of the porcupine, with the mouth and peculiar generic character of the ant-eater.

The flesh of the great ant-eater (*Myrmecophaga jubata*, Linn.) is esteemed a delicacy by the Indians and negro slaves in Brazil, and, though black and of a strong musky flavour, is sometimes even met with at the tables of Europeans.

The armadillo, remarkable for its laminated shell, when baked in its scaly coat is a good treat, the flesh being considered delicate eating, somewhat like a rabbit in taste and colour. The flesh of the large twelve-banded Brazilian one (*Dasypus Tatouay*) is said to be the best of all. In South America there are several species of armadillo, all of which are used for food when met with.

Mr. Gosse states, that this animal feeds upon soft ground fruits and roots, and also on carrion, whenever it can find it; and a large proportion of the sustenance of this, as well as of other species, is derived from the numberless wild cattle which are caught and slaughtered on the Pampas for the sake of their hides and tallow, the carcases being left as valueless to decay, or to become the prey of wild animals. Notwithstanding the filthy nature of their food, the armadillos, being very fat, are eagerly sought for by the inhabitants of European descent, as well as by the Indians. The animal is roasted in its shell, and is esteemed one of the greatest delicacies of the country; the flesh is said to resemble that of a sucking pig.

PACHYDERMATA, OR THICK-SKINNED ANIMALS

What do our African brethren consider tit-bits? Ask Gordon Cumming. He will enumerate a list longer than you can remember. Study his 'Adventures,' and you will become learned in the mystery of African culinary operations. What are sheep's-trotters and insipid boiled calves' feet compared to baked elephants' paws?

Listen to his description of the whole art and mystery of the process of preparing them:—

'The four feet are amputated at the fetlock joint, and the trunk, which at the base is about two feet in thickness, is cut into convenient lengths. Trunk and feet are then baked, preparatory to their removal to headquarters. The manner in which this is done is as follows:—A party, provided with sharp-pointed sticks, dig a hole in the ground for each foot and a portion of the trunk. These holes are about two feet deep and a yard in width; the excavated earth is embanked around the margin of the holes. This work being completed, they next collect an immense quantity of dry branches and trunks of trees, of which there is always a profusion scattered around, having been broken by the elephants in former years. These they pile above the holes to the height of eight or nine feet, and then set fire to the heap. When these strong fires have burnt down, and the whole of the wood is reduced to ashes, the holes and the surrounding earth are heated to a high degree. Ten or twelve men then stand round the pit and take out the ashes with a pole about sixteen feet in length, having a hook at the end. They relieve one another in quick succession, each man running in and raking the ashes for a few seconds, and then pitching the pole to his comrade, and retreating, since the heat is so intense that it is scarcely to be endured. When all the ashes are thus raked out beyond the surrounding bank of earth, each elephant's foot and portion of the trunk is lifted by two athletic men, standing side by side, who place it on their shoulders, and, approaching the pit together, they heave it into it. The long pole is now again resumed, and with it they shove in the heated bank of earth upon the foot, shoving and raking until it is completely buried in the earth. The hot embers, of which there is always a great supply, are then raked into a heap above the foot, and another bonfire is kindled over each, which is allowed to burn down and die a natural death; by which time the enormous foot or trunk will be found to be equally baked throughout its inmost parts. When the foot is supposed to be ready, it is taken out of the ground with pointed sticks, and is first well beaten, and then scraped with an assagai, whereby adhering particles of sand are got rid of. The outside is then pared off, and it is transfixed with a sharp stake for facility of carriage. The feet thus cooked are excellent, as is also the trunk, which very much resembles buffalo's tongue.'

Elephants' petit(?) toes, pickled in strong toddy vinegar and cayenne pepper, are considered in Ceylon an Apician luxury. As soon as it is known that an elephant has been killed in Africa, every man in the neighbourhood sets off with his knife and basket for the place, and takes home as much of the carcase as he can manage to carry. The flesh is not only eaten when fresh, but is dried and kept for months, and is then highly esteemed.

The manner in which the elephant is cut up is thus described by the author and sportsman I have already quoted:—'The rough outer skin is first removed, in large sheets, from the side which lies uppermost. Several coats of an under skin are then met with. The skin is of a tough and pliant nature, and is used by the natives for making water-bags, in which they convey supplies of water from the nearest *vey*, or fountain (which is often ten miles distant), to the elephant. They remove this inner skin with caution, taking care not to cut it with the assagai; and it is formed into water bags by gathering the corners and edges, and transfixing the whole on a pointed wand. The flesh is then removed in enormous sheets from the ribs, when the hatchets come into play, with which they chop through and remove individually each colossal rib. The bowels are thus laid bare; and in the removal of these the leading men take a lively interest and active part, for it is throughout and around the bowels that the fat of the elephant is mainly found. There are few things which a Bechuana prizes so highly as fat of any description; they will go an amazing distance for a small portion of it. They use it principally in cooking their sun-dried biltongue, and they also eat it with their corn. The fat of the elephant lies in extensive layers and sheets in his inside, and the quantity which is obtained from a full-grown bull, in high condition, is very great. Before it can be obtained, the greater part of the bowels must be removed. To accomplish this, several men eventually enter the immense cavity of his inside, where they continue mining away with their assagais, and handing the fat to their comrades outside till all is bare. While this is transpiring with the sides and bowels, other parties are equally active in removing the skin and flesh from the remaining parts of the carcase.

'In Northern Cachar, India, the flesh of the elephant is generally eaten. The Kookies encamp in the neighbourhood of the carcase until they have entirely consumed it, or are driven away by the effluvia of decomposition. Portions of the flesh that they cannot immediately eat are dried and smoked to be kept for future consumption.

'Fat of any kind is a complete godsend to the Bechuana and other tribes of Southern Africa; and the slaughter of an elephant affords them a rich harvest in disembowelling the carcase, and mining their way into the interior of the huge cavity to remove the immense layers furnished by such a large animal if in good condition.'

Galton, the African traveller, in his hints for bush cooking, tells us:—

'The dish called *beatee* is handy to make. It is a kind of haggis made with blood, a good quantity of fat shred small, some of the tenderest of the flesh, together with the heart and lungs of the animal, cut or torn into small shivers, all of which is put into the stomach and roasted, by being suspended before the fire with a string. Care must be taken that it does not get too much heat at first, or it will burst. It is a most delicious morsel, even without pepper, salt, or any seasoning.'

In all the large rivers of Southern Africa, and especially towards the mouths, the hippopotami abound. The colonists give them the name of sea-cows. The capture of one of these huge beasts, weighing, as they sometimes do, as much as four or five large oxen, is an immense prize to the hungry Bushman or Koranna, as the flesh is by no means unpalatable; and the fat, with which these animals are always covered, is considered delicious. When salted it is called zee-koe speck, is very much like excellent fat bacon, and is greatly prized by the Dutch colonists, not only for the table, but for the reputed medicinal qualities which are attributed to it. In Abyssinia, hippopotamus meat is commonly eaten.

The hog is one of those animals that are doomed to clear the earth of refuse and filth, and that convert the most nauseous offal into the nicest nutriment in its flesh. It has not altogether been unaptly compared to a miser, who is useless and rapacious in his life, but at his death becomes of public use by the very effects of his sordid manners. During his life he renders little service to mankind, except in removing that filth which other animals reject.

A delicate sucking pig, a Bath chap, or a good rasher of bacon are, however, tit-bits not to be despised.

Lord Brougham hoped to see the day when every man in the United Kingdom would read Bacon. 'It would be much better to the purpose,' said Cobbett, 'if his lordship would use his influence that every man in the kingdom could eat bacon.'

In British India, only Europeans and the low Hindoos eat pork, but wild hogs are very abundant, and afford good sport to the hunter. The avoidance of pork arises as much from religious scruples as the deep-rooted aversion to the domestic swine all must imbibe who have only seen it in the East, where it is a tall, gaunt, half famished, and half ferocious-looking brute, which performs the office of scavenger.

The legend which ascribes to the eating of human flesh the origin of one of the most loathsome of diseases, scarce offers a more horrible picture to the imagination than is presented by a letter recently published in the *Ceylon Examiner*. The beautiful islands of Mauritius and Bourbon are largely supplied with pork from Patna, a province of Hindostan that has been over-run by the cholera. Both there and at Calcutta the bodies of the natives are consigned to the Ganges, instead of being interred. 'Let any person,' says the writer in the Ceylon paper, 'at daybreak start from the gates of Government House, Calcutta, and, whether his walk will be to the banks of the river or to the banks of the canals which on three sides surround the city, he will see pigs feeding on the dead bodies of the natives that have been thrown there during the night. During the day the river police clear away and sink all that remains of the bodies. Bad as is the metropolis of India it is nothing compared to Patna. Hundreds upon hundreds of human corpses are there strewed along the strand; and fattening, ghoule-like, upon these are droves upon droves of swine. These swine are slaughtered, cut up, and salted into hams, bacon, and pickled pork, and then despatched to Calcutta.... The great market for this poisonous swine produce is the Mauritius and Bourbon, where it is foisted on the inhabitants as the produce of Europe. Moreover, as these swine are sold in Calcutta at 3s. or 4s. each carcase, it is stated that the inferior class of homeward-bound vessels are provisioned with them, and thus this human-fed pork is introduced into Europe and America.'

Pork-eaters may believe as much of the following remarks as they please. 'It is said that the Jews, Turks, Arabians, and all those who observe the precept of avoiding blood and swine's flesh, are infinitely more free from disease than Christians; more especially do they escape those opprobria of the medical art, gout, scrofula, consumption, and madness. The Turks eat great quantities of honey and pastry, and much sugar; they also eat largely, and are indolent, and yet do not suffer from dyspepsia as Christians do. The swine-fed natives of Christendom suffer greater devastation from a tubercular disease of the bowels (dysentery) than from any other cause. Those persons who abstain from swine's flesh and blood are infinitely more healthy and free from humors, glandular diseases, dyspepsia, and consumption; while in those districts, and among those classes, of men, where the pig makes the chief article of diet, tubercle in all its forms of eruptions, sore legs, bad eyes, abscesses, must prevail.'

These are the remarks of an American journalist, which, however, have not, I conceive, the shadow of foundation.

'It appears somewhat singular,' remarks Mr. Richardson, in his history of the pig, 'that the flesh of the hog was prohibited in the ceremonial of the Jewish law; the same prohibition being afterwards borrowed by Mahomet, and introduced into the Koran.' Great difference of opinion prevails as to the cause of this prohibition; some alleging that this food was unsuited to the land inhabited by the Jews. As, however, the kinds of food to be eaten and rejected—doubtless to prevent that luxurious epicurism unsuited to a growing and prosperous nation—were to have a limit, this limit was fixed by two distinctive marks: they must 'divide the hoof, and chew the cud;' that principle of restriction admitting only a limited range to the food permitted. The pig, the horse, and the camel were excluded. It was only in a state of low nationality, or in times of great degeneracy, that the Jew ever tasted pork.

The food of the hog varies in different localities, and probably materially influences the flavour of the meat. In the River Plata provinces they feed them on mutton. After describing the purchase—8,000 at *eighteenpence per dozen* (?)—by a Mr. M. Handy, a traveller adds, 'As soon as the sheep became fattened on his own lands, he killed about a thousand, sold the fleeces at five shillings per dozen, and with the mutton he fed a herd of swine. Mentioning this fact to a large party of Europeans, at the dinner table of Lord Howden, when in Buenos Ayres, my statement was received with a murmur of scepticism; but I offered to accompany the incredulous to the pastures, where the remainder of the sheep were then feeding.'—(*Two Thousand Miles' Ride through the Argentine Provinces.*) But the Yankees beat this, according to a late American paper. In North America they generally feed them on maize, but in some of the States, apples form a principal portion of their food, and the 'apple sauce' thus becomes incorporated with the flesh. A gentleman travelling down East, overtook a farmer dragging a lean, wretched-looking, horned sheep along the road. 'Where are you going with that miserable animal?' asked the traveller. 'I am taking him to the mutton mill, to have him ground over,' said the farmer. 'The *mutton mill*? I never heard of such a thing. I will go with you and witness the process.' They arrived at the mill; the sheep was thrown alive into the hopper, and almost immediately disappeared. They descended to a lower apartment, and, in a few moments, there was ejected from a spout in the ceiling four quarters of excellent mutton, two sides of morocco leather, a wool hat of the first quality, a sheep's head handsomely dressed, and two elegantly-carved powder horns.'

In America they speak of hogs as other countries do of their sugar, coffee, and general exportable staple crops; and even when packed and cured they occasionally compute the produce by the acre. Thus, the *Louisville Courier* stated recently, that there were five or six *acres* of barrelled pork piled up three tiers high, in open lots, and not less than six acres more not packed, which would make eighteen acres of barrels if laid side by side, exclusive of lard in barrels, and pork bulked down in the curing houses, sheds, &c. Besides the above slaughtered hogs, there were five or six acres more of live hogs in pens, waiting their destiny.

In the Western States pork is the great idea, and the largest owner of pigs is the hero of the prairie. What coal has been to England, wheat to the Nile or the Danube, coffee to Ceylon, gold to California and Victoria, and sheep to the Cape and Australia, pork has been to the West in America.

The phrase, 'Going the whole hog,' must have originated in Ohio, for there they use up the entire carcases of about three-quarters of a million of pigs, and the inhabitants are the most 'hoggish' community of the entire Union. What crocodiles were in Egypt, what cows are in Bengal, or storks in Holland, pigs are in Cincinnati, with this trifling difference, their sacredness of character lasts but as long as their mortal coil; and this is abbreviated without ceremony, and from the most worldly motives. In life, the pig is free, is honored; he ranges the streets, he reposes in thoroughfares, he walks beneath your horse's legs, or your own; he is everywhere respected; but let the thread of his existence be severed, and—shade of Mahomet!—what a change! They think in Cincinnati of nothing but making the most of him.

Historically, socially, gastronomically, the pig demands our careful attention. The connection with commerce, with the cuisine, and even with the great interest of fire insurance, have all made him an object of particular regard. In the early days of the Celestial Empire—as we learn from the veracious writings of the witty and voracious essayist, Charles Lamb—a wealthy Chinaman was so unfortunate as to have his dwelling destroyed by fire. Prowling around the smoking ruins, and seeking to save some of his valuables which the conflagration might have spared, his hand came in contact with the smoking remains of a poor pig which had perished in the flames; instantly, smarting with the pain, he carried his hand to his mouth, when a peculiar flavour greeted his palate, such as the gods (Chinese ones I mean, of course,) might in vain have sighed for. Regardless of pain he applied himself once more, and drew forth from the smoking cinders the remains of the pig. Carefully brushing off the ashes, he regaled himself with the feast before him, but closely preserved the secret he had learned. In a few short months, however, the taste for roast pig came back so strong, that John Chinaman's house was burned down again, and again was a pig found in the ashes. This was repeated so often that the neighbours grew suspicious, and watched until they ascertained that the reason for the conflagration was the feast that invariably followed. Once out, the secret spread like wildfire; every hill-top shone with the flames of a burning habitation—every valley was blackened with the ashes of a homestead; but roast pig was dearer to a Chinaman than home or honour, and still the work of destruction went on. Alarmed at a course which bid fair to ruin every insurance office in the empire, the directors petitioned in a body to the General Court of China, for the passing of an Act that should arrest the evil and avert their threatened ruin; and a careful examination of the revised statutes of China would probably show stringent resolutions against the crime of burning houses for the sake of roasting pigs.

Since the invention of the modern cooking stove, however, although incendiarism has decreased only in a slight degree, still it has ceased to be attributed to this cause, and a juicy crackling is no longer suggestive of fallen rafters, or a houseless family.

'There is an old adage, 'Give a dog a bad name, and his ruin is accomplished.' Such may be true of the canine race; but the noble family of animals of which I am treating, furnishes a striking illustration that the proverb applies not to their numbers. A goose, it is said, saved lordly Rome by its cackling; and had not their list of Divinities just then been full, a grateful people would have found for him a sedgy pool and quiet nest in Olympus. How did the ancestors of that same people repay the pig for a service scarcely less important?

'The veriest smatterer in the classics knows, that, when from flaming Troy 'Æneas the great Anchises bore,' seeking in strange lands a new home for his conquered people, a white sow, attended by thirty white little pigs, pure as herself, pointed out to him the scene of his future empire. But what did he and his people do for the pig in return? Did they load him with honours? Did they cherish him with corn? Did they treat him with respect? No! with black ingratitude, which still merits the indignation of every admirer of the pig, they affixed to the animal the appellation of *Porcus*; and 'poor cuss' the pig would have been to the present day, had not the Latin tongue long since ceased to be the language of the world. But, 'poor cuss' he is no longer, when in Worcester county he spurns his classic name, and, adopting the vernacular, he 'grows the whole hog,' that he may 'pork us,' in return for the care which we bestow upon him.

'For the sake of our farmers, who are anxious to make a profit from pig-raising, it is greatly to be regretted that the thirty-at-a-litter breed has disappeared from the face of the earth. Breeding swine with such a rate of increase must be almost as profitable as 'shaving' notes at two per cent. per month; but still the impression is irresistibly forced upon us, that, in a family so numerous, those who came last to dinner, at least in their infant days, would not have gained flesh very rapidly. Indeed, in such a family it would seem almost impossible to dispense with the services of a wet nurse, in order to bring up profitably the rising generation.

'The course of the pig, like that of the Star of Empire, has ever tended westward. From China we trace him to Italy, the gloomy mountains of the Hartz, the broad plains of Westphalia, the fertile valleys of France, and to the waving forests of 'Merrie England;' all have known him since the days when their bold barons and hungry retainers sat down to feast on the juicy chine of the wild boar, and the savoury haunch of venison. In green Erin, piggy has been an important member of society; true, he has shared his master's meal, and basked in the comfortable warmth of his cabin; but, like a 'gintleman' as he is, he has ever paid the 'rint;' and St. Patrick, in the plenitude of his power and influence, never saw the day he could have banished him from that 'gem of the ocean.'

'When the pig first crossed to this western world remains in doubt. Whether he came with the Pilgrims, pressing with the foot of a pioneer the Blarney-stone of New England, and scanning with fearless eye the cheerless prospect before him, or whether, regardless of liberty of conscience, and careful only of his own comfort, he waited till the first trials and toils of a new settlement had been met and overcome, we have no record; enough for us that he is here; how or where he came concerns us not. He is among us and of us. From souse to sausage we have loved him; from ham to harslet we have honoured him; from chine to chops we have cherished him. The care we have shown him has been repaid a hundred-fold. He has loaded our tables, and lighted our fire-sides, and smiling plenty has followed in his steps, where hungry famine would have stalked in his absence.

'But still further towards the setting sun has been the arena of the pig's greatest triumphs; there have been the fields of his widest influence. Beneath the vast forests of Ohio, raining to the ground their yearly harvests of mast—through her broad corn-fields, stretching as far as the eye can see, he has roamed, and fed, and fattened. From him, and the commercial interests he has mainly contributed to establish, has grown a mighty State, scarcely second to any in this confederacy; from his ashes has arisen a new order in society—the 'Bristleocracy of the great West.'

'A broad levee bustling with business, lofty and spacious stores and slaughter-houses, crowded pens, and a river bearing on its bosom steamboats in fleets—all attest the interest which the pig has exerted on the agricultural and commercial interests of the great State of Ohio. He has filled the coffers of her bankers, and has bought the silks which cover her belles. He has built the beautiful palaces which adorn the 'Queen City of the West,' and feeds the princely luxury of those who inhabit them. *There* he is almost an object of worship, and his position is considered as about equivalent to a patent of nobility. Fancy dimly paints the picture, when a few years hence, the wealthy pork merchant, who justly boasts his numerous *quarterings*, shall, in the true spirit of heraldry, paint on the pannel of his carriage, and on the escutcheon over his door-way, a lustrous shield, bearing in brilliant colours a single pig, his bristles all *rampant*, his tail closely *curlant*, and his mouth widely *opant*, till the lions, the griffins, and the unicorns of the Old World shall fade into insignificance before the heraldic devices of the New.'[7]

'Your Spanish pig, who, by the way, is a no less important character in his country than is his cousin in Ireland, is not raised for the vulgar purpose of being fried to lard, or salted down to pork. He has, in fact, no more fat than he has hair on him. He is a long-legged, long-snouted, and long-tailed fellow, and would have been described by Plato as an animal without hairs. But though the pickings on his ribs be small, they are sweet. The Spaniard rolls the morsels under his tongue as he does his easily-besetting sins. It is nut-fed flesh; and has the flavour of acorns. This taste is as much prized in the roasted joint as that of the skin in the sherry. Pig is game in Spain. The porker does not live there in the chimney corner, and sit in the best arm-chair, as in Paddy's cabin; but he roams the fields, and goes a-nutting with the boys and girls. He eats grass, as there are no cows to eat it; and would milk the goats, doubtless, if they would let him. He evidently knows more than the same animal in other countries; and is, in consequence, more willing to be driven. He will squeal when he feels the knife, but for no other reason. Nor is his squeal the same as that heard at the North. There are more vowel sounds in it. It is also less through the nose than in New England; and has some gutturals even farther down the throat than those of a Dutchman. Your wild boar is a monster compared with him. The flesh of the latter is to that of the former as the crisp brown of roast pig is to the tanned hide in your riding saddle. Accordingly, to refuse pork at a Spanish table is to pronounce yourself 'of the circumcision;' and should you decline a cut of a particularly nice ham, you would be set down as no better than a heathen. However, you never would do it—particularly after having read this essay. I assure you that when you may have eaten up all the chickens which were stowed away in your saddle bags, you cannot do better than to attack your landlord's roast pig—provided you can get it. Only it may cost you dear in the reckoning, as it is thought a dish to set before the king. You may like pork, or you may not; but one thing is certain, it is the only meat in the

Peninsula which has juices in it. Mutton may have a very little; and should you travel far in the country, you would see the day when you would be glad of a leg of it. But the beef is dry as 'whittlings.' An entire joint of roast beef would kill a man as effectually as a joist of timber. Whoever should undertake to live on Spanish beef a twelvemonth, would become at the end of that time what he was, in fact, at the beginning—wooden-headed. Make up your mind, therefore, to eat the meat of the uncircumcised, if you have any thought of going to Spain. You will often have to take your choice between that and nothing; and my word for it, 'tis much preferable. For the land is leaner far than pork; and happy is that traveller, who, when he is reduced to pickings, can find a spare-rib to work upon. Forewarned—forearmed.[8]'

Pork is the great food of the Brazilian people. It is prepared and eaten, according to Dr. Walshe, in a peculiar manner. When the pig is killed, the butcher dexterously scoops out the bones and muscular flesh, leaving behind only the covering of fat. In this state it is salted, folded up, and sent in great quantities to Rio, where it is called *toucinho*. All the stores and *vendas* are full of it, and it is used commonly for culinary purposes, and forms an ingredient in every Brazilian article of cookery.

The flesh of the peccary (after cutting away the fetid orifice on its back) and of the wild or musk hog, both known under the Indian appellation of quanco in Trinidad, is much preferable to that of the domestic swine.

The flesh of the rhinoceros is eaten in Abyssinia, and by some of the Dutch settlers in the Cape Colony, and is in high esteem. The flesh of the hippopotamus used also to be eaten on the east coast of Africa, roasted or boiled, and fetched a high price as a delicacy. The fat was used in making puddings, instead of butter. The Portuguese settlers were permitted by the priests to eat the flesh of this animal in Lent, passing it off as *fish* from its amphibious habits, and hence their consciences were at ease.

The flesh of the tapir, when roasted, closely resembles beef, especially if it be young; and that of the water hare is also considered excellent food, being white and delicate, and much of the same flavour as that of the tapir.

HORSE-FLESH

At Paris, where all eccentricities are found, and even encouraged, one of the latest gastronomic innovations is the use of horse-flesh. The French are always adding to their dietetic regimen by introducing new articles of food. This social phenomenon of making the horse contribute to the nourishment of the human race, is not altogether new. The ancient Germans and Scandinavians had a marked liking for horse-flesh. The nomade tribes of Northern Asia make horse-flesh their favorite food. It has long been authorized and publicly sold in Copenhagen.

With the high ruling prices of butcher's meat, what think you, gentlemen and housekeepers, of horse-flesh as a substitute for beef and mutton? Are you innocently ignorant of the French treatise of that eminent naturalist and professor of zoology, M. St. Hilaire, upon horse for food? Banquets of horse-flesh are at present the rage in Paris, Toulouse, and Berlin. The veterinary schools there pronounce horse-bone soup preferable beyond measure to the old-fashioned beef-bone liquid, and much more economical.

Horse-flesh steak without sauce, and cold, is cited as a morsel superior to the finest game that flies! and cut, too, from a horse nearly a quarter of a century old; one of the labouring cavalry kind who pranced at the sound of the trumpet, and snuffed the battle from afar off, little dreaming he was doomed to steaks, soup, and washing-day hashes. Horse-flesh pie, too, eaten cold, is a dainty now at Berlin and Toulouse, and boiled horse, *rechauffé*, has usurped the place of ragouts and secondary dishes! What a theme, hippophology, to write upon. We shall soon hear in our city dining rooms, 'A piece o' horse, my kingdom for a piece of horse!' 'Waiter! a cut from the fore-shoulder, well done.' 'A horse sandwich and ale, and the morning paper.' Our witty friend *Punch* had its horse-laugh recently upon the subject of the sensation this movement has created in equestrian circles.

A Frenchman, observes a recent writer, was one day remonstrating against the contempt expressed by Englishmen for French beef, the inferiority of which he would not admit. 'I have been two times in England,' said he, 'but I nevere find the beef so supérieur to ours. I find it vary convenient that they bring it you on leetle pieces of stick for one penny, but I do not find the beef supérieur.' 'Good gracious!' exclaimed the Englishman, 'you have been eating cats' meat for beef.' What this Frenchman did in the innocence of his heart, his countrymen now do, it seems, with *malice prepense*.

And a Frenchman of considerable reputation, in a letter on alimentary substances, and especially upon the flesh of the horse, calls upon the whole world to put aside, what he considers, an ancient and absurd prejudice, and to realize at home that famous sentence in the geography we used to read at school, which, under the head of Norway, informed us 'horse-flesh is publicly sold in the markets.'

'M. Isidore St. Hilaire is very serious. He does not merely advocate the fillet of horse-flesh—the mare soup and fricasseed colt—in sarcastic allusion to the practice of Parisian restaurants. He comes gravely forward, with chapters of scientific evidence and argument, to contend that, while animal food is absolutely necessary to the proper nourishment of the human race, millions of Frenchmen eat no animal food, and every year millions of pounds of excellent meat are wasted. He knows how the cause he advocates lends itself to ridicule—he knows how difficult it has always been to get rid of a prejudice—he knows the fate of innovators; but, though a Frenchman, he braves ridicule, brings a heavy battery of facts to destroy what he deems a prejudice, and is already experiencing some of the triumph which follows a hard-won victory. For seven years he has been advocating the desirableness of eating horse-flesh—for seven or eight years he has been collecting evidence and gaining converts—and now he feels strong enough to appeal to the European public in a small volume.[9]

'Since then, Germany has had its 'Banquets of Horse-flesh' for the wits to ridicule—public feastings at which 'cats' meat' was served in various forms, as soup, as bouilli, as fillet, as cutlet; and all the feasters left the table converted hippophagists. In 1841, horse-flesh was adopted at Ochsenhausen and Wurtemburg, where it is now publicly sold under the surveillance of the police. Every week five or six horses are brought to market. At the Lake of Constance, a large quantity of this meat is also sold. In 1842, a banquet of 150 persons inaugurated its public use at Königsbaden, near Stuttgard. In 1846, the police of Baden authorized its public sale, and Schaffhausen followed in the same year. In 1847, at Detmold and at Weimar, public horse-flesh banquets were held with great *éclat*—in Karlsbad (Bohemia) and its environs, the new beef came into general use—and at Zittau, 200 horses are eaten annually. At Ling, after one of these banquets, the police permitted the sale of horse-flesh, which is now general in Austria, Bohemia, Saxony, Hanover, Switzerland, and Belgium. The innovation made rapid converts. In 1853, Berlin had no less than five *abattoirs*, where 150 horses were killed and sold. At Vienna, in 1853, there was a riot to prevent one of these banquets; but in 1854, such progress had been made, that 32,000 pounds weight were sold in fifteen days, and at least 10,000 of the inhabitants habitually ate horse-flesh.' And now Parisian banquets of horse-flesh are common.

These facts are at all events curious. Think of the prejudices to be overcome, and think how unreasoning is the stomach!

Young horses are too valuable to be brought to the shambles, unless killed by accident. But our worn-out hacks, of which 250 or 300 die or are killed weekly in the metropolis,—old horses used up, are capable, we are assured, of furnishing good meat. An old horse, which had done duty for twenty-five years, was the substance of a learned gastronomic feast at Paris.

M. St. Hilaire, the champion of this new addition to our food resources, reasons in this fashion:—'Horse-flesh has long been regarded as of a sweetish disagreeable taste, very tough, and not to be eaten without difficulty. So many different facts are opposed to this prejudice, that it is impossible not to recognize its slight foundation. The free or wild horse is hunted as game in all parts of the world where it exists—Asia, Africa, and America—and formerly, and perhaps even now, in Europe. The domestic horse itself is made use of as alimentary as well as auxiliary—in some cases altogether alimentary—in Africa, America, Asia, and in some parts of Europe.

'Its flesh is relished by people the most different in their manner of life, and of races the most diverse, negro, Mongol, Malay, American, Caucasian. It was much esteemed up to the eighth century among the ancestors of some of the greatest nations of Western Europe, who had it in general use, and gave it up with regret. Soldiers to whom it has been served out, and people in towns who have bought it in markets, have frequently taken it for beef. Still more often, and indeed habitually, it has been sold in restaurants, even in the best, as venison, and without the customers ever suspecting the fraud or complaining of it.

'And further, if horse-flesh has been often accepted as good under a false name, it has also been pronounced good by those who, to judge of its qualities, have submitted it to careful experiment, and by all who have tasted it in a proper condition, that is, when taken from a sound and rested horse, and kept sufficiently long. It is then excellent roasted; and if it be not so acceptable as *bouilli*, it is precisely because it furnishes one of the best soups—perhaps the best that is known.

'It is good also, as experiments prove made by myself as well as others, when taken from old horses not fattened, whose age was 16, 19, 20, and even 23 years, animals thought worth no more than a few francs beyond the value of their skin.

'This is a capital fact, since it shows the possibility of utilizing a second time, for their flesh, horses which have already been utilized up to old age for their strength; and, consequently, of obtaining a further and almost gratuitous profit at the end of their life, after they had well nigh paid the cost of their rearing and keep by their labour.'

Let us see what additional evidence M. St. Hilaire has to adduce. First, he appeals to his long experience at the *Jardin des Plantes*, where the greater part of the *carnivora* are habitually fed on horse-flesh, which keeps them healthy in spite of many unfavourable conditions. But this will not carry much weight with it. Our digestion is not quite so good as that of a lion. The condor has been known to eat, with satisfaction, food which Mrs. Brown would find little to her taste. No dietetic rule for men can be deduced from the digestions of tigers. We prefer the experience of human stomachs. Fortunately this is not wanting, and M. St. Hilaire collects an imposing mass of evidence. Huzard, the celebrated veterinary surgeon, records, that during the revolution, the population of Paris was for six months dieted with horse-flesh, without any ill effects. Some complaints, indeed, were made when it was found that the *beef* came from horses; but, in spite of prejudice and the terrors such a discovery may have raised, no single case of illness was attributed to the food. Larrey, the great army surgeon, declares that on very many occasions during the campaigns, he administered horse-flesh to the soldiers, and to the soldiers sick in the hospital; and instead of finding it injurious, it powerfully contributed to the convalescence of the sick, and drove away a scorbutic epidemic which attacked the men. The testimony of Parent Duchâtelet is also quoted to the same effect. M. St. Hilaire feels himself abundantly authorized to declare that horse-flesh, far from being unwholesome, is one of the most nutritious and wholesome of alimentary substances: and, to support this declaration, he adduces the testimony of historians and travellers, showing how whole tribes and nations have habitually eaten and highly esteemed it.

Having thus, as he considers, satisfactorily settled the question of wholesomeness, M. St. Hilaire proceeds to deal with the question of agreeableness. Is wholesome horse-flesh agreeable enough to tempt men, not starving, to eat it? It is, of course, of little use that historians and travellers tell of hippophagists—it is nothing to the purpose that soldiers in a campaign, or citizens during a siege, have eaten horses with considerable relish. Under such circumstances, one's old shoe is not to be despised as a *pièce de résistance*; and one's grandmother may be a toothsome morsel. The real point to be settled in the European mind is this—apart from all conditions which must bias the judgment, is horse-flesh pleasant to the taste? M. St. Hilaire cites the evidence of eminent men who, having eaten it knowing what it was, pronounced it excellent—all declaring that it was better than cow-beef, and some that there was little difference between it and ox-beef.

But perhaps the reader, having eaten German beef, has a not ill-grounded suspicion that horse-flesh might bear honourable comparison with such meat, and yet be at best of mediocre savour. Let us, therefore, says a writer in the *Saturday Review*, cite the example of Parisian banquets, where the convives were men accustomed to the *Trois Frères, Philippe's,* and the *Café de Paris.* M. Renault, the director of the great Veterinary College at Alfort, had a horse brought to him with an incurable paralysis of the hinder extremities. It was killed, and three days afterwards, on the 1st December, 1855, eleven guests were invited—physicians, journalists, veterinary surgeons, and *employés* of the government. Side by side were dishes prepared by the same cook, in precisely the same manner, and with the same pieces taken respectively from this horse and from an ox of good quality. The *bouillon* of beef was flanked by a *bouillon* of horse, the *bouilli* of beef by a *bouilli* of horse, the fillet of roast beef by a fillet of roast horse; and a comparison was to be made of their qualities. Dr. Amédée Latour thus writes:—

'*Bouillon de cheval.*—Surprise générale! C'est parfait, c'est excellent, c'est nourri, c'est corse, c'est aromatique, c'est riche de goût.

'Le bouillon de *bœuf* est bon, mais *comparativement inférieur*, moins accentué de goût, moins parfumé, moins résistant de sapidité.'

The jury unanimously pronounced the horse *bouillon* superior to that of the ox. The *bouilli*, on the contrary, they thought inferior to that of good beef, although superior to ordinary beef, and certainly superior to all cow-beef. The roast fillet, again, they found superior to that of the ox; and M. Latour thus sums up the experiment:—

Un bouillon supérieur;
Un bouilli bon et très-mangeable;
Un rôti exquis.

Similar experiments have been subsequently tried, several times in Paris and in the provinces. They have been tried under three different conditions. First, the guests have known what they were going to eat; secondly, they have been totally ignorant; and thirdly, they have been warned that they were going to eat something quite novel. Yet in every case, we are told, the result has been the same. It is right to add, that the author anticipates the objection that the animals selected were young horses in splendid condition, and that such horses are too valuable to be sent to the butcher. The majority of these experiments have, we are assured, been made at veterinary colleges, upon horses incapacitated by age or accident from further work. The horse which M. Renault served up to his friends had already *vingt-trois ans de bons et loyaux services*. He was in good 'condition'—that is to say, well-fleshed, although paralysed. In fact, all the horses, it is asserted, were such as are sold for fifteen or twenty francs—not such as are the pride of our stables. The younger the horse, the better his flesh; and as young horses die daily from accidents, these, we presume, would form the 'prime cuts.' But old horses, used up, unfit even for cabs, if allowed a little rest, are capable, we are assured, of furnishing beef better than cow-beef. But this serving up of horse-flesh is equalled by that of the maître de cuisine to the Maréchal Strezzi, who, at the siege of Leith, according to Monsieur Beaujeu, 'made out of the hind quarter of one salted horse forty-five *couverts*, that the English and Scottish officers and nobility who had the honour to dine with the Monseigneur, upon the rendition, could not tell what the devil any one of them were made upon at all.' M. St. Hilaire discusses at great length many other objections, with which we need not here trouble ourselves. But the taste is spreading and the advocates increasing. The public use of horse-flesh as human food is spoken of approvingly in *Blackwood*.

The *New York Tribune* thus endorses the fanatical idea of the French *savans*, (more properly *ravens*,) as to the propriety of eating horse-flesh:—

'In the horse we have an animal which is much cleaner in its habits than the hog, herbivorous like the ox or sheep, whose flesh is rich in nitrogen, and as pleasant to the taste as that of either of the above-named animals. What prevents horse-flesh from being found on our tables? Nothing but a popular prejudice, which recent investigations in Paris show is entirely without any foundation whatever.

'8,000 horses die, it is said, in New York annually, or about 22 per day' (a great exaggeration no doubt); 'but instead of fetching 17 or 18 dollars to press the carcase for grease, and to feed the hogs on to make pork for export, the prices will be greatly enhanced for meat for home consumption.'

Thus writes the Paris correspondent of the *Indépendance Belge*:—'You know what interest is attached to-day—and very naturally so—to all questions relating to the public food. In connexion therewith, I have to mention a fact which is both curious and odd; it is, that there is being formed in Paris a society of economists, naturalists, and hardy gourmands, having for aim the introduction of horse-flesh into the category of butchers' meat. It may perhaps be said, that this social phenomenon is not altogether new. Ten years ago, *hippophagy* made some noise in Germany, and, if I remember right, a society of eaters of the horse was formed, and attempted a public festival, at which all the meat should be of that quadruped, but were interrupted by the public, who, feeling their prejudices wounded, broke the tables to pieces. At Paris, where all eccentricities are found, and even encouraged, there is nothing of that kind to fear. Accordingly, *hippophagy* progresses. Do not consider this an exaggeration. The last number of the *Revue des Cours Publics* will prove to you, by means of a summary, that M. Geoffroy de St. Hilaire has made the subject the theme of one of his recent lectures, and that the learned professor was greatly applauded. I should add that his auditors included economists, agriculturists, and heads of benevolent institutions. When the orator concluded by saying that the day was come when the horse ought to contribute to the nourishment of the human race, as well as the ox, the sheep, and the pig, a hundred voices cried in chorus, '*Oui! oui! très bien!*' This question, strange at first sight, has been raised, and it will not sleep again. I predict that it will have not only numerous adherents, but eloquent fanatics. As a commencement, many of the auditors wished to eat horse soup, horse steaks, and the same flesh under other forms.' At the time at which I write, dissertations are made, *brochures* written, the regulations of a *hippophagic* society drawn up, and the establishment of horse shambles demanded. In 1832, M. Alphonse Karr, mocking the extreme zeal of the society for protection, exclaimed—'Philanthropists! the horse has carried man long enough; it is now for man to carry the horse!'

There is very little doubt that horse-flesh, besides its application for 'cats' meat,' enters, even now, largely into surreptitious use in certain quarters in this country as food for bipeds. Thus, a Blackburn paper tells us that 'on Monday last Mr. Laverty seized and confiscated the carcase of a horse. The animal had been stuck and bled, and was taken very near to the premises of a noted brawn and black-pudding maker. We understand that horse-flesh is used in this town by a certain vender and manufacturer of brawn.'

Hoffman and Burns, makers and venders of horse-meat sausages, at Philadelphia, were recently tried, convicted, and sentenced to eighteen months' imprisonment. *Apropos* of sausages, judging from the following anecdote, home-made ones are the more attractive.

'A minister in one of our orthodox churches, while on his way to preach a funeral sermon in the country, called to see one of his members, an old widow lady, who lived near the road he was travelling. The old lady had just been making sausages, and she felt proud of them—they were so plump, round, and sweet. Of course she insisted on her minister taking some of the links home to his family. He objected on account of not having his portmanteau along with him. This objection was soon over-ruled, and the old lady, after wrapping them in a rag, carefully placed a bundle in either pocket of the preacher's capacious great coat. Thus equipped, he started for the funeral.

'While attending to the solemn ceremonies of the grave, some hungry dogs scented the sausages, and were not long in tracking them to the pockets of the good man's over-coat. Of course this was a great annoyance, and he was several times under the necessity of kicking these whelps away. The obsequies at the grave completed, the minister and congregation re-passed to the church, where the funeral discourse was to be preached.

'After the sermon was finished, the minister halted to make some remarks to his congregation, when a brother who wished to have an appointment given out, ascended the steps of the pulpit, and gave the minister's coat a hitch to get his attention. The divine, thinking it a dog having designs upon his pocket, raised his foot, gave a sudden kick, and sent the good brother sprawling down the steps!

'You will excuse me, brethren and sisters,' said the minister, confusedly, and without looking at the work he had just done, 'for I could not avoid it—I have sausages in my pocket, and that dog has been trying to grab them ever since I came upon the premises!'[10]

The reader may judge of the effect such an announcement would have at a funeral. Tears of sorrow were suddenly exchanged for smiles of merriment.

Mr. Richardson, officer of the Local Board of Health of Newton Heath, near Manchester, gave the following evidence before Mr. Scholefield's Committee on Adulteration, before whom I was also examined as a witness.

'We have in Newton five knackers' yards, and there is only one in Manchester. The reason is, that they have so much toleration in Newton; and it has been a great source of profit to them, because they have the means of selling the best portions of the horse-flesh to mix with the potted meats.

'I can say for a fact, that the tongues of horses particularly, and the best portions, such as the hind quarters of horses, are generally sold to mix with collared brawn, or pigs' heads, as they are called with us, and for sausages and polonies. I understand, also, from those who have been in the habit of making them, that horse-flesh materially assists the making of sausages; It is a hard fibrin, and it mixes better, and keeps them hard, and they last longer in the shop window before they are sold, because otherwise the sausages run to water, and become soft and pulpy. I believe horse-flesh also materially assists German sausages; it keeps them hard.'

The instinct of the dog, the cat, and the rat, are so well known that one anecdote will suffice to illustrate the three. A terrier and a tom cat were pursuing a large rat down a street. The rat was almost caught, when it dodged suddenly and ran into a sausage shop. The cat and dog stopped convulsively at the door; and, looking at the sausages, hung their heads, and slunk away terror-stricken.

But in other quarters than England, unwholesome and infected meat is vended, for a year or two ago the editor of the *Madras Athenæum* thus wrote:—

'We question whether since the days of Pelops a more filthy dish was ever offered to human beings, than those which are daily served up to the European inhabitants of Madras. With respect to the state of our market, we have never seen a more disgusting receptacle of all kinds of abominations than that market presents.

'A lazar house it seemed, wherein were laid
Numbers of all diseased.'

'Unfortunate beings in the worst stages of leprosy, naked, and covered all over with the livid spots of that hideous disease, standing at the stalls, handling the meat, and talking with the butchers, is a sight as common as it is horrible. As for the small-pox, that is almost too abundant to allow of any cases being particularly noticed. It is very conspicuous on the native, on account of the pustules being white. The only disease bearing any resemblance to it is the itch. We have ourselves observed a dirty fellow, with his hands covered all over with one of these nauseous eruptions, coolly walking down the whole length of a set of stalls, and clapping those abominable hands, in a lazy manner, upon every piece of meat within his reach. Faugh! The very thought smells. When we were last there, the place swarmed with pariah dogs, the effect of which was to render the stench and filth accumulated round the stalls perfectly unbearable. We are aware the subject is a nasty one, but at the risk of spoiling the breakfast of Brown, Jones, or Robinson, as they take up our damp sheet this morning, we make the evil conspicuous, and bring it plainly into notice, that measures may be taken to sink it into oblivion ever after. If one could jest upon such a subject, one might say, that the market of Madras is as much the morning lounge of the filthiest wretches in the place, as the stables of Taylor and Co. are the morning rendezvous of the rank and fashion, who there do congregate, to look at the Australians and Arabs ushered to their notice under the winning smile of the worthy head partner. Is not the thought horrible, too, that the fairer part of the creation, who should be fed on

'Sugar and spice

'And all that's nice,

are offered such filthy and infected stuff?

'We should also recommend attention being called to the practice, which we are afraid prevails, of 'blowing the meat,' to give it a good appearance. This is a cognizable offence, and butchers have, on occasion, most deservedly received a dozen or two for it; but the inducement to make their meat look tempting by filling it with breath, not quite so 'fragrant as the flower of Amrou,' is too profitable, we fear, to be disregarded upon the vague and distant contingency of a flogging or a fine. If the functionaries who are employed to superintend the market are insufficient in number, it would surely be poor economy not to increase them. If they are inattentive and remiss, discharge them. It would be pennywise, indeed, for a few paltry rupees a month, to allow a Secretary to Government, or a Member of Council, whose wisdom and experience have been purchased at an immense cost to the country, to be poisoned, which at present they are liable to be, by infected meat.

'If by calling attention to the subject, some improvement is made, our object will be attained. We will gladly run the chance of spoiling a few dinners. Jones of the club, as he takes the cover off one of Maltby's best *entrées*, may for once think of the leprous hand that has handled it; Brown may fancy for once he will catch small-pox from his beef-steak; Robinson may think of the dog licking the leg of mutton from which his whack is taken, and all may heartily anathematise the *Athenæum* for telling them the truth, but we will cheerfully put up with their wry faces and abuse, if the necessary reform we advocate be attained.'

Sam Slick, in his truthful, but satirical vein, alludes to the disguises of fashionable cookery.—'Veal' (he says) 'to be good, must look like anything else but veal. You mustn't know it when you see it, or it's vulgar; mutton must be incog, too; beef must have a mask on; any thin' that looks solid, take a spoon to; any thin' that looks light, cut with a knife; if a thing looks like fish, you take your oath it is flesh; and if it seems real flesh, it's only disguised, for it's sure to be fish; nothin' must be nateral—natur is out of fashion here. This is a manufacturin' country; everything is done by machinery, and *that* that aint, must be made to look like it; and I must say, the dinner machinery is perfect.'

If horses are eaten, why not donkeys? The animal is more rare, and hence it would be the greater delicacy. The Greeks ate donkeys, and we must suppose they had their reasons for it. Has any modern stomach in Europe been courageous enough, knowingly, to try it?

The flesh of the common ass, though never eaten by us, is esteemed a delicacy in some countries, particularly in Tartary. The northern climate, pasturage, and freedom may have some effect on the flesh.

Travellers affirm that dogs' flesh, which with us is intolerable, is one of the most savoury meats, when the animal has been kept for some time in the warm, tropical regions. This cannot, however, apply to the brutish pariah dogs that infest the streets of Madras, Constantinople, and other eastern towns.

The Roman peasants found the flesh of the ass palatable, and the celebrated Mæcenas having tasted it, introduced it to the tables of the great and rich, but the fashion of eating it lasted no longer than his life. Galen compares the flesh of the ass to that of the stag. It is said to be eaten plentifully in the low eating-houses of Paris, under the denomination of veal. The flesh of the wild ass is eaten by the Tartars, and is said to be very delicate and good, but when killed in a tame state, it is hard and unfit for food.

The wild ass, called Koulan by the Persians, is still common in many parts of Central Asia, from the 48° of North latitude to the confines of India. The Persians and Tartars hold its flesh in high esteem, and hunt it in preference to all other descriptions of game. Olearius assures us, that he saw no fewer than 32 wild asses slain in one day, by the Shah of Persia and his court, the bodies of which were sent to the royal kitchens at Ispahan; and we know from Martial, that the epicures of Rome held the flesh of the Onager, or wild ass, in the same estimation as we do venison.

Cum tener est *Onager*, solaque lalisio matre

Pascitur; hoc infans, sed breve nomen habet.

[Martial, xiii. 97.]

From a passage in Pliny (lib. viii., c. 44), it would appear, that the Onager inhabited Africa; and that the most delicate and best flavoured *lalisiones*, or fat foals, were brought from that continent to the Roman markets. Leo Africanus repeats the same story of wild asses being found in Africa, but no traveller has since met with them; and, as far as we at present know, the species is confined to Asia.

The quaggas (*Asinus Quagga*) are often hunted in Africa by the Dutch for their skins, of which they make large bags to hold their grain, and by the Hottentots and other natives, who are very fond of their flesh.

Lieutenant Moodie (*Ten Years in South Africa*) says, 'Being one morning at the house of a neighbouring farmer who had just shot one of these animals, I requested that he would have a piece of the flesh cooked for my breakfast. His 'frow' expressed some disgust at my proposal, but ordered a small bit to be grilled, with butter and pepper. I did not find it at all unpalatable, and certainly it was better than horse-flesh, to which I had been treated in the hospital at Bergen-op-Zoom in 1814, when lying wounded there, after the unfortunate failure of that well-planned attack.'

RUMINANTIA

The ruminants furnish, as is well known, the largest portion of our animal food, being consumed by man alike in civilized or unsettled countries. The domestic animals require little notice at our hands. There are, however, some whose flesh is eaten in different countries that are less familiar. Thus the bison and musk-ox of North America, the reindeer of Greenland and Northern Europe—the various antelopes, the gnu, the giraffe, and the camel of Africa, and the alpaca tribe of South America, supply much of the animal food of the people in the districts where they are common.

The flesh of the camel is dry and hard, but not unpalatable. Heliogabalus had camels' flesh and camels' feet served up at his banquets. In Barbary, the tongues are salted and smoked for exportation to Italy and other countries, and they form a very good dish. The flesh is little esteemed by the Tartars, but they use the hump cut into slices, which, dissolved in tea, serves the purpose of butter.

The flesh of the Axis deer (*Cervus axis*, or *Axis maculata*) is not much esteemed in Ceylon, having little fat upon it, and being very dry. The India samver, or musk deer, is eaten there.

The flesh of the great moose deer or elk, of North America, the carcase of which weighs 1,000 or 1,200 lbs., is as valuable for food as beef, but from its immense size, much of the flesh is usually left in the forest.

It is more relished by the Indians and persons resident in the fur countries, than that of any other animal, and bears a greater resemblance in its flavour to beef than to venison. It is said that the external fat is soft like that of a breast of mutton, and when put into a bladder is as fine as marrow.

The flesh of the caribboo, a smaller animal, rarely exceeding 400 lbs., is less palatable than moose venison. Nor is the flesh of the red or Virginian deer much better, although the venison dried is very good.

Venison is not 'meat' in the parlance of the backwoodsman; that term, as Sam Slick tells us, is reserved *par excellence* for pork; and he is frequently too indolent or too much occupied otherwise, to hunt, although deer tracks may be seen in every direction around the scene of his daily rail-splitting operations. He considers it cheaper to buy venison of the Indians, when there are any Indians in the locality. But venison has some solid value even in those parts, and if salted and smoked, would be entitled to a place among the articles of household thrift.

Of the Arctic quadrupeds, the reindeer (*Cervus tarandus*) is most valuable, its flesh being juicy, nutritious, and well-flavoured, and easy of digestion. They abound in Greenland, and are tolerably numerous in Melville Island.

In Sweden, roast reindeer steaks and game are dressed in a manner preferable to that which prevails with us. The flesh is first perforated, and little bits of lard inserted; and, after being baked in an oven, it is served in a quantity of white sauce.

The flesh of the young giraffe is said to be good eating. The Hottentots hunt the animal principally on account of its marrow, which, as a delicacy, they set a high value on.

The Hottentots have a curious mode of cooking their antelope venison, which renders it, however, exceedingly palatable. After stewing the meat in a very small quantity of water, they take it out of the pot and pound it between two stones until reduced to the consistency of pap, when they mix it with a considerable quantity of sheep's fat, and then stew it for a short time longer. This is an excellent way of preparing dry flesh of any kind.

'On one occasion' (says Lieut. Moodie), 'after I had taken out my share of this mess, the Hottentots added a larger quantity of fat to it to please their own palates; and one of them ate so heartily of the greasy mixture, that he became seriously unwell, but recovered by chewing dry roots of the sweet-scented flag (*Calamus aromaticus*). This plant is very much used by the Dutch for stomach complaints, and they generally cultivate some of it in wet places in their gardens.'

The eland of Africa (*Boselaphus Oreas*) is the largest of the antelope tribe, its size being indicated by its generic name. The bulls attain to the height of nineteen hands at the shoulder, and frequently exceed 1,000 lbs. in weight. It fattens readily on the most meagre herbage of the desert, and to the delicious, tender, juicy, and wholesome nature of its flesh every hunter will bear witness, who has regaled himself on the steaks broiled in the homely style of South African cookery, with some of the usual condiments or spices to give them an unnatural relish. The flesh has a peculiar sweetness, and is tender and fit for use the moment the animal is killed.

It is hunted with avidity, on account of the delicacy of its flesh, but is very rarely found within the limits of the Cape Colony, having been driven beyond the Orange River by the progress of colonization.

The hartebeest, an antelope of the size of the Scotch red deer, though now rather rare, is much prized by the African sportsman. It is also called caama by the Dutch farmers, and is a favourite object of pursuit with both natives and colonists. The flesh is rather dry, but of a fine grain, more nearly resembling the beef of the ox than that of any other antelope, except, perhaps, the so-called eland or elk of the colonists (*A. oreas*, Pallas), and it has a high game flavour which makes it universally esteemed.

The meat of the sassaby (*A. lunata*, Burchell), a rare species, is tender and well tasted. The flesh of the ourebi of Southern Africa (*A. scoparia*, Schreber), though dry and destitute of fat, is esteemed one of the best venisons of the country.

The flesh of the bosh-bok, or bush goat, as its colonial name implies (*A. sylvatica*, Sparrman), makes good venison, that of the breast being particularly esteemed. The flesh of the rheebok (*A. capreolus*, Lichstenstein) is dry and insipid, and relished less than that of any other of the numerous Cape antelopes. The bush antelope (*A. silvicultrix*, Afzelius) affords excellent venison, and is much sought after on that account. The flesh of the ahu (*A. subgutturosa*, Guldenstaedt) is excellent, and of an agreeable taste. That of the gnu of South Africa is in great repute both among the natives and Dutch settlers. Though the meat has a wildish flavour, it is more juicy than that of most of the antelope tribe, and very much like beef.

The flesh of the alpaca and guanaco is sold in the public shambles of Peru, Chili, &c.

Sheep's milk is a common beverage in Toorkistan, where the sheep are milked regularly three times a day. Goats are very scarce; cows not to be seen; but the sheep's milk affords nourishment in various forms, of which the most common is a kind of sour cheese, being little better than curdled milk and salt.

If we think ox tails a delicacy, Australians (as we have seen) like kangaroo tails, and the Cape colonists have fat sheep's tails requiring a barrow or a cart on which to support them. The broad fat tail, which often composes one-third of the weight of the animal, is entirely composed of a substance betwixt marrow and fat, which serves very often for culinary purposes instead of butter; and being cut into small pieces, makes an ingredient in various dishes.

The dried flesh of the argali, or wild sheep, is in Kamtschatka an article of commerce.

The domestic goat's flesh is not in much favour anywhere, although that of a young kid, three or four months old, is very tender and delicate. Some of the goats are eaten in the Cape Colony, but the flesh is generally lean and tough. The Malabar goat is a delicate animal, that browzes on the rocks. It is more sought after than any game in Ceylon, for, contrary to the general nature of the goat, its flesh is tender and excellent when broiled.

Bison beef, especially that of the female, is rather coarser grained than that of the domestic ox, but is considered by hunters and travellers as superior in tenderness and flavour. The hump, which is highly celebrated for its richness and delicacy, is said, when properly cooked, to resemble marrow. The flesh of the buffalo, as it is misnamed, is the principal, sometimes the only, food of numerous tribes of North American Indians. It is eaten fresh on the prairies during the hunt, and dried in their winter villages.

The musk-ox (*Ovibos moschatus*) is of much importance from its size and palatable rich meat. It has occasionally furnished a rich meal to arctic explorers. When they are fat, the flesh is well flavoured, but smells strongly of musk.

CETACEA

The flesh of the manatus is white and delicate, and tastes like young pork eaten fresh or salted, while the fat forms excellent lard. The cured flesh keeps long without corruption, and it will continue good several weeks, even in the hot climate of which it is a native, when other meat would not resist putrefaction for as many days. The fibres and the lean part of the flesh are like beef, but more red; it takes a very long time boiling. The fat of the young one is like pork, and can scarcely be distinguished from it, while the lean eats like veal. The fat, which lies between the entrails and skin has a pleasant smell, and tastes like the oil of sweet almonds. It makes an admirable substitute for butter, and does not turn rancid in the sun. The fat of the tail is of a firmer consistence, and when boiled is more delicate than the other.

Manatees, or sea calves, are found in certain parts of British Honduras in great numbers. They are, according to my friend, Chief Justice Temple, frequently caught and brought to the market of Belize, where they are snapped up with the greatest avidity. He states the flesh to be white and delicate, something between pork and veal. The tail, which is very fat, is most esteemed. This caudal luxury is generally soused or pickled. I do not, myself, fancy the flesh of this brute, for it is so inhumanly human— it reminds one so much of a mermaid, or of one of the fifty daughters of Nereus, that to eat it seems to me to be an approximation to cannibalism. It appears horrible to chew and swallow the flesh of an animal which holds its young (it has never more than one at a litter) to its breast, which is formed exactly like that of a woman, with paws resembling human hands. But these notions would be considered highly fantastic by those who masticate a monkey with the greatest relish, partake with gusto of rattlesnake soup, and voraciously devour an alligator stew. The manatus is commonly found in shallow water, at the mouths of rivers, where it feeds upon the marine herbage which there grows in great luxuriance. It has no teeth, but two thick, smooth, hard, unserrated bones run from one side of the mouth to the other. I am inclined to think that these bones might be used as a substitute for ivory.[11]

Mr. P. H. Gosse, in his interesting little manual on the *Natural History of the Mammalia*, remarks:—

'From personal experience we can confirm Hernandez's statement of the excellence of the flesh of the manatee; he truly compares it to well fatted pork, of pleasant flavour. The pursuit of it, on this account, has rendered it scarce in many localities, where it was formerly numerous; in the vicinity of Cayenne, it was at one time so common, that a large boat might be filled with them in a day, and the flesh was sold at 3*d*. per pound. About the middle of the last century it fetched, at Port Royal in Jamaica, 15*d*. currency per pound.'

The tongue of the sea-lion (*Phoca jubata*) is very good eating, and some seamen prefer it to that of an ox or calf. Thus Dr. Pernetty (*Voyage to the Falkland Islands*) says,—'For a trial we cut off the tip of the tongue hanging out of the mouth of one of these lions which was just killed. About sixteen or eighteen of us ate each a pretty large piece, and we all thought it so good that we regretted we could not eat more of it.

'It is said that their flesh is not absolutely disagreeable. I have not tasted it, but the oil which is extracted from their grease is of great use. This oil is extracted in two ways; either by cutting the fat in pieces and melting it in large caldrons upon the fire, or by cutting it in the same manner upon hurdles or pieces of board, and exposing them to the sun, or only to the air. This grease dissolves of itself and runs into vessels placed underneath to receive it. Some of our seamen pretended that this last sort of oil, when it is fresh, is very good for kitchen uses. It is preferred to that of the whale; is always clear, and leaves no sediment.'

Walrus meat is strong, coarse, and of a game-like flavour. Seal flesh is exceedingly oily, and not very palatable; but by practice, residents in the northern regions learn to relish both exceedingly.

The large tongue, the heart, and liver of the walrus (*Trichecus rosmarus*), are often eaten by whalers for want of better fresh provisions, and are passably good.

Commodore Anson's party killed many sea-lions for food, using, particularly, the hearts and tongues, which they thought excellent eating, and preferable even to those of bullocks. The flesh of the female sea-bear (*Phoca ursina*, Lin.) they found very delicate, having the taste of lamb; while that of the cub could scarcely be distinguished from roasted pig.

Sir Edward Parry was once asked, at a dinner where Lord Erskine was present, what he and his crew had lived upon when they were frozen in in the Polar Seas. Parry said they lived upon seals. 'A very good living, too,' exclaimed the Chancellor, 'if you keep them long enough.'

One of the ordinary acts of hospitality and civility on the part of the Esquimaux ladies, is to take a bird, or piece of seal-flesh, chew it up very nicely, and hand it to the visitor, who is expected to be overcome with gratitude, and finish the operation of chewing and digesting the delicate morsel.

The carcase and blubber of the whale at Bahia, in Brazil, are reduced to food by the poor.

To most of the rude littoral tribes of Northern Asia and America, the whale and seal furnish, not only food and clothing, but many other useful materials. The Esquimaux will eat the raw flesh of the whale with the same apparent relish, when newly killed, or after it has been buried in the ground for several months.

The whales on the coasts of Japan not only afford oil in great abundance, but their flesh, which is there considered very wholesome and nutritious, is largely consumed. No part of them, indeed, is thrown away; all is made available to some useful purpose or another. The skin, which is generally black, the flesh, which is red and looks like coarse beef, the intestines and all the inward parts, besides the fat or blubber, which is boiled into oil, and the bone, which is converted into innumerable uses, — all is made available to purposes of profit.

Both sperm and black whales abound on the coast of Western Australia. Sometimes a dead whale is thrown on the shore, and affords luxurious living to the natives. They do not, however, eat the shark.

The natives of New Zealand, when short of food, will not scruple to eat the flesh of the whale, when caught in their vicinity.

The deep has many food dainties as well as the land, as we shall shortly have to notice, and among these is the porpoise, which the reader may probably have seen dashing up our rivers, or, during a long voyage, disporting itself amid the briny waves, and rolling gracefully near the sides of the ship. This sea pig sometimes serves for a feast. When caught, it is cut into steaks, dried, and put into the ship's coppers, with a *quantum suf.* of spices and condiments which nearly overpower the oily taste. The steaks turn blackish on being exposed to the air, but this is 'a matter of nothing' to those whose daily diet is usually limited to hard biscuits and salt junk. Landsmen may question the niceness of the palate which partakes of this dainty, but the old adage holds true everywhere, 'de gustibus non disputandum.' There is no disputing about tastes.

According to ancient records, salted porpoises were formerly used for food in this country.

In the olden times, when glass windows were considered an effeminate luxury, and rushes supplied the place of carpets, the flesh of the porpoise constituted one of the standard delicacies of a public feast. It was occasionally served up at the tables of the old English nobility as a sumptuous article of food, and eaten with a sauce composed of sugar, vinegar, and crumbs of fine bread. But tastes have altered, and even sailors will scarcely touch the flesh now. M. de Bouganville, in his voyage to the Falkland Islands, writes—'We had some of the porpoise served up at dinner the day it was taken, which several others at the table besides myself thought by no means so ill-tasted as it is generally said to be.'

Porpoises are rather dangerous enemies to the shoals of fish. A porpoise, before taking in a barrel of herrings for its dinner, will often whet its appetite with a cod's head and shoulders, leaving the tail part for some poor fisherman.

BIRDS

Leaving now our passing survey of the food supplies derived from animals, we come next to birds, and, in the first order, we do not find that any are eaten, at least, as far as my knowledge extends; indeed, these carnivorous birds, from their habits and their food, would not be very tempting. This, however, as we have seen in the case of predatory animals, is no safe criterion to judge from. Probably, the man who would feast on the flesh of a lion, or a polecat, would have a stomach strong enough to digest slices of a John Crow carrion vulture, an eagle, or a hawk.

In the order of Insessores, or perching birds, I may mention first—

The becafico, or fig-eater (*Sylvia hortensis*), a bird about the size of a linnet, which is highly prized by the Italians for the delicacy of its flesh, particularly in autumn, when it is in excellent condition for the table.

There is a curious food product obtained, (not exactly, however, from the bird,) which is in high repute in China; and that is the edible nest of a species of swallow extensively obtained in some of the islands of the Eastern Archipelago.

These nests are attached to the sides of rocks like those of our martin and swallow to walls, and look like so many watch-pockets. The eggs are white, with a slight pinkish tinge, and are generally two in number. The nests are either white, red, or black, and the natives maintain that these are built by three distinct species, with a white, red, and black breast, but this is erroneous. The Malays assert frequently, moreover, that the nests are formed from the bodies of certain sea snakes, but the food is, without doubt, insects. The subjoined accounts furnish the most detailed information known respecting the collection and trade in these birdsnests.

The following description of the birdsnests' rocks, in the district of Karang Bollong, on the southerly sea-coast of Java, is given in the first volume of the *Journal of the Indian Archipelago*, published at Singapore.

'The gathering of these nests takes place three times a year—in the end of April, the middle of August, and in December. The yearly produce is commonly between 50 and 60 piculs of 133⅓ lbs. The business of collection is opened with great ceremony by the natives. By the assistance of ladders and stages made of rattan, the collectors descend the rocks and cliffs, provided with the requisite bags to contain the nests, which are taken from the wall by the hand, and those which are on the roof by an iron hook made fast to a long bamboo. The birds feed upon different kinds of bloodless insects, hovering above the stagnant waters, for which their wide open beak is very useful. They form their nests by vomiting the strongest and best fragments of the food which they have eaten. The nests are weighed and packed in hampers (of 25 catties each), and labelled with the net weight, mark of the overseer, &c., and then further preserved and secured with strips of bark, leaves, and matting.

'The edible birdsnests, which owe their celebrity only to the whimsical luxury of the Chinese, are brought principally from Java and Sumatra, though they are found on most of the rocky islets of the Indian Archipelago. The nest is the habitation of a small swallow, named (from the circumstance of having an edible house) *Hirundo esculenta*. They are composed of a mucilaginous substance, but as yet they have never been analyzed with sufficient accuracy to show the constituents. Externally, they resemble ill-concocted, fibrous isinglass, and are of a white colour, inclining to red. Their thickness is little more than that of a silver spoon, and the weight from a quarter to half an ounce. When dry they are brittle and wrinkled; the size is nearly that of a goose's egg. Those that are dry, white, and clean, are the most valuable. They are packed in bundles, with split rattans run through them to preserve the shape. Those procured after the young are fledged, are not saleable in China. The quality of the nest varies according to the situation and extent of the caves, and the time at which they are taken. If procured before the young are fledged, the nests are of the best kind; if they contain eggs only, they are still valuable; but if the young are in the nests, or have left them, the whole are then nearly worthless, being dark-coloured, streaked with blood, and intermixed with feathers and dirt. These nests are procurable twice every year; the best are found in deep, damp caves, which, if not injured, will continue to produce indefinitely. It was once thought that the caves near the sea-coast were the most productive; but some of the most profitable yet found are situated 50 miles in the interior. This fact seems to be against the opinion that the nests are composed of the spawn of fish, or of *bêche-de-mer*. The method of procuring these nests is not unattended with danger. Some of the caves are so precipitous, that no one but those accustomed to the employment from their youth can obtain the nests, being only approachable by a perpendicular descent of many hundred feet, by ladders of bamboo and rattan, over a sea rolling violently against the rocks. When the mouth of the cave is attained, the perilous task of taking the nests must often be performed by torchlight, by penetrating into recesses of the rock; where the slightest slip would be instantly fatal to the adventurers, who see nothing below them but the turbulent surf, making its way into the chasms of the rock—such is the price paid to gratify luxury. After the nests are obtained, they are separated from feathers and dirt, are carefully dried and packed, and are then fit for the market. The Chinese, who are the only people that purchase them for their own use, bring them in junks to this market, where they command extravagant prices; the best, or *white* kind, often being worth four thousand dollars per picul (a Chinese weight, equal to 133⅓ lbs. avoirdupois), which is nearly twice their weight in silver. The middling kind is worth from twelve to eighteen hundred, and the worst, or those procured after fledging, one hundred and fifty to two hundred dollars per picul. The majority of the best kind are sent to Pekin, for the use of the court. It appears, therefore, that this curious dish is only an article of expensive luxury amongst the Chinese; the Japanese do not use it at all, and how the former people acquired the habit of indulging in it, is only less singular than their persevering in it. They consider the edible birdsnest as a great stimulant, tonic, and aphrodisiac, but its best quality, perhaps, is its being perfectly harmless. The labour bestowed to render it fit for the table is enormous; every feather, stick, or impurity of any kind is carefully removed; and then, after undergoing many washings and preparations, it is made into a soft, delicious jelly. The sale of birdsnests is a monopoly with all the governments in whose dominions they are found. About two hundred and fifty thousand piculs, of the value of one million four hundred thousand dollars, are annually brought to Canton. These come from the islands of Java, Sumatra, Macassar, and those of the Sooloo group. Java alone sends about thirty thousand pounds, mostly of the first quality, estimated at seventy thousand dollars.'[12]

Mr. J. H. Moor, in his notices of the *Indian Archipelago*, published at Singapore some years ago, states, that 'one of the principal and most valuable articles of exportation is the edible birdsnests, white and black. These are found in much greater abundance in and about the Coti, more than any other part of Borneo, or from what we at present know on the subject, all parts put together. On the western coast they are scarcely known to exist; about Banjermassin and Bagottan there are none; at Bataliching and Passier they are found in considerable quantities. At Browe there is abundance of the black kind of a very superior quality, but little of the white. At Seboo, and all the parts to the north of Borneo, we know there is none, as I have seen many letters from different Rajahs of those countries averring the fact, and begging the Sultan of Coti to exchange his edible nests for their most valuable commodities, and at his own price. Nor ought this to create surprise, when we consider, not only the large consumption of this article by the Cambojans, who almost exclusively inhabit some of the largest Sooloo Islands, and the northern parts of Borneo, but the amazing demand on the whole coast of Cambodia, particularly of Cochin China, the principal inhabitants of which countries are as partial to this luxury as their more northern neighbours—the Chinese. There are in Coti and adjacent Dyak countries perhaps eighty known places, or what the natives term holes, which produce the white nests. I have seen the names of forty-three. There can, however, be no doubt there are many more likewise known to the Dyaks, who keep the knowledge to themselves, lest the Bugis should dispossess them, which they know from experience is invariably the case.

'According to the accounts of the Sultan, rendered by Saib Abdulla, the bandarree in 1834 yielded 134 piculs. The usual price in money to the Coti traders is 23 reals per catty from the Dyaks, and 25 in barter. The black nests may be procured in great abundance. The best kinds come from Cinculeram and Baley Papang. The latter mountain alone yields 230 piculs (of 113⅓ lbs.). Cinculeram gives nearly as much. There are several other parts of Coti which produce them, besides the quantity brought down by the Dyaks. Last year, 130 piculs paid duty to the Sultan; these left the large Coti river. Those from Cinculeram and Bongan were taken to Browe and Seboo. The bandarree's book averages the annual weight of those collected in the lower part of Coti at 820 piculs (about 1,025 cwts.)

'The Pangeran Sierpa and the Sultan say they could collect 2,700 piculs of black nests, if the bandarree and capella-campong would behave honestly. The Sultan, however, seldom gets any account of what is sent to Browe, Seboo, and the Sooloo Islands, the quality of which is far superior to any sent to European ports.'

The exports of birdsnests from Java, between 1823 and 1832, averaged about 250 piculs a year; in 1832, 322 piculs; but of late years the exports have not averaged half that amount; and in 1853 and 1854 there were only about 35 or 40 piculs shipped.

In the third order, Scansores, there are very few edible birds.

In the mountain of Tumeriquiri, in the government of Cumana, is the immense cavern of Guacharo, famous among the Indians. It serves as a habitation for millions of nocturnal birds (*Steatornis caripensis*, a new species of the *Caprimulgis*, of Linnæus), whose fat yields the oil of Guacharo.

Once a year, near midsummer, this cavern is entered by the Indians. Armed with poles, they ransack the greater part of the nests, while the old birds hover over the heads of the robbers as if to defend their brood, uttering horrible cries. The young which fall down are opened on the spot. The peritoneum is found loaded with fat, and a layer of the same substance reaches from the abdomen to the vent, forming a kind of cushion between the hind legs. Humboldt remarks that this quantity of fat in frugivorous animals, not exposed to the light, and exerting but little muscular motion, brings to mind what has been long observed in the fattening of geese and oxen. 'It is well known,' he adds, 'how favourable darkness and repose are to this process.'

At the period above mentioned, which is generally known at Carissa by the designation of 'the oil harvest,' huts are built by the Indians, with palm leaves, near the entrance and even in the very porch of the cavern. There the fat of the young birds just killed is melted in clay pots, over a brushwood fire, and this fat is named butter or oil of the Guacharo. It is half liquid, transparent, inodorous, and so pure that it will keep above a year without turning rancid.[13]

There is a curious bird met with in caves in the West India Islands—as at Dominica, and the gulf of Paria, the diablotin or goat-sucker, which, if eaten when taken from the nest, is pronounced by epicures unrivalled; and the flesh is also considered a delicacy when salted.

It has received its popular cognomen from its ugliness, but I have not been able to trace its scientific name.

The bird is nearly the size of a duck, and web-footed, with a big round head and crooked bill like a hawk, and large full eyes like an owl; the head, part of the neck, and chief feathers of the wing and tail, are black, while the other parts of its body are covered with a fine milk-white down; the whole appearance being very singular. The diablotin only leaves its haunts at night time, flying with hideous screams like the owl, which it resembles in its dislike to day-light. The nests are made in holes in the mountains. When the palms are in fruit, the bird becomes one lump of fat. The hideous appearance of the bird and the strong scent once got over, it is said to be a delicious morsel.

We have our delicate tit-bits in spitted larks, and as many as four thousand dozen have been known to be taken in the neighbourhood of Dunstable between September and February. What the number sold in our metropolitan markets is annually, it is impossible to say. But larks are taken in much larger numbers in Germany, where there is an excise upon them, which has yielded as much as £1,000 a year in Leipsic—the larks of which place are famous all over Germany as being of a most delicate flavour.

In the Italian markets, besides carrion crows, strings of thrushes, larks, and even robin redbreasts are sold.

Young rooks, when skinned and made into pies are much esteemed by some persons, but they are very coarse eating.

One of the most delicious birds is the rice-bunting of South Carolina (*Dolichonyx oryzivorus*).

The rice-bunting migrates over the continent of America, from Labrador to Mexico, and over the great Antilles, appearing in the southern extremity of the United States about the end of March. Towards the middle and close of August, they enter New York, and Pennsylvania on their way to the south. There, along the shores of the large rivers lined with floating fields of wild rice, they find abundant subsistence, grow fat, and their flesh becomes little inferior in flavour to that of the European ortolan, on which account the reed, or rice birds, as they are then called, are shot in great numbers. When the cool nights in October commence, they move still farther south, till they reach the islands of Jamaica and Cuba in prodigious numbers to feed on the seeds of the guinea grass. Epicures compare the plump and juicy flesh of this delicacy to the ortolan.

On the shores of the Mediterranean there are feathered delicacies in the shape of the quail and the ortolan. Thousands of ortolans used to be shipped from the island of Cyprus, packed in casks of 300 or 400, prepared with spice and vinegar. When specially fattened for the table, they are regarded as most delicious; but, being merely lumps of fat, are so rich as soon to satiate the appetite of even a professed gourmand. In the West India Islands and the Southern States of America, the rice-bunting, as we have seen, takes its place, and is, occasionally, found in prodigious numbers, and greatly esteemed.

The bluish flesh of the toucan, notwithstanding its enormous and unsightly beak, is a wholesome and delicate meat; and there are no birds that give the Trinidad epicure a more delicious morsel. It is one of the most omnivorous of birds, and its powers of digestion and impunity to poisons are remarkable.

Parrot pie is said to be pretty good; at least, it may be so when other animal food is scarce.

Among the gallinaceous fowls, large numbers contribute to the food delicacies of man. Some, like the turkey, peacock, &c., of considerable size; others, as the pigeon tribe, form smaller tit-bits.

The game birds, the pheasant, partridge, grouse, &c., and the quail, guinea fowl, and jungle fowl, are bagged whenever they can be obtained by the sportsman.

The peacock enkakyll 'was one of the famous dishes at the costly royal banquets of old, and the receipt for dressing it is thus given:—

'Take and flay off the skin with the feathers, tail, and the neck and head thereon; then take the skin and all the feathers and lay it on the table abroad, and strew thereon ground cumin; then take the peacock and roast him, and baste him with raw yolks of eggs; and when he is roasted, take him off and let him cool awhile, then take him and sew him in his skin, and gild his comb, and so serve him forth with the last course.'

As far as my own experience goes, with all the basting and sauces, the peacock is, at best, a dry and tough eating bird.

The domestic fowls and the tame turkey require no notice here, there being nothing curious about them, however delicate eating they may be when properly fattened and brought to table; but there is a species of wild turkey found in New Granada, weighing from 12 to 16 lbs., and called the iowanen, which is described by Mr. W. Purdie of Trinidad as the most delicate article of food he ever tasted.

Dear as fowls, ducks, and eggs comparatively are, they meet, as every one knows, with a ready sale. When we find our imports of eggs, chiefly from France, amount to about 130,000,000 a year, besides our nominal 'new laid,' or home produce, — when we learn that the foreign poultry we receive (mixed up with not a few Ostend rabbits) is valued at 39,000*l*., and that Ireland supplies us with about 150,000,000 of eggs, we begin to perceive that fowls, ducks, geese, and turkeys must be a profitable investment to some persons, and the capital of about 4,000,000*l*. we lay out on these various products serves to gladden the heart of many a poultry breeder.

There are sent to market about nine or ten million head of poultry in a year to supply the whole population of the United Kingdom, shipping and all, which is not more than one-third of a fowl to each person annually. Now, were every one to have a fowl as part food once a month, it would require 330,000,000 more fowls or other poultry than are at present sold.

I copy the following from what I believe to be the first fixed tariff of provisions, in the City of London, about the second year of Edward I. (1272.) The people had at that time great cause to complain of the exorbitant prices demanded of them for provisions, by hucksters and dealers, and a fixed price was found necessary by the Mayor: —

The best hen	three half-pence
Pullet	three half-pence
Capon	two pence
Goose	five pence
Wild goose	four pence

Pigeons, three for	one penny
Mallard, three for	a half-penny
Plover	one penny
Partridge	three half-pence
Larks, per dozen	one penny half-penny
Pheasant	four pence
Heron	six pence
Swan	three shillings
Crane	three shillings, and by
a subsequent Act	one shilling
The best peacock	one penny
The best coney, with skin	four pence
Ditto, without skin	three pence
The best hare, with skin	three pence half-penny
The best lamb, from Christmas to Lent	six pence
At other times of the year	four pence.

In the time of Edward II., 1313, eggs were 20 a penny, and pigeons sold at three for a penny.

It is curious, even to notice the London prices of poultry, two or three centuries ago, although regard must of course be had to the difference in the value of money now and then.

Sir James Hawes, during his mayoralty, in the year 1575, fixed the following prices within the City of London:—

	s.	d.
Blackbirds, per dozen	0	10
The best capon, large and fat	1	8
Ditto, second best, being fat	1	4
The best green goose, until Whitsuntide	0	8
Ditto ditto, after Whitsuntide	0	10
Ditto, in winter, being fat	1	2
Pigeons, per dozen	1	4
Chickens, the largest, each	0	4
Ditto, second sort	0	3

	s.	d.
The best coney rabbit, from and after the summer	0	5
Eggs, four	0	1
Cygnets, fat until Allhalloweentide, each	6	0
Ditto, from then to Shrovetide	7	0
Cranes, the best, each	6	0
The best heron, pheasant, shoveller (duck), and bittern, each	2	6
Turkey-cock, fat and large	3	0
Turkey chicken, fat and large	1	4
Woodcocks, each	0	6
Snipes, each	0	2½
Hens, being fat and the best, each	0	9
Ditto, second sort	0	7
Green plovers, fat	0	4
The best wild mallard	0	6
Teals, each	0	3

At a feast given at Ely House, by the serjeants-at-law, November, 1531, (23rd of Henry VIII.) on the occasion of making eleven new serjeants, open house was kept for five successive days. On the fourth day, King Henry, his Queen, the Foreign Ambassadors, the Judges, and Lord Mayor and Aldermen, were feasted, as also numerous guests, knights, and gentlemen. Stow particularizes the following articles and prices, in order to furnish *data* for computing the relative value of money at different periods:—

	s.	d.
Great beeves, from the shambles (twenty-four) each	26	8
One carcase of an ox	24	0
Fat muttons (one hundred), each	2	10
Great veals (fifty-one), each	4	8
Porks (thirty-four), each	3	8
Pigs (ninety-one), each	0	6
Capons of Greece (of one poulterer, for they had three) ten dozen, each capon	1	8

Capons of Kent (nine dozen and six), each	1	0
Capons, coarse (nineteen dozen), each	1	0
Cocks of grouse (seven dozen and nine), each cock	0	8
Cocks, coarse (fourteen dozen and eight)	0	3
Pullets, the best, each	0	2½
Other pullets, each	0	2
Pigeons (thirty-seven dozen), at per dozen	0	10
Swans (twenty-four dozen)	no price	
Larks (340 dozen), per dozen	0	6

The consumption of liquids, pastry, and *trifles*, can easily be guessed at.

Here is an ancient receipt for making a Christmas game pie, found in the books of the Salter's Company, which is presumed to have often furnished an annual treat to the members in the olden times; and when made after this receipt, by the Company's cook in modern days, has been found to be excellent.

'For to make a mooste choyce paaste of Gamys to be etin at ye Feste of Chrystemasse.

'(17th Richard II., A.D. 1394.)

'Take Fesaunt, Haare, and Chykenne, or Capounne, of eche oone; wᵗ. ij. Partruchis, ij. Pygeounes, and ij. Conynggys; and smyte hem on peces and pyke clene awaye p'fro (*therefrom*) alle pᵉ (*the*) boonys pᵗ (*that*) ye maye, and p'wt (*therewith*) do hem y̲nto a Foyle (*a shield or case*) of gode paste, made craftily ynne pᵉ lykenes of a byrde's bodye, wᵗ pᵉ lyuours and hertys, ij. kydneis of shepe and farcys (*seasonings or forced meats*) and eyren (*eggs*) made ynto balles. Caste p'to (*thereto*) poudre of pepyr, salte, spyce, eysell,[14] and funges (*mushrooms*) pykled; and panne (*then*) take pᵉ boonys and let hem seethe ynne a pot to make a gode brothe p' for (*for it*) and do yᵗ ynto pᵉ foyle of paste and close hit uppe faste, and bake yᵗ wel, and so s'ue (*serve*) yᵗ forthe: wt pᵉ hede of oone of pᵉ byrdes, stucke at pᵉ oone ende of pᵉ foyle, and a grete tayle at pᵉ op' and dyvers of hys longe fedyrs sette ynne connynglye alle aboute hym.'

Marrow bones seem to have been in favour at an early date. 2,000 marrow bones were among the requisites for the Goldsmiths' Company's feast, on St. Dunstan's day, 1449.

In the reign of Edward VI., 1548, a time of plague and scarcity, the king thought it prudent to fix the price of cattle, &c., sold in the several seasons of the year:—

	£	s.	d.
The best fat ox, from Midsummer to Michaelmas, at	2	5	0
One of inferior sort	1	8	0
The best fat ox, from Hallowmas to Christmas	2	6	8
One of inferior sort	1	19	8
The best fat ox, from Christmas to Shrovetide	2	8	4
One of inferior sort	2	6	8
The best fat wether, from shearing time to Michaelmas	0	4	0
One of ditto, shorn	0	3	0
The best fat ewe	0	2	6
One ditto, *shorn*	0	2	0
The best fat wether, from Michaelmas to Shrovetide	0	4	4
One ditto, *shorn*	0	3	0
Essex barrelled butter, per pound	0	0	0¾
All sorts of other barrelled butter, per pound	0	0	0½
Essex cheese, per pound	0	0	0¾
All other sorts	0	0	0½

We are not quite such prodigious devourers of eggs as our French neighbours, having a greater amount of meat or solid animal food to fall back upon, and fewer fast days. Another reason is, that we cannot, like the French, get them so fresh and cheap; but as an alimentary substance, eggs are always in demand at a ratio proportionate to the prices at which they can be obtained. In Paris the consumption of eggs is at least 175 per annum to every head of the population; in the departments it is more than double that amount; eggs entering into almost every article of food, and butchers' meat being scarce and dear. If we only use, in London, half the number of eggs the Parisians do, there must be a sale of about 173 millions a year; and the consumption throughout the kingdom would be fully 2,000 millions. Although smaller in size, and not equal to a new-laid egg, the French eggs arrive in pretty good condition, and, if sold off quickly, are well adapted for ordinary culinary purposes. Few are wasted, for even when not very fresh, they are sold for frying fish, and to the lower class of confectioners for pastry. Fried eggs, boiled eggs chopped up with salad, egg sauce for fish, &c., eggs for puddings, for omelets, and pancakes, all contribute to the sale. Omelets, sweet or flavoured with herbs, are much less patronized in this country than they are in France.

The sixty wholesale egg merchants and salesmen in the metropolis, whose itinerant carts are kept constantly occupied in distributing their brittle ware, might probably enlighten us as to the extent and increasing character of the trade, and the remunerative nature of the profits. Railways and steamers bring up large crates, and carefully packed boxes of eggs, for the ravenous maws of young and old, who fatten on this dainty and easily digested food. The various city markets dispose of two millions of fowls, one million of game birds, half a million of ducks, and about one hundred and fifty thousand turkeys, every year. But even if we doubled this supply, what would it be among the three million souls of the great metropolis requiring daily food.

Ireland and the continent contribute largely to our supply of poultry and eggs. Immense pens of poultry, purchased in the Irish market, are shipped by the steamers to Glasgow and Liverpool. Commerce owes much to the influence of steam, but agriculture is no less indebted to the same power. Taking everything into account, and examining all the advantages derived by cheap and rapid transit, the manufacturer of food is quite as much indebted to the steam-ship and the locomotive as the manufacturer of clothing.

There is no difficulty whatever in testing eggs; they are mostly examined by a candle. Another way to tell good eggs is to put them in a pail of water, and if they are good they will *lie on their sides*, always; if bad, they will stand on their small ends, the large ends always uppermost, unless they have been shaken considerably, when they will stand either end up. Therefore, a bad egg can be told by the way it rests in water—always end up, never on its side. Any egg that lies flat is good to eat, and can be depended upon.

An ordinary mode is to take them into a room moderately dark and hold them between the eye and a candle or lamp. If the egg be good—that is, if the albumen is still unaffected—the light will shine through with a reddish glow; while, if affected, it will be opaque, or dark.

In Fulton and Washington market, New York, a man may be seen testing eggs at almost any time of the year. He has a tallow candle placed under a counter or desk, and taking up the eggs, three in each hand, passes them rapidly before the candle, and deposits them in another box. His practised eye quickly perceives the least want of clearness in the eggs, and suspicious ones are re-examined and thrown away, or passed into a 'doubtful' box. The process is so rapid that eggs are inspected perfectly at the rate of 100 to 200 per minute, or as fast as they can be shifted from one box to another, six at a time.

The preservation of eggs for use on ship board has always occupied a large share of attention. They have been usually smeared with oil or grease, and packed in bran or sawdust. A plan recommended by M. Appert for preserving eggs is to put them in a jar with bran, to prevent their breaking; cork and hermetically seal the jar; and put it into a vessel of water, heated to 200 degrees Fahrenheit, or 12 degrees below boiling. The vessel with water being taken from the fire, the water must cool till the finger may be borne in it; then remove the jar. The eggs may then be taken out, and will keep for six months.

Salted ducks' eggs are an article in great demand in some parts of the East, for transport by the trading junks. The Malays salt them as they do their meat; but the Chinese mix a red unctuous earth with the brine, which no doubt stops the pores of the shell, and preserves them better. They are put into this mixture at night, and taken out during the day to be dried in the sun, which is, in fact, a half roasting process in a tropical climate.

Pickled eggs, while they constitute a somewhat novel feature in the catalogue of condiments, are at the same time particularly relishing. When eggs are plentiful, farmers' wives, in some localities, take four to six dozen of such as are newly laid, and boil them hard; then, divesting them of the shells, they place them in large-mouthed earthen jars, and pour upon them scalded vinegar, well seasoned with whole pepper, allspice, ginger, and a few cloves of garlic. When this pickle is cold, the jars are closed, and the eggs are fit for use in a month afterwards. Eggs thus treated are held in high esteem by all the farm-house epicures.

Fowls' eggs, variously coloured, and having flowers and other matters upon them, formed by the colouring matter being picked off so as to expose the white shell of the egg, are a part of all the Malay entertainments in Borneo. The eggs eaten by the Dyaks are frequently nearly hatched when taken from the nest, as they enjoy them just as well as when fresh.

An article called 'condensed egg' is now sold in the shops. It consists of the whole substance of the fresh uncooked egg, very delicately and finely granulated by patent processes, after the watery particles, which the egg naturally contains, have been completely exhausted and withdrawn, without further alteration of its constituents. It contains all the nutritious properties of the egg in its natural state, and must be valuable to shipmasters, emigrants, and others. One ounce of it is said to be equal to three eggs.

The ancient Romans, though not great beef-eaters, were particular as to poultry. Dr. Daubeny, in his *Lectures on Roman Husbandry*, says—'The ancient Romans had large preserves, not only of poultry and pigeons, but even of thrushes and quails enclosed in pens which were called 'ornithones,' from which they could draw their supply for the table at pleasure. We are told, indeed, of two sorts of ornithones, the one merely aviaries stocked with birds for the amusement of the proprietor; the other kind, constructed with a view to profit, which were often of vast extent, to supply the demands of the Roman market for such articles of luxury. In the Sabine country particularly, we read of extensive pens, filled with birds for the latter purpose. For thrushes alone there were large rooms provided, each capable of holding several thousand birds. As they were put in to be fattened, the place had only just light enough to enable the birds to see their food, but there was a good supply of fresh water accessible. And I may remark that, whilst nothing is said by the Roman writers about the fattening of oxen and sheep, particular directions are given for fattening poultry and other birds—a strong additional argument of the little importance they attached to the larger animals as articles of food.'

The following may be enumerated as the sportsman's game in Jamaica:—

1. The pintado, or wild guinea fowl (*Numida Meleagris*), a bird now domesticated in our poultry-yards. In its wild state the flesh is considered by many persons to equal that of the pheasant.

2. The quail (*Perdix coturnix*).

3. Wild pigeons, namely, ring-tail, bald-pate, pea-dove, white-breast, white-wing, mountain-witch, ground dove, and red-legged partridge.

4. Snipe (*Scolopax gallinago*).

5. Wild duck, or mallard (*Anas boschas*).

6. Gray, or Gadwall duck (*Anas strepera*).

7. The common teal (*Anas crecca*), the flesh of which was so much prized by the Roman epicures, and is still in request for the table.

8. Widgeon (*Anas Penelope*).

9. Gray and ring plover (*Charadrius minor*, and *hiaticula*).

If we are out shooting in Canada we may easily add to our mess the ruffled grouse (*Tetrao umbellus*), although these, like many other birds, are partridges with the settlers—this variety being termed the birch partridge.

Another species, the spruce partridge of the colonists (*T. Canadensis*), is less palatable, for, unfortunately, it has a habit of feeding upon laurel leaves. But here is something to make amends—a fine Esquimaux curlew, as large as an English partridge, and a mud-sucker, *id est* snipe.

Let me note a Canadian receipt for cooking a partridge, which may be useful to sportsmen and travellers:—

'Expedition is the maxim of all sylvan cookery, and as plucking the feathers of a partridge would be too great a tax on the time and patience of the voyageur, the method most in vogue is to run your hunting knife round his throat and ancles and down his breast, when, taking a leg in each hand, and pressing your thumb into his back, you pop him out of his skin, as you would a pea from its pod. Then make a spread-eagle of him on a forked twig, the other extremity of which is thrust into the ground, and after wrapping a rasher of bacon around his neck and under his wings, as ladies wear a scarf, you incline him to the fire, turning the spit in the ground, and you will have a result such as Soyer might be proud of. When your other avocations will not afford time even for the skinning process, an alternative mode is to make a paste of ashes and water, and roll up your bird therein, with the feathers, and all the appurtenances thereof, and thrust the performance in the fire. In due time, on breaking the cemented shell (which is like a sugared almond), the feathers, skin, &c., adhere to it, and then you have the pure kernel of poultry within.'

The red-legged partridge is common in the Greek islands, on the continent of Asia, and in the southern countries of Europe. In some of the Cyclades, where the inhabitants are too poor to expend money on powder, they chase the birds on foot, till they are so wearied, as to be easily taken with the hand.

Of all the European birds, the quail (*Coturnix vulgaris*) is the most remarkable, on account of the vast numbers which congregate on the shores of the Mediterranean in the spring, coming from Asia Minor and Northern Africa, to avoid the excessive heat. For a few weeks in the month of April, when they first begin to arrive in Sicily, everybody is a sportsman. Arriving always in the night, although not a quail could be seen the evening before, the report of guns the next morning, in all directions, attests their number and the havoc that has begun upon them. Such prodigious numbers have appeared on the western coasts of the kingdom of Naples, that a hundred thousand have been taken in a day, within the space of four or five miles.

The flesh of the turtle dove is considered much superior to that of the wild pigeon.

The passenger pigeon (*Columba migratoria*) of America, is a very large and well flavoured variety, being 16 inches long, and 24 inches in the spread of its wings; its hue chiefly slate-colour. They migrate at certain seasons in millions, and feed on acorns and fresh mast. They travel in the morning and evening, and repose about mid-day in the forests. Their passage, whether in spring or autumn, lasts from 15 to 20 days, after which they are met with in the centre of the United States. The Indians often watch the roosting places of these birds, and knocking them on the head in the night, bring them away by thousands. They preserve the oil or fat, which they use instead of butter. There was formerly scarcely any little Indian village in the interior, where a hundred gallons of this oil might not at any time be purchased.

These pigeons spread over the whole of North America, abounding round Hudson's Bay, where they remain till December. They arrive in the fur countries in the latter end of May, and depart in October. They are met with as far south as the Gulf of Mexico, but do not extend their range westward of the Rocky Mountains. Stray passenger pigeons have been taken both in Norway and in Russia; and this bird has found a place in the British fauna, from a solitary bird having been shot in Westhall, Fifeshire, on the 31st December, 1825. Like other pigeons, this genus makes a slender platform nest of sticks and straws, but, unlike other pigeons, prolific as it is, it lays but one egg. The female builds the nest, the male bird fetches the materials. The time of incubation is 16 days, and the male relieves the female in sitting during that period. The immense number of these birds baffles all computation. Those eminent ornithologists, Wilson and Audubon, describe flocks seen by them to contain respectively from thousands of millions to upwards of a billion in each, the daily food required to sustain which would be at least 60,000 bushels; and the New York *Evening Post* informs us that, on one day, seven tons of these pigeons were brought into the New York market by the Erie railroad.

In their breeding places, herds of hogs are fed on the young pigeons or 'squabs,' which are also melted down by the settlers, as a substitute for butter or lard. The felling a single tree often produces 200 squabs, nearly as large as the old ones, and almost one mass of fat. When the flocks of full grown pigeons enter a district, clap-nets and guns are in great requisition. Pennant, in his *Arctic Zoology*, says, Sir William Johnstone told him, that at one shot, he brought down with a blunderbuss above a hundred and twenty pigeons. Wagon loads of them are poured into the towns, and sold as cheap as a half-penny up to two-pence the dozen. The flesh tastes like the common wild blue pigeon, but is, if anything, better flavoured. Why (it has been asked) could not this large pigeon, whose migratory habits are principally caused by search for food, be introduced into this country as a tame variety, or by crossing with our native breeds enlarge the size; or, in the same way as fresh mutton was sent from Australia, be sent in casks potted in their own fat, to supply us with cheap pigeon pies? And the same with a cross with the large Texan rabbit, or the wild American turkey, the latter being far superior in size and appearance to its degenerate descendant, the tame turkey, sometimes as much as four feet in length, and five feet from wing to wing? The canvas-back ducks of America are there boasted of exceedingly as a delicacy, yet, although a great variety of useless water-fowl has been introduced merely as an ornament to the ponds and streams of our gentry, no attempt has been made to bring this kind to our farm-yards and tables; and even if it was found impossible to tame the pure breed, a cross with our own might be effected. In the capercailzie, or *cock of the wood*, a bird of the grouse species, but nearly as large as a turkey, once indigenous to Scotland, but now only found in the north of Europe, and in the *bustard*, the largest European land-bird, the cock weighing from 25 to 27 lbs., we have examples of two fowls well worth the trial of domesticating by the amateur or intelligent agriculturist, a trial which, if successful, would probably repay quite as well as competition about the colour of a feather, or the shortness of a tail, and in time would be the means of affording a constant, certain, and moderately-priced supply, which is never the case while animals remain in a wild or half-wild state.

Although the forests of New Zealand are not thickly inhabited by the feathered tribes, there are many birds to be met with. Among others are the following, which are excellent eating.—The wild pigeon, which is very large and common; the parrot or ka-ka; and the *tui* or mocking bird, which is about the size of the English black-bird, and of the same colour, but with two bunches of white feathers under the neck—his notes are few, but very melodious, resembling the tinkling of small bells, which harmonize together as they are delivered. The bronze-winged pigeon of Australia is most delicate eating. It abounds in summer, when the acacia seeds are ripe.

GRALLATORES

From the order of grallatores, waders or stilt-birds, we find many which yield choice dainties, whether it be the ostrich or emu for their eggs, the bustard and bittern, the flamingo for its tongue, the plover, dotterel, curlew, snipe, woodcock, rail, &c., for the table.

An ostrich egg is considered as equal in its contents to 24 of the domestic hen. When taken fresh from the nest, they are very palatable, and are wholesome, though somewhat heavy food. The best mode of cooking them is that practised by the Hottentots, who place one end of the egg in the hot ashes, and making a small orifice at the other, keep stirring the contents with a stick till they are sufficiently roasted; and thus, with a seasoning of salt and pepper, you have a very nice omelet. The nest sometimes contains as many as 24 eggs, and the difficulty the sportsman has is how to carry away his spoil. The usual plan is to denude himself of his upper or lower garments, and, tying up the orifices of leg-holes or arm-holes, to make an impromptu sack, in which he can bear away his prize. If he leaves them, he will be sure to find on his return that the ostrich has broken the eggs, because they have been disturbed.

The eggs of the emu of South America are large, and, although the food which they afford is coarse, it is not unpalatable.

The emu, or New Holland cassowary, is becoming rarer as settlements advance. The same remark applies also to the kangaroo and other animals against whom a war of extermination seems to have been declared.

The emu is easily domesticated when taken young, and becomes very familiar with, and attached to, the dogs, which generally leads to the death of a tame one. A full-grown one, when erect, stands seven feet high. The natives creep on them and spear them. The eggs are of a tea green colour, with a watered appearance on the surface. There is a singularity in the growth of the feathers—two of them spring from one quill. The bird is principally valued for its oil. The skin of a full-grown bird produces six or seven quarts of oil, clear, and of a beautiful bright yellow colour. The method of extracting or 'trying' out the oil is to pluck the feathers, cut the skin into pieces, and boil it; but the aborigines prefer the flesh with the skin upon it, regarding it as the Esquimaux do the flesh of whales and seals, as a highly luscious treat. The flesh is eaten by Europeans, and preferred by some to the kangaroo; the rump part is considered as delicate as fowl; the legs coarser, like beef, but still tender.

Bustards are plentiful in many parts of the Cape Colony, and the smaller sorts, called *koerhans*, are approachable in a bush country; but the larger kinds, called *paws*, are a great prize, as they are found on plains, and are generally shot with ball. In Australia, the bustard is called, colonially, the wild turkey. It is a fine large bird, frequently weighing 12 to 15 lbs., and extending full six feet, from tip to tip of the wings. There it is declared excellent for eating, but its flesh is much too gamey for ordinary palates.

Don Pernetty, in his *Historical Journal of the Voyage to the Falkland Islands*, under the command of M. de Bouganville, says, they found the bustard 'exquisite either boiled, roasted, or fricasseed. It appeared from the account we kept that we ate 1,500. It is, indeed, hardly to be conceived that the ship's company of our two frigates, consisting of a hundred and fifty men, all in perfect health and with good stomachs, should have found a quantity of these birds sufficient for their subsistence during a stay of more than two months, within a tract of country not exceeding three leagues.'

But they also tried other descriptions of feathered game. The wild ducks were found, in general, to have the taste of mussels. Of a kind of grey goose, weighing about 19 or 20 lbs., it is reported: 'Its flesh was oily, had a disagreeable smell and a fenny taste; but it was eaten by the ships' companies when no bustards were given them.'

The clucking hen of Jamaica (*Ardea scolopacea*), on the authority of Browne and Robinson, is looked upon as the best wild fowl in the country, although the latter writer tells us it feeds upon snakes, toads, and lizards, as well as wood snails and gully crabs. The flavour is, however, represented to be remarkably fine—a compound of ham, partridge, and pigeon. The flesh is of a peculiarly close and compact texture, and very tender.

The mangrove hen (*Rallus Virginianus*), indigenous to the watery marshes of Jamaica, greatly resembles the dappled grey variety of the common fowl. At the pullet age, the young birds are run down, when feeding on the mud, with great facility. At this time, I have found them to be delicious eating. Persons, on whose taste reliance may be placed, say that, though a plover be undoubtedly a fine bird for the table, and the sanderling a great delicacy, the young mangrove hen exceeds both, as it combines all their peculiarity of flavour with the fleshiness of the quail. This is no small commendation.

But much depends upon your *cuisinier*; if he is a good *artiste*—a man of undoubted talents, it matters little what the materials be.

The *Rallus crex* is another esteemed dainty of no ordinary kind, and a most delicious bird.

In the reign of Henry the Eighth, the bittern was held in great esteem at the tables of the great. Its flesh has much the flavour of hare, and is far from being unpleasant.

Snipe of all kinds, from the 'teeterer,' that hovers about the edge of the surf, to the jack snipe (*Scolopax gallinula*), half-brother to the woodcock, are in high esteem for the table. The 'green' sportsman finds these birds the most perplexing of all feathered game when on the wing. Their catter-cornered, worm-fence line of flight renders them very difficult to hit, until long practice has rendered the marksman's eye familiar with their erratic movements. Some sportsmen take them at an angle; others after they have made their tack; and others, again, seem to blaze away at them without any particular aim, and yet always bring down their bird. The yellow-legged snipe is in America considered the best species for the table. They should be larded and roasted in bunches of three, and served in gravy made from their own unctuous drippings. There are few side-dishes more popular with epicures than snipe on toast. Some cooks stuff them with a composition of bread crumbs and egg, highly seasoned; but, in my opinion, they are far better without this kind of 'trimmings.'

While the trail of the woodcock is a choice morsel with the English epicure, the inhabitants of the North of Europe, to whose forests the woodcocks retire in the summer, never eat the birds, esteeming their flesh unwholesome, from the circumstance of their having no crops. But they are particularly fond of the eggs, which the boors offer for sale in large quantities in the principal markets, and this contributes, possibly, to make the birds so scarce.

The semi-palmated snipe, better known by its common sobriquet of 'pill-will-willet,' the loud shrill note which it emits, is at certain periods of the year esteemed an excellent bird in America. It ought to be served up in the mode that snipes usually are, and for these delicious viands it is esteemed a tolerable substitute when in good order.

Dampier, nearly two centuries ago, speaking of the flamingo, says: 'Their flesh is lean and black, but not ill-tasted. They have large tongues, and near the root of them a piece of fat, which is accounted a great dainty.'

The flamingo was much esteemed by the Romans at their sumptuous entertainments. Their flesh is thought tolerably good food, and the tongue was looked upon by the ancients as among the most delicate of all eatables. Pliny, Martial, and many other writers, speak of it in the highest terms of commendation. Many who have tried it, consider the flesh extremely rich, much like that of the wild duck, but with a strong fishy taste. The tongue is certainly delicate, but scarcely worthy the high encomiums bestowed on it by the ancients.

During the surveying expedition of Captain Owen, on the east coast of Africa, the sailors used to shoot hundreds of these beautiful birds for the purpose of making a dish of the tongues alone. The remainder of the bird— in imitation of the Roman epicures—being thrown away.

NATATORES

The Natatores, or swimming birds, supply us with very choice food. Even many of the coarse sea fowl are not rejected by voyagers.

The Chinese shoot sea-gulls in large numbers, which add to their stock of food. A man is constantly engaged in the bay of San Francisco, California, shooting sea-gulls, which he sells to the Chinese at the rate of 25 cents each. The *San Francisco Evening News* says,—'This bird is a slow and steady mover, of large size, and flies at a convenient distance over the head of the sportsman. The man in the skiff was armed with a double-barrelled shot gun, both barrels of which he would load, and taking a dead gull would throw it high in the air and allow it to fall at some distance from the boat. This would naturally attract a flock of gulls, and as they made their slow circuit around the spot, the gunner raised his piece and generally succeeded in bringing down a bird for both barrels. He would then re-load as fast as possible, and if a gull was in range, another shot was fired and another trophy won.'

The flesh of sea-fowl is generally too rancid to find much favour with fastidious palates. Sailors indeed eat the livers and hearts of the penguins, which are exceedingly palatable, but the black flesh of the body is rank and oily, and has rather a perfumed taste. Some voyagers, however, tell us, that eaten in ragouts, they are good as that made from a hare.

The young puffins, having gorged themselves with sprats and crustacea, when pickled with spices, are by some considered dainties, and they are, occasionally, potted in the North. But when it has attained its ugly full developed bill, like a short, thick plough coulter, this bird does not look very prepossessing. Besides making use of them for food, some of the islanders use them for fire-wood. They split them open, dry them, and then burn them feathers and all.

There is a species of puffin, the *Puffinus urinatrix* or *P. brevicaudis*, popularly termed the mutton-bird by Tasmanian colonists, which is met with on some of the New Zealand islands. It forms the principal food for the native inhabitants of Foveaux Straits, and by them is called the *titi*. It is a sea bird of black colour,[15] in its usual condition smaller than the common duck. Like all sea birds it has thin, slender legs, with webbed feet: the wings are long, with many joints, I forget how many: the bill is a little hooked at the point. They are generally in large flocks, covering the ocean as far as the eye can reach; sometimes flying all in the same direction, at other times crossing through each other like swarming bees. They breed on the small uninhabited islands scattered round the coasts of Stewart's Island. These islands have a loose, dry, peatish soil, on a stony bottom. Their being exposed to the stormy winds, loaded with the salt spray of the sea, prevents the growth of a forest, except patches of stunted bushes intermixed with a sort of soft, light green fern. The loose soil is perforated with numberless birdholes, like a piece of worm-eaten wood, running from two to four feet underground in a horizontal direction, at the farthest end of which is the nest. Each female lays only one egg, which is nearly as big as a goose egg, on which they sit—it is believed male and female alternately—many weeks. The young bird is full grown in the month of April, which corresponds to October in Europe. At that time, almost all the inhabitants of Foveaux Straits, old and young—the infirm only excepted—repair to the Titi Islands, and take the young birds out of their nests, which amount to many thousands, and a great many still escape. They put a stick in the hole to feel where the bird is, which generally betrays itself by biting the stick. If the hole is so long that the bird cannot be reached by the hand, a hole is dug over it, the bird taken out and killed by breaking its head, and the broken hole covered with rubbish and earth, so that it may be used again the next year. Afterwards the birds are plucked, and, to clean the skin from the hairy down, it is moistened and held over the fire, when it is easily wiped quite clean. Then the neck, wings, and legs are cut off, the breast is opened, the entrails are taken out, and the body is laid flat, either to be salted or to be boiled in its own fat, and preserved in air-tight kelp bags. Though it cannot be said that the young birds suffer, they being killed so quickly, yet it might seem cruel to rob the parents of their young ones on so large a scale, and one would fancy a great deal of fluttering and screaming of the old ones, bewailing the bereavement of their offspring. But that is not the case. None of the old birds make their appearance in the day-time. They are all out at sea, and come only to their nests in the evening when it gets dark, and are off again at day-break. But yet it would seem the parents would be distressed at finding their nests robbed. Not so. It would seem as if Providence had ordered it so that man should go and take the young birds for his food without hurting the feelings of the parents. When the young birds are full grown, then they are neglected by their parents, in order to starve them to get thin, else they would never be able to fly for the heaviness of their fat. It seems that at the time when they are taken by men, they are already forsaken by the old birds; and those that are not taken are compelled by hunger, when they have been starved thin and light, to leave their holes and go to sea. The old birds are tough and lean, but the young ones, which are nearly twice as big, contain, when the legs, wings, neck, and entrails are taken off, three-fourths of pure white fat, and one-fourth of red meat and tender bones. The flavour is rather fishy, but, if once used to it, not bad at all, only rather too fat. They eat best when salted and smoked a little, and then boiled a short time, and afterwards eaten cold. If properly salted, they might make an article of trade, like herrings in Europe. The fat when clean is quite white, and looks just like goose fat, but the taste is rather oily; however, it may be used for a good many other purposes than for food. It burns very well on small shallow tin lamps, which get warmed by the light and melt the fat. The feathers are very soft, and would make excellent beds if they could be cured of the oily smell, which it is likely they can.

The following remarks on the articles of food found in the arctic regions are by one of the officers of the *Assistance*:—

'To the feathered tribe we are chiefly indebted, and foremost in the list for flavour and delicacy of fibre stand the ptarmigan (*Lagopus mutus*) and the willow grouse (*Tetrao saliceti*). The flesh is dark-coloured, and has somewhat the flavour of the hare. These may be used in pie, stewed, boiled, or roast, at pleasure, and are easily shot. Next in gustatory joys, the small birds rank, a kind of snipe, and a curlew sandpiper; both are, however, rarely met with, and do not repay the trouble of procuring them.

'The brent goose (*Anser torquatus*) is excellent eating, and its flesh is free from fishy taste. Then follow the little auk or rotge (*Alca alle*), the dovekey, or black guillemot (*Uria grylle*), the loon, or thick-billed guillemot (*Uria Brunnichii*). The first two are better baked with a crust, and the last makes, with spices and wine, a soup but little inferior to that of English hare. All these are found together in flocks, but the easiest method of obtaining them is either to shoot them at the cliffs where they breed, or as they fly to and fro from their feeding ground.

'The ducks now come upon the table, and are placed in the following order by most Polar epicures. The long-tailed duck (*Fuliluga glacialis*), the king duck (*Anas spectabilis*), and the eider duck (*A. mollissima*). They require to be skinned before roasting or boiling, and are then eatable, but are always more or less fishy.

'The divers are by some thought superior for the table to the ducks, but the difference is very slight. The red-throated diver was most frequently seen, but few were shot; and of the great northern divers (*Colymbus glacialis*) none were brought to table, two only having been seen. Some of the gulls were eaten, and pronounced equal to the other sea birds; they were the kittiwake, the tern, and the herring or silver gull.

'The denizens of the sea have fallen little under our notice, and they may be dismissed with the remark, that curried narwhal's skin can be tolerated, but not recommended. Some fresh-water fish were caught, and proved to be very good; they are said to be a kind of trout.'

The eggs of sea-fowl, although much eaten on the coasts, are seldom brought to market for consumption in our large English towns, and yet they form a considerable article of traffic in several parts of the world, and are procured in immense quantities about the lands near the North and South Poles.

The precipitous cliffs of England are occasionally searched for the eggs of the razor-billed auk, which are esteemed a delicacy, for salads especially.

A correspondent at San Francisco informs me that an important trade is carried on in that city in the eggs of sea birds. He states, that the Farallones de los Frayles, a group of rocky islets, lying a little more than twenty miles west of the entrance to the Bay of San Francisco, are the resort of innumerable sea-fowl, known by the fishermen as 'murres.' These islands are almost inaccessible, and, with a single exception, are uninhabited. They, therefore, very naturally afford a resort for great multitudes of birds. Some time since a company was organized in San Francisco for the purpose of bringing the eggs of the murres to market. An imperfect idea of the numbers of these birds may be formed from the fact, that this company sold in that city the last season (a period of less than two months, July and parts of June and August) *more than five hundred thousand eggs*! All these were gathered on a single one of these islands; and, in the opinion of the eggers, not more than one egg in six of those deposited on that island was gathered. My correspondent informs me that he was told by those familiar with the islands that all the eggs brought in were laid by birds of a single kind. Yet they exhibit astonishing variations in size, in form, and in colouring. There is no reason to suppose that he was misinformed in regard to these eggs being deposited by a single species. The men could have had no motive for deception, and similar facts are observable on the Labrador coast and in the islands north of Scotland. Besides, the writer ascertained from other sources, that all the eggs brought to the market were obtained from a limited portion of the island, known as the Great Farallone—called the Rookery, where a single species swarm in myriads, and where no other kind of bird is found. Naturalists, who have received specimens of these birds, pronounce them to be the thick-billed or Brunnich's guillemot, or murre, of Labrador and Northern Europe. The eggs are three and a half inches in length, and are esteemed a great delicacy.

There is a small island off the Cape of Good Hope, named Dassen Island, about six miles from the mainland, which is one and a half mile long by one broad, from which 24,000 eggs of penguins and gulls are collected every fortnight, and sold at Cape Town for a half-penny each.

The late Lieut. Ruxton, R.N., speaking of the Island of Ichaboe, on the Western Coast of Africa, says, 'Notwithstanding that the island had been occupied for nearly two years, during which time thousands upon thousands of penguins had been wantonly destroyed, on the cessation of work these birds again flocked to their old haunts, where they had again commenced laying their eggs. The rocks round the island are literally covered with penguins, cormorants, and albatrosses. The former, wedged together in a dense phalanx, have no more dread of man than ducks in a poultry-yard, although they have met with such persecution on the island; and any number might be taken by the hand without any difficulty. The sailors eat the livers and hearts, which are exceedingly palatable, but the flesh of the body is rank and oily.'[16]

Captain Morrell, also writing of Ichaboe (*Nautical Magazine*, vol. 13, p. 374), tells us, 'Eggs may be obtained here in great quantities. In the months of October and November this island is literally covered with jackass-penguins and gannets, which convene here for the purpose of laying and incubation. The nests of the gannets are formed like those of the albatross, but are not so much elevated; while the jackass-penguins lay their eggs in holes in the ground from twelve to thirty inches in depth, which they guard with the strictest vigilance. They frequently lay three or four eggs, but the gannet seldom lays more than two.'

A correspondent, writing from Tristan d'Acunha, in September, gives an account of his adventures in taking penguins' eggs. 'This is now the time for penguins' eggs. They get great numbers of them. There are two rookeries, as they call them; one on the east, and one on the west, of us. To the one on the west, they go over land, beyond Elephant Bay. I went there last year, when I saw the great sea elephant and the penguins for the first time. But this year I have been disappointed, the weather has been so unsettled. But yesterday was a fine day, and they were going in the boat to the other, to which they can go only by water; so I went with them. It was a good day, and we landed easily, though it is a very bad beach. Fancy the scene—a long, very narrow strip of land, at the foot of a great rock, covered with the thick tussac grass, far higher than my head; the whole place swarming with these penguins—pretty to look at, but the most ungainly creatures in their movements that I ever saw? They stand almost upright. The breast is glossy white, the rest is gray. A couple of tufts of those pretty yellow feathers, of which I sent home a few, adorn each side of the head and give them a very lively appearance. They have no wings, but instead, a couple of flippers, as they call them, like arms, which they use about as gracefully as Punch does his. And then the way in which they hop along! Talk of the motion of a frog! it is elegance itself compared with them. Altogether, they are the most interesting, curious things in Tristan. They are about as big, and twice as noisy, as a duck. Fancy going into the midst of thick grass higher than your head, with thousands of them round you, all croaking out in a harsh, loud, quick note, 'Cover up! cover up!' and then kicking them right and left, quickly, taking care they do not get hold of you,—seizing their great eggs, till you have got some hundreds of them in your bosom. The men wear a large shirt, tied round their waist, so as to form a large loose bag in front, and so pop them in as fast as they can pick them up. The men will gather two or three hundred in this way, and the boys from one to two; and from the other rookery carry them the whole way home—no little load. The eggs vary much in size, from a large hen's egg to a goose's. They mostly lay two at once. Their nests are sometimes close together, so you can soon pick up a lot. They stand in pairs, each couple at their nest to defend it, and some will not give up till they have been kicked away two or three times. They can give a good sharp bite, if they get hold of you. The men found me a spot where the eggs were very thick, and very little tussac, and though I was a new hand at the work, and therefore obliged to look sharp to escape a bite, I managed to collect more than a hundred of them in a short time. Fancy what work, to stand amid hundreds of the birds, all screaming round you, so as almost to deafen you, tumbling them here and there, and picking up their eggs as fast as you can gather them! It is really amusing sport. I must remind you the kicking them over with our soft moccasins (shoes) does not hurt them in the least, and the next day they will have just as many eggs.

'Six of the men went round in the boat. We were there about four hours, and gathered about four thousand—pretty near a boat's load; and could have got more if we had chosen. It was a pleasant day, and we had a good row back.'

An interesting account which recently appeared in a Jamaica paper, respecting egg gathering, is also worth quoting.

The annual egg gathering visit, which the boatmen of Port Royal make to the Pedro Keys, we may set down as a remnant of Indian life. In the work entitled *The Discovery of America by Christopher Columbus, compiled from his papers by his son Don Ferdinand*, we are informed, that on the 13th of November, 1492, the discovery squadron weighing from the Rio de Mares, Cuba, stood to the eastward, to search for the island called Bohio by the Indians, and coming to an anchor among some high raised islets on the coast, found them to be places visited by the Indians at certain seasons of the year, for supplies of fish and birds. 'The islands,' Columbus says, 'were not inhabited, but there were seen the remains of many fires which had been made by the fishermen; for it afterwards appeared that the people were in use to go over in great numbers in their canoes to these islands, and to a great number of other uninhabited islets in these seas, to live upon fish, which they catch in great abundance, and upon birds and crabs, and other things which they find on the land. The Indians follow this employment of fishing and bird-catching according to the seasons, sometimes in one island sometimes in another, as a person changes his diet, when weary of living on one kind of food.'[17]

'From the lighthouse on the Port Royal palisades to Portland in Vere, a line encloses a system of coast islands, reefs, banks, and shoals colonized by numerous birds and fishes. Each kind has its own locality. Pelican Key and Pigeon Island never interchange inhabitants, and the bank that gives the king-fish furnishes neither the snapper nor the grouper. Southward from Portland, at a distance of some few leagues, the great Pedro bank is reached, stretching near 100 miles. There are islets at each extremity, but the group that attracts the egg gatherers every year, are the Keys, distinguished as the Pedros, at its eastern end. We shall loiter a little to describe a living world there that must have been a great attraction to the aboriginal Indians, in those periodical junketings that came under the notice of Columbus.

'The Port Royal boats bound for the egg harvest, bring to, at the outermost of the Portland Keys, and start at midnight from there, to gain with a favourable breeze in 14 or 15 hours the shelter of the Pedros, and to be snug at anchor long before sundown. The vessels in their voyage steer for a single rock in fathomless water, the Isla Sola of the Spanish maps. It rises about 30 or 40 feet out of the sea like a castle in ruins, over which the surf breaks fiercely; and in about five or six hours after making it, they anchor within what are properly called the Keys.

'There are numerous outlying rocks just above and beneath the water, between the Pedro shoal and the open sea, on which the winds and the currents roll a heavy surf. The spots properly called the islands are seven in number, and vary from forty to some three or four acres in size. They are upthrown masses of broken coral and shell cemented by calcareous sand, washed upon rocky ledges above the sea. The breakers shift with the shifting winds, rolling these fragmentary deposits on before them. By the regularity of their change of action, they have done the work of accumulation pretty equally on all sides: they have raised a wall all round the islands, and left the centres hollow.

'From time to time storms of unusual violence have carried the heaped-up coral and sand suddenly, and in thick layers, over portions of the islands where the dung of the sea birds had accumulated for years, and these irruptions have made intermediate deposits of animal matter and cemented rock. It is evident from the prevalence of this succession of deposits within the hollow centres of the islets, that the sea has washed in the fragmentary materials of the outer margins, by a more than ordinary rise of the waters, and laid them in pretty equal strata at distant intervals of time, so that the centres have risen in height as the sea walls have been built and cemented up. The animal deposits, which may be characterized as loosely cohering urate of lime, are sometimes found two feet beneath the strata of cemented coral and shells, and run about an inch or an inch and a half thick.

'Immediately within the islands, the waters shoal, and make a bank called the Vibora by the Spaniards. It runs to the Cascabel rock, 90 odd miles westward, bristled with reefs and sunken rocks, having a depth of from 7 to 17 fathoms. Easterly winds, that is, the trade winds, veering southward and northward, for determinate portions of the year, roll constant billows over it. Westerly breezes, varying northerly and southerly, bring tremendous gales and heavy swells. The rough agency of all these movements has heaped up the sands, and the corals, and shells, cementing them into rock, and giving the island an elevation of from 15 to 20 feet.

'The vegetation on these islands is stunted surianas, among whose tough and twisted branches the birds find nestling places. To these lonely islets resort thousands and tens of thousands of sea-fowl. As soon as visitors land, myriads of birds are upon the wing in all directions. Some flocks rise in circling flight high up into the air, and descending again in the same dense numbers as they rose, settle in more remote places; others break away hurriedly, and fly in a wide sweep far around, but return again hastily to the rocks they had quitted, reconciled to bear with the disturbance. The turmoil and hubbub of the thousands of birds thus suddenly put upon the wing, overpower for a moment the roar of the breakers, and darken the air like the sudden passing of a cloud.

'The constant inhabitants of the rocks are several species of the booby, gannets, terns, gulls, and petrels—and the frigate pelican. The frigate-birds preserve their predilection for rapine amid the teeming plenty of the waters, and subsist by pillaging the gulls and gannets. The migratory visitors are ducks, herons, plovers, snipes, sandpipers, curlews, and ibises, with the several falcons that follow them. In the autumnal movement of these birds towards the equatorial regions, they would be found steering from north to south, but at the time when the egg gatherers visit the islets, they are seen coming from the south, just resting and departing north. The successive months of March, April, and May, are those of the egg harvest.

'The Keys are open to all adventurers, but the egg gathering is regulated by a custom which recognises the first coming vessel as commanding for the season. The second vessel in seniority is called the Commodore, the first being styled the Admiral. They have a code of laws, to which, in a spirit of honourable compliance, all are expected to show obedience; and in case of any infraction of the obligations thus voluntarily imposed upon themselves, a jury selected from the several vessels tries complaints, and with due formality inflicts punishment for offences.

'The south-west is the principal of the Pedro Keys. The stay of the birds that resort there to breed is prolonged by the successive loss of the eggs they lay. Each loss is a stimulus to a fresh act of pairing; a new lot of eggs being the result, possibly in number equal to the former lot, but probably less, as the latter deposits are a forced production, at the expense of the vigour of the bird, without any additional strength to the constitution by the increased nourishment of food, the process by which domesticated birds, in changing their habits, are led to lay a continuance of eggs for a long season. The egg gatherers are careful observers of the progress of incubation, and take only the eggs they know to be fresh laid. These are a part of the regulations they require to be observed, or the constant depredations committed on the birds would fatally thin their numbers.

'Without going into the discussion of naturalists, who see in the different colours of eggs a certain relation to circumstances favourable to concealment, it may be observed that the blotched egg, laid by the *Hydrochelidon fuliginosa*, properly distinguished as the *egg-bird*, is found among sticks and dried leaves of the suriana, whilst the white eggs of the boobies and petrels are deposited in hollows of the coral rocks, amid sand and chalky dung. There is one curious coincidence between the eggs of the noddy, *Sterna stolida*, and the peculiarities of the nest, that must not, however, be unremarked. The elaborate pile of sticks slightly hollowed, in which they deposit their eggs, is always embellished with broken sea shells, speckled and spotted like the eggs. Audubon records the same occurrence in the nests of the noddy terns he inspected in the Florida Keys. The obvious suggestion for this curious prevalence of instinct is deceptiveness, arising from similarity between the egg shell and the sea shell. The nests are pillaged by what is called the laughing gull (the *Larus atricilla*, not the *ridibundus*); the numerous empty shells lying among the rocks being always set down to the predatory visits of the laughing gull.

'South-west Key, and the other sandy islets around it, are beside, annually resorted to by the fishermen in the turtling season for a different harvest of eggs. The turtles (*Chelone midas*) visit these shoals to deposit their eggs in the dry sand, and leave them to the fostering influence of the sun. They repeat their layings thrice, at the interval of two or three weeks, laying a hundred at a time. Some experience is necessary to trace the place of deposit, for the eggs are always laid in the night; but few of them escape the detection of the turtler.'

Geese are reared in large numbers in Alsace, the livers of which are used in making the famous Strasburg pies. In Denmark, geese and ducks are salted down for winter use.

In Greenland, the snow goose affords great subsistence to the natives, and the feathers are an article of commerce. Each family will kill thousands in a season; these, after being plucked and gutted, are flung in heaps into holes dug for that purpose, and are covered only with earth. The mould presses, and forms over them an arch; and whenever the family have occasion to open one of these magazines, they find their provisions perfectly sweet and good.

In Captain Sir John Ross's *Arctic Voyage to Regent Inlet*, it is recorded, that when they discovered that the wild geese had begun to lay on the margin of the lakes, their eggs formed a dainty and wholesome repast. 'The eggs on being weighed were found on an average to be 4½ ounces—of a dingy white, faintly speckled. The discovery of a goose's nest, where the process of incubation had not begun, was regarded by them in the light of a treasure. To the natives, however, it appeared to be a matter of very trifling import whether the egg were freshly laid, or whether it were within a few days of being hatched. Half-a-dozen eggs beaten up with the young ones, in all stages of their growth, from the first development of the form to the complete formation of the foetus, proved to the natives what a dish of callipash and callipee is to the gourmandizing alderman; nor were they very particular as to the embryos being wholly divested of the shells, for the latter appeared to be nearly of the same use as beans to the food of a horse, to force him to masticate the oats more thoroughly.'

The cygnet, or young of the swan, was formerly much esteemed; at Norwich they were fattened for the corporation. The flesh of the old birds is hard and ill tasted.

The pintail (*Anas acuta*) is a very choice bird—the very 'ring tail' of the duck tribe. They are undoubtedly a *recherché morceau*, for, being essentially grain feeders, they have no fishy flavour.

Widgeon and teal are in great favour when in good condition.

REPTILIA

We find various reptiles, *Chelonian, Saurian,* and *Ophidian,* still forming articles of food in many quarters of the world, and some so repulsive in their appearance, that it seems difficult to conceive how they could first have been tasted.

In the class Reptilia, we have in the first order *Chelonia* or *tortoises,* comprising the following which are used as food:—1, several of the terrestrial tortoises, genus *Testudo*; 2, some of the marsh tortoises or Emydes, the chelodina, matamata, &c.; 3, the cryptopus or river tortoise; and 4, the marine tortoises or turtles.

In the second order Sauria or lizards, we find—1, crocodiles and alligators contributing to the sustenance of man; 2, several of the iguarians.

In the third order, Ophidia or serpents, the rattlesnake, boas and pythons, and several other snakes.

In the fourth order, Amphibia, some of the edible and tree frogs.

We know not, observes a recent writer, why the flesh of the vegetable-feeding tortoises should not be adopted, as well as that of the green turtle, among the various articles which are in request for the table. There is much in habit and association of ideas; and though persons who would not refuse turtle might turn from tortoise with disgust, they may rest assured that in Sicily and Italy these land tortoises are sold in the markets, principally for being made into soup, which dish is more esteemed than the flesh prepared in any other way.

The flesh of a tortoise, called the matamata by the aborigines of Cayenne (*Chelys matamata,* Dumeril, *C. fimbriata,* Spix), is said to be highly esteemed in various parts of Guiana.

There is a great variety of land tortoises in Trinidad and some of the other West Indian Islands, which in general are as delicious as the best green turtle.

The eggs of the close tortoise (*Testudo clausa*) of North America, are reckoned a delicacy, and are about the size of pigeons' eggs.

The gopher tortoise (*Testudo Carolina*, of Leconte) occasionally makes considerable depredations in the potato fields of the farmer, and in gardens and other cultivated grounds, but its flesh is excellent, and hence it is sought after for the table.

The flesh of the Carolina terrapin or box tortoise (*Cistudo Carolina*) is occasionally eaten, but it is held in low estimation; the eggs, however, which are about as large as those of a pigeon, are accounted excellent, and are much sought after.

The flesh of the European box tortoise (*Cistudo Europæa*), though not very delicate, is nevertheless eaten on the Continent; it is said, however, to be greatly improved by feeding the animals for some time on grains, bran, and other vegetable aliment. The salt water terrapin (*Emys concentrica*), which is found both in North and South America, is in great request, its flesh being highly esteemed as a delicacy for the table, especially at the close of the summer, when the animals have returned to their winter dormitory. They are then fat, and considered as a luxury.

The eggs of the terrapin are not provided with a hard shell, but a skin like that purest of all parchments, parchment just before it receives the ink of law upon it.

The general method of killing these animals is a most barbarous one. They are laid upon their backs, either close to the fire, or upon the red wood-ashes, until the thick shell becomes so hot to the animal within that he desperately stretches out both legs and neck, in the vainest of endeavours to extricate himself from the walls of his burning house. The tender-hearted cook watches his opportunity, and when it is evident that, in ordinary phrase, the poor terrapin 'cannot contain itself,' or in other words, will no longer draw back his head into such a living furnace—the knife descends, and the head is cut away. The late Mr. Charles Hooton told me, that he had seen such heads at least half-an-hour after being cut off, attempt, on being touched, to bite with sufficient force to take the piece out of the finger. During this time the eyes will occasionally open, though generally they remain shut.

The flesh of the Indian Cryptopus, a river or fluviatile tortoise (*Cryptopus granosus*, Bibr., *Testudo scabra*, Latr.) is eaten in Pondicherry and Coromandel, where it lives in large sheets of fresh water or lagoons.

The flesh of the soft tortoise of America (*Trionyx ferox*, Cuvier), which inhabit the rivers of Carolina and Georgia, is eaten.

The curious New Holland tortoise (*Chelodina longicollis*), first described by Shaw, which, as far as the head and neck is concerned, reminds one rather of a snake than a tortoise, is abundant in some of the lakes of Western Australia, and is considered by the natives a great treat, as are also the snakes and lizards.

Chief Justice Temple, of Honduras, from whose lively and interesting letters to the Society of Arts I have already quoted, says—'Another article which might be preserved and exported, and which would, I have little doubt, be highly prized by epicures in England, is the liver of the hiccatee. The hiccatee is the fresh water turtle or tortoise, and is, I believe, altogether unknown in Europe. It never approaches anything like the size of the large turtles. The weight of the hiccatee seldom exceeds 20 lbs. It has not got fins like a turtle, or to be more correct, the sea tortoise, but round, webbed-feet, each having five claws, like those of a duck. It is made for the land, therefore, as well as the water. It does not, however, make the former its home, and its feet are evidently intended merely to enable it, when one pool becomes dry, to travel in search of another. The hiccatee is generally caught in the dry season, when going across the country in pursuit of water. The feet when dressed are gelatinous, but the flesh is dry and fibrous. It is, however, the liver which renders this species of tortoise so highly estimable. It is a dark olive colour, and immensely large. If this were preserved in oil with truffles, it would be considered far superior to the goose's liver of which the *pâté de foie gras* is made.'

The following way of effectually shooting a turtle may be interesting to the sporting world generally, and aldermen in particular. 'The soft-shell turtle is found throughout the south, and abounds in the rivers and bayous of Louisiana, where they are esteemed a delicacy. They are so shy as to elude the various inventions which are adopted to capture them; the rifle has, therefore, been resorted to; and, though easily killed by a fair marksman, when he finds them sunning themselves on the floating or projecting trunk of some old tree, he still often fails to secure his prize, since they drop into the bayous, are swept down into the current, and scarcely, if ever, secured. To remedy this, a gentleman of Louisiana adopted the following method successfully. He cut a piece of wood, one inch long, and rounded it so as to fit easily in his rifle; around the middle, crosswise, he cut a small groove, so as to secure to it a twine some six or seven inches long; at the other end of this string he attached the ball, by passing the string through a bore in the ball, and then knotting the end of the string. The ball is first inserted in the rifle; the string and wood follow, and all are rammed down. The turtle is now shot, and as the ball passes through the turtle, it enters the tree or log some one or two inches; the piece of wood, being too light to enter the shell of the turtle, is left suspended. So that, at a single shot, the game is killed, strung, and hung up.' Of course, this is from an American paper.

The flesh of the land tortoise is largely used for food, both fresh and when salted, in the Gallipagos Archipelago and other islands of the Pacific; and a beautifully clear oil is prepared from their fat. They are eaten in Australia by the aborigines; and in Russia, on the shores of the Mediterranean, and some parts of Germany, are fattened for the table, and are esteemed a great delicacy. Wallace, in his journeys up the Amazon, says he found the land tortoise for dinner as good as turtle.

Captain Dampier, when he visited the Gallipagos, in 1684, records 'That there is no place in the world so much stored with guanoes and land tortoises as these isles. The first are fat and of an extraordinary size, and exceeding tame; and the land tortoises so numerous, that some hundred men may subsist on them for a considerable time, being very fat, and as pleasant food as a pullet, and of such bigness that one of them weighs 150 or 200 lbs.; and are from two feet to two feet six inches over the belly; whereas, in any other places, I never met with any above 30 lbs. weight, though I have heard them say that at St. Lawrence or Madagascar there are also very large ones.'

Wafer, another old voyager, when at these islands, salted the flesh of the land tortoise for use on shipboard, and fried the fat and converted it into lard or oil, of which they secured 60 large jars.

Tortoises of an immense size are found on many of the islands of the Pacific. Mr. Lawson, a vice-governor of the Gallipagos Archipelago, states that he has seen several so large that it required six or eight men to lift them from the ground; and that some had afforded as much as 200 lbs. of meat. Dr. Darwin remarks: 'I was always amused when overtaking one of these great monsters, as it was quietly pacing along, to see how suddenly, the instant I passed, it would draw in its head and legs, and, uttering a deep hiss, fall to the ground with a heavy sound, as if struck dead. I frequently got on their backs, and then giving a few raps on the hinder part of their shells, they would rise up and walk away; but I found it very difficult to keep my balance. The flesh of this animal is largely employed, both fresh and salted; and a beautifully clear oil is prepared from the fat. When a tortoise is caught, the man makes a slit in the skin near its tail, so as to see inside its body, whether the fat under the dorsal plate is thick. If it is not, the animal is liberated; and it is said to recover soon from this strange operation.

In chasing the turtle, a man standing ready in the bow of the boat dashes through the water upon the turtle's back; then clinging with both hands by the shell of its neck, he is carried away till the animal becomes exhausted and is secured. In the Chagos Archipelago, the natives, by a horrible process, take the shell from the back of the living turtle. It is covered with burning charcoal, which causes the outer shell to curl upwards; it is then forced off with a knife, and before it becomes cold flattened between two boards. After this barbarous process, the animal is suffered to regain its native element, where, after a certain time, a new shell is formed; it is, however, too thin to be of any service, and the animal always appears languishing and sickly.

Dampier, in 1684, speaks of three or four kinds of land tortoises being eaten in the West Indies. 'One,' he says, 'is called by the Spaniards *Hackatee*, which keep most in fresh-water ponds; they have small legs and long necks, and flat feet, and commonly weigh betwixt ten and fifteen pounds. The second sort they call *Tenopen* (terrapin?), much less than the former, and something rounder; but for the rest not unlike them, except that the shell on their backs is naturally coloured with a curious carved work. Both sorts afford very good meat, and these last delight in low marshy places, and are in vast numbers at the Isle of Pines, near Cuba, among the woods.'

Turtle would seem to have been first introduced in England, as an article of food, about the middle of the 17th century, for a record in the *Gentleman's Magazine*, under date August 31, 1753, shows that it was then a rarity. 'A turtle, weighing 350 lbs., was ate at the King's Arms tavern, Pall Mall; the mouth of an oven was taken down to admit the part to be baked.' The locality for eating them now has been transferred principally to the city; and the Ship and Turtle, the London Tavern, Birch's (in Cornhill), and the Guildhall or Mansion-house, are perhaps the largest depôts of consumption. Steam communication has greatly increased the imports, which amount to about 15,000 in the year, weighing from one quarter to three hundred weight, and valued at, probably, £8,000. Not that all these shielded animals can be called 'lively' turtle, for the voyage has very often a damaging effect upon them.

Turtling is much resorted to by the inhabitants of Grand Cayman, 160 miles north-west from Jamaica. The turtle are now chiefly caught on the Mosquito coast, or on the South Keys of Cuba, and sold either in Jamaica or to homeward-bound vessels. Formerly, these valuable animals were abundant at Grand Cayman itself, but the very reprehensible practice which has prevailed there, for some years past of making use of large quantities of their eggs deposited on the shore, has almost frightened them entirely away.

In an account of Jamaica, published in 1683, we find the following statement respecting turtle hunting and other articles of food:—

'Tortoise are taken much on this coast, but chiefly at the island of Caymanos, thirty leagues to the west of this island, whither the vessels go May, June, and July, to load of their flesh, that they pickle in bulk, and take them in that season when they come on shore to lay their eggs, which they do, and cover them with sand, that hatches them; and then by instinct they crawl to the sea, where they live, and feed on weed that grows in the bottom or floats. In many rivers and ponds of Jamaica, there is vast numbers of crocodiles or allegators, that is an amphibious creature, and breeds an egg, hatch'd by the sun in the sand. A tortoise egg is just like the yolk of a hen egg, of which she lays near a peck at a time; but the allegator but a few, and are like a turkey's. Their flesh is not good; they are voracious, and live on fowls and beasts that they catch by surprise, but seldom or never hurt any man.

'Here's an Indian coney, called racoon, that is good meat; but of a distasteful shape, being something like an overgrown rat. The snakes in this island are not at all hurtful, but were eaten by the Indians as regular as the guanaes are by the Spaniards; it is but small, and of the shape of an allegator, and the flesh is sweet and tender.'

I was told a story not long ago of a distinguished American politician from the rural districts, who came to New York, and resolved to give a splendid dinner to some of his party friends. In order to make sure that everything should be of the very best quality, he went to the market himself, and bought first a *turtle*. After taking great pains to select one of the finest specimens in the lot, and ordering it to be sent home, he said to the tradesman, by way of making it quite right, 'This is a right down genuine turtle, aint it?'

'Oh, certainly,' was the reply, 'one of the very best.'

'Because,' he added, 'although I ain't been in the city long, I ain't to be humbugged: it won't do for you to try to put off any of your confounded *mock* turtles on me!'

The turtle dealer stood astounded at his customer's sharpness.

Sir James E. Alexander calls Ascension 'the headquarters of the finest turtle in the world,' and his account of the operations connected with turtling in that locality is so interesting that I must copy it.

'We walked down to the turtle ponds, two large enclosures near the sea, which flowed in and out through a breakwater of large stones. A gallows was erected between the two ponds, where the turtle are slaughtered for shipping, by suspending them by the hind flippers and then cutting their throats. About 300 turtle of four and five hundred pounds each lay on the sand or swam about in the ponds—a sight to set an alderman mad with delight!

'In the hot weather of January, February, March, and April, the females land at night, and waddling over the sands in the various bays of the island, far above high-water mark,—for by a pole in the ponds, the tide only rises here four feet,—they scrape up, by alternate scoops of their flippers, a hole deep enough to cover their bodies. Into this they get, sighing heavily, and deposit from 150 to 200 eggs, cover them up, leaving them to the sun to hatch; and then waddle again towards the sea. Two stout hands are, meanwhile, on the look out, watching the movements of the unfortunate turtle; and, running up to her after the completion of her task, one seizes a fore flipper and dexterously shoves it under her belly to serve as a purchase; whilst the other, avoiding a stroke which might lame him, cants the turtle over on her back, where she lies helpless. From fifteen to thirty are thus turned in a night; and 600 had been so captured in the season of 1834.

'In the bays, when the surf of heavy rollers prevents the boats being beached to take on board the turtle when caught, they are hauled out to them by ropes.

'No ships' crews are now allowed to turn turtle, which is converted into a government monopoly; and £2 10s. is the fixed price for each. Strange to say, from the time that the young turtle, the size of a dollar, are observed scuttling down to the water, they are never seen again here until they are four or five hundred pounds weight; and how long they take to attain this great size, and where they spend the intermediate time, is as yet a mystery. I was surprised to hear that turtle are kept in the ponds for a year and upwards without a morsel of food of any kind. They sometimes deposit their eggs in the sand, on the sides of the ponds; and in due time the little animals are allowed to make their escape to the sea.

'One old female called 'Nelson,' because one of her flippers had been carried off by a shark, was kept, out of respect, for two or three years in the ponds. She contrived, however, one night to crawl round the enclosure and make her escape; but she was turned next year in Clarence Bay. Another turtle was also turned there a short time since, on the back of which was carved the name of a mate of a British vessel, who had bought it and sailed with it three weeks before; it is probable that, imagining it to be dead, he had thrown it overboard.

'The best way to send home turtle from Ascension is, to head them up in a *sealed* cask, and have the water changed daily by the bung hole and a cork. Turtle, though the extremes of heat and cold are equally injurious to them, should always arrive in hot weather in England. Thus, an unfortunate captain, on one occasion, took from Ascension 200 turtle, and timing his arrival badly, brought only four alive to Bristol!'

Humboldt, in his *Personal Narrative*, speaks of the expertness of the jaguars of South America, who turn the turtle on the beach and devour them at their ease, emptying the double armour of the arraus, by the introduction of their supple paws, with greater ingenuity than the most skilful naturalist could do. They also eat the eggs.

The eggs are of a globular shape, with a soft semi-transparent calcareous shell. These are much prized whenever they can be procured as articles of food, both by natives and Europeans. A native will consume in Brazil as many as twenty or thirty eggs at one meal, and an European sometimes eats a dozen for breakfast.

Scarcely a thirtieth of the number of young turtles, even if the eggs are all hatched, reach the sea, or live after they have gained that element. Birds, and beasts, and alligators, and rapacious fishes, all prey upon them.

The flesh of the female is held in the greatest estimation, and it is considered to be in perfection at the time she is about depositing her eggs. The flesh, the eggs, and certain portions of the intestines, are often salted and barrelled for shipment to a distance. The eggs of the turtle, although oily, are very savory, and make an excellent omelet. The shell does not harden, but is leathery; and the white never coagulates, but is thrown away and the yolk only eaten. The Indians of Brazil frequently eat the eggs raw, mixed with their cassava farinha.

Captain William Dampier, in his voyages, tells us, the flesh of the hawk's-bill turtle is eaten. 'The flesh' (he remarks) 'is but indifferent, yet somewhat better than that of the loggerhead. Those taken betwixt the Sambellas and Portobello, make those that eat their flesh vomit and purge vehemently. The flesh however differs according to their food, for those that feed upon moss among the rocks have a much yellower fat and flesh, and are not so well tasted as those that feed upon grass.'

Soon after the fall of the waters of the Orinoco, which begins in February, millions of turtle deposit their eggs among the sand, and the Indians obtain a rich harvest of food. From the eggs they procure a rich oil termed '*mantega*,' which is preserved in pots. A good deal is sent down the Amazon, fully to the value of £2,000, and several thousand persons are occupied in its preparation.

The eggs are not very large, but about the size of a bantam's egg. The stratum of eggs in the sand is ascertained by a pole thrust in, the mean depth being about three feet, and the harvest of eggs is estimated like the produce of a well cultivated acre; an acre, accurately measured, of 120 feet long, and 30 wide, having been known to yield 100 jars of oil. The eggs, when collected, are thrown into long troughs of water, and being broken and stirred with shovels, they remain exposed to the sun till the yolk, the oily part, is collected on the surface, and has time to inspissate; as fast as this oily part is collected on the surface of the water, it is taken off and boiled over a quick fire. This animal oil, or tortoise grease, when prepared, is limpid, inodorous, and scarcely yellow. It is used, not merely to burn in lamps, but in dressing victuals, to which it imparts no disagreeable taste. It is not easy, however, to produce oil of turtle's eggs quite pure. It has generally a putrid smell, owing to the mixture of addled eggs. The total gathering of the three shores, between the junction of the Orinoco with the Apure, where the collection of eggs is annually made, is 5,000 jars, and it takes about 5,000 eggs to furnish one jar of oil.

In the Comarca of the Rio Nigro, the value of the turtle oil imported in 1840 was 6,000 dollars; and from the small town of Barra, on the Amazon, in 1850, turtle oil of the value of 1818 dollars was sent. It is filled in pots, of which 1628 were made in Santarrem, a mile above the mouth of the Tapajos.

Turtle oil is employed for various purposes. In some of the West India islands, it is used when fresh in the place of butter, or salad oil, and also for lamps.

The eggs of most of the species are excellent, being both nutritive and agreeable to the taste; those of the green turtle are especially fine. The white, or albuminous portion, does not, however, harden on boiling.

The large tree lizard, popularly termed the guana, (*Iguana tuberculata,* Laur. Syn. 49) is certainly not very attractive in appearance, and yet by most persons its flesh is highly esteemed, being reckoned as delicate as chicken, and but little inferior to turtle in flavour.

It is about three feet long, from the head to the extremity of the tail, and covered with a soft skin of a bluish green colour on the back and legs; on the sides and belly, nearly white. It has a pouch of loose skin under its throat, of a light green; eyes black; and claws, of which there are three or five on each foot, sharply pointed. A fringed skin, or kind of mane, runs along from the head to the tail, which it erects when irritated, and will then snap hold of anything with great tenacity; but it is perfectly harmless if undisturbed. The bite is painful, but is not dangerous.

This ugly-looking tree lizard, which looks like an alligator in miniature, is considered a great delicacy in most tropical countries. However white and tender the flesh may be when cooked, when one of its fore paws happens to stick up in the dish, it reminds one too much of the allegator to eat it with any great relish.

I know no animal, or rather reptile, whose appearance is so little calculated to tempt man to eat of its flesh; and yet, despite the repugnance that results from its looks, neither Ude nor Soyer could have compounded any dish that would compare to the delicacy of a well-dressed iguana.

We all know that the turtle is most delicious, yet did we see it for the first time, we might call it with the rustic 'a great sea toad.' The appearance of the turtle does not carry a letter of recommendation to the kitchen; accordingly, his introduction to the Lord Mayor's table was rather tardy, and we learn from Sir Hans Sloane that, at the beginning of the last century, turtle was only eaten in Jamaica by the poor.

The poet Gay hath sung, that he must have been a bold man who first swallowed an oyster:

'The man had sure a palate covered o'er

With steel or brass, that on the rocky shore

First ope'd the oozy oyster's pearly coat,

And risked the living morsel down his throat.'

Yet neither turtle nor oyster looks so repugnant, yet tastes so delicious, as an iguana.

Although often roasted or fricasseed, a frequent native mode of cooking the iguana is to boil it, taking out the leaves of fat, which are melted and clarified, and put into a calabash or dish, into which they dip the flesh of the guana as they eat it.

It was long before the Spaniards could conquer their repugnance to the guana, the favourite delicacy of the Indians, but which the former regarded with disgust as a species of serpent. They found it however to be highly palatable and delicate, and from that time forward, the guana was held in repute among Spanish epicures. The story is thus related by Peter Martyn: —

'These serpentes are like unto crocodiles, saving in bygness; they call them guanas. Unto that day none of oure men durste adventure to taste of them, by reason of they're horrible deformitie and lothsomnes. Yet the Adelantado being entysed by the pleasantnes of the king's sister Anacaona, determined to taste the serpentes. But when he felte the flesh thereof to be so delycate to his tongue, he fell to amayne without al feare. The which thynge his companions perceiving, were not behynde hym in greedynesse: insomuche that they had now none other talke than of the sweetnesse of these serpentes, which they affirm to be of more pleasant taste than eyther our phesantes or partriches.'

Pierre Labat gives a minute account of the mode of catching this reptile, and if the reader has no objection to accompany the good father à la chasse, he may participate in the diversion as follows:—'We were attended,' says he, 'by a negro who carried a long rod; at one end of which was a piece of whipcord with a running knot. After beating the bushes for some time, the negro discovered our game basking in the sun on the dry limb of a tree. Hereupon he began whistling with all his might, to which the guana was wonderfully attentive, stretching out his neck, and turning his head as if to enjoy it more fully. The negro now approached, still whistling, and advancing his rod gently, began tickling with the end of it the sides and throat of the guana, who seemed mightily pleased with the operation, for he turned on his back and stretched himself out like a cat before the fire, and at length fell fairly asleep; which the negro perceiving, dexterously slipt the noose over his head, and with a jerk brought him to the ground; and good sport it afforded to see the creature swell like a turkey-cock at finding himself entrapped. We caught others in the same way, and kept one of them alive seven or eight days; but,' continues the reverend historian, 'it grieved me to the heart to find that he thereby lost much delicious fat.'

Guanas are very large and plentiful on the outlying cays and islands of the Bahamas. They are hunted with a small kind of hound, and if taken alive, the mouth is sewed up with twine, and they keep alive a month or six weeks without food. Nassau, New Providence, the capital is chiefly supplied from these islands with the guana.

There are several varieties of this reptile in Australia, but that which is most common is from four to six feet in length, and from about a foot and a half to two feet across the broadest part of the back, with a rough dark skin, enlivened by yellow spots. Although perfectly harmless, as far as the human race are concerned, this huge lizard is a terrible foe to the smaller quadrupeds—opossums, bandicoots, kangaroo-rats, &c.,—on which it preys. It is very destructive also among hen roosts, and often takes up its quarters in the vicinity of a farm-house for the convenience of supping on the hens and their eggs.

The guana is much sought for and esteemed by the blacks as an article of food, and is frequently presented as a great delicacy to the young 'gins.' By the settlers it is not often eaten, owing to the natural feeling of dislike which is created by its form and habits. Those, however, who do not entertain these feelings, or are able to overcome them, find the flesh of the creature really excellent. It is not unlike that of a rabbit, to which, in flavour, it is fully equal, and eats best when stewed or curried.

The guana usually lives in trees, and, on the approach of man, it invariably makes off with great alacrity, scrambling rapidly up the nearest trunk; but it is easily brought down by a shot.

Captain Keppel tells us, 'that while out on a shooting excursion at Port Essington, he observed a native plucking the feathers off a goose; while so employed his eye caught the tip-end of the tail of an iguana, an animal of the lizard kind, about four feet long, which was creeping up the opposite side of a tree; he tossed the goose, without further preparation, on to the fire, and ascended the tree as easily as Jack would run up the well-rattled rigging of a man-of-war. He almost immediately returned with the poor animal struggling in his scientific grasp. It was the work of a minute to secure it to a stick of about the same length as itself to prevent its running away, when it was made to change places with the goose, which, being warm through, was considered to be sufficiently done. The whole goose he devoured, making no bones, but spitting out the feathers. Then came the iguana's turn, which, although less tender, was not the less relished. It appeared to require great muscular strength to detach the flesh from the skin. The operation being finished, he lay down to sleep. His wife, having sprinkled him with dirt to keep the flies off, was proceeding to eat the skin of the iguana, when the arrival of some more geese offered her a more satisfactory repast.'

The iguana is, I believe, the Talagowa of the natives of Ceylon—*le Monitor terrestre d'Egypte* of M. Cuvier. The Indian monitor (*Monitor dracæna*, Gray) is found in great abundance in all the maritime provinces of Ceylon. The natives are partial to its flesh. Dr. Kelaart states that he once tasted some excellent soup made from a tender guana, which was not unlike hare soup. At Trincomalee they are hunted down by dogs, and sold in the market for 6d. each. They feed on the smaller reptiles and insects, and measure, when large, four feet five inches. Despite its repulsive appearance, the iguana is eagerly hunted for food by the natives of Africa, Australia, America, and Asia.

The eggs of the guana are another article deserving the attention of gourmands. One of these lizards sometimes contains as many as four-score eggs. These are about the size of a pigeon's egg, with a very soft shell, which contains only a very small quantity of the albumen. The yolk, unlike that of other eggs, does not become hard and dry when boiled, but is soft and melting as marrow.

It would be a refreshing sight to see Alderman A., or Sheriff B., or any other civic dignitary who has gone the round of all the dishes which native and foreign skill have been able to produce, and to whom a new combination would convey as much delight as a black tulip or a blue dahlia would to a horticulturist, partaking for the first time of *pâté de foie gras de l'hiccatee*, or a dish of the eggs of the iguana garnished with anchovies. The inhabitants of some of the Pacific islands esteem the large oval eggs of the lizards as food.

The meat of the *Amblyrynchus subcristatus*, another lizard, when cooked, is white, and by those whose stomachs rise above all prejudices it is relished as very good. Humboldt has remarked, that in intertropical South America, all lizards which inhabit dry regions are esteemed delicacies for the table.

There are an almost innumerable variety of lizards, properly so called, in all parts of the colony of New South Wales, and the whole of the larger kinds are used for food by the blacks, although but very rarely eaten by the settlers. Those who have eaten them, state that their flesh resembles that of a fowl. The dragon lizard, or as it is sometimes called, the frilled lizard, is the most remarkable, being provided with a large frill, which it has the power of extending suddenly, and in a rather startling manner, when attacked or alarmed; it is usually about a foot and a half or two feet long. The Jew lizards are dark coloured, with a dewlapped and puffy appearance about the throat and neck, varying in size, but seldom exceeding two feet in length. The scaly lizards are fierce looking, although harmless, reptiles, with a spotted scaly hide, generally about a foot long, and remarkable for having small round club-shaped tails. They are easily domesticated, but as their appearance is far from attractive, they are seldom made pets of. The large spiny-backed rock lizard resembles a guana, the only material points of difference being that it has a heavy dewlap beneath its chin, and a row of spines along the back from the head to the tail. The flat-tailed lizard, called by the natives the Rock Scorpion, is imagined by them to be venomous, although in reality it is perfectly harmless; it is nocturnal in its habits, and possesses to a peculiar extent the singular power, which is more or less vested in all the lizard family, of leaving its tail in the hands of any one who attempts to capture it by laying hold of that appendage, and of making off apparently scatheless. The sleeping lizard is in body, as well as in its sluggish habits, exactly like the terrible death adder, from which it is only to be distinguished by its short feet.

Many of the lizard family are believed by the settlers to be venomous, but such is not the case; I believe in fact that no four-footed reptile has yet been discovered which is possessed of venom.

A remarkable power possessed by the guana, and perhaps by others of the lizard family, is its power of resisting the poison, ordinarily most destructive to animal life, — prussic acid. A middling sized guana took a small bottle of prussic acid, and seemed rather to have been exhilarated by it than otherwise; it was killed, however, by a dose of arsenic and spirits of wine.

There is a large, ugly, amphibious lizard, about three feet long, met with in Guiana, known as the Salempenta, or *El Matêo*, which is thought (particularly by the Indians) good eating, the flesh being white and tender. It is, however, much more ugly in appearance than the guana.

Occasionally large lizards of other kinds, two or three feet in length, are brought to the Rio market, and they are said to be excellent eating.

In the reign of Cheops, as an Egyptian gentleman curious in poultry, and famous even there for his success in producing strange birds, was walking by the river Nile, he met with an egg, which, from its appearance, he thought promised results out of the common way; so, picking it up, he took it home, and gave directions for hatching it. But some time after, on visiting his poultry yard, he found that all his pets had disappeared, a few feathers only lying scattered about, whilst a fearful animal rushed upon him open-mouthed. The fact was, *he had hatched a crocodile.*

Mr. Joseph, in his *History of Trinidad*, tells us, that he has eaten the eggs of the cayman or alligator, (without knowing what eggs they were), and found them good. In form and taste they much resemble the eggs of the domestic hen.

Dr. Buckland, the distinguished geologist, one day gave a dinner, after dissecting a Mississippi alligator, having asked a good many of the most distinguished of his classes to dine with him. His house and his establishment were in good style and taste. His guests congregated. The dinner-table looked splendid, with glass, china, and plate, and the meal commenced with excellent soup. 'How do you like the soup?' asked the doctor, after having finished his own plate, addressing a famous gourmand of the day. 'Very good, indeed,' answered the other; 'turtle, is it not? I only ask because I do not find any green fat.' The doctor shook his head. 'I think it has something of a musky taste,' said another; 'not unpleasant, but peculiar.' 'All alligators have,' replied Buckland; 'the cayman particularly so. The fellow whom I dissected this morning— —' At this stage there was a general rout of the whole guests. Every one turned pale. Half-a-dozen started up from the table; two or three ran out of the room; and only those who had stout stomachs remained to the close of an excellent entertainment. 'See what imagination is!' said Buckland. 'If I had told them it was turtle, or tarrapen, or birdsnest soup, salt-water amphibia or fresh, or the gluten of a fish, or the maw of a sea bird, they would have pronounced it excellent, and their digestion been none the worse. Such is prejudice.' 'But was it really an alligator?' asked a lady. 'As good a calf's head as ever wore a coronet,' answered Buckland.

The Australian crocodile is more closely allied to the gavial of India (*Gavialis gangeticus*), but is now often termed, like the American species, an alligator. It is large and formidable; one captured by Captain Stokes, in the Victoria River, and described in his published journal, was fifteen feet long, and some have been taken still larger than this. Like all animals of its class, the Australian crocodile is a much more formidable enemy in the water than on shore; but even in the latter position, it is by no means to be despised, for it progresses with tolerable speed; and, although it seldom or never attacks a man openly when out of its own proper element, still it is believed to have a strong liking for human flesh, when that delicacy can safely be obtained. One of these creatures paid a visit to a seaman, who was asleep in his hammock on shore after a hard day's labour, and being unable to get conveniently at the man, it managed to drag off and carry away the blanket which covered him; the sailor at first charged his comrade with having made him the subject of a practical joke, but the foot-prints of the huge reptile, and the discovery of the abstracted blanket in the water, soon showed him the real character of his nocturnal visitant.

The flesh of the crocodile is white and delicate, resembling veal. It was a favourite dish among the Port Essington settlers, and among the seamen employed in the surveys of the northern coast and rivers of Australia. It is frequently pursued and killed for food by the aborigines of that part of the country: the plan which they adopt is to hunt it into some blind creek, when the reptile, finding itself closely pressed, and no water near, usually forces its head, and perhaps the upper part of its body in some sand-hole, fancying that it has, by so doing, concealed itself from its pursuers. In this position it is despatched with comparative ease. The crocodile makes a terrible noise by snapping its jaws, particularly when in pain, or when it is annoyed by the buzzing about its mouth and eyes of the mosquitoes or other insects, which are found in myriads among the swamps, creeks, and shallow waters, where it abides; this snapping noise is often a startling sound to explorers encamping near waters frequented by the monster.

The aboriginal tribes far to the southward of the localities in which the crocodile has its habitation, have an imperfect knowledge of the animal; stories of its voracity and fierceness have probably been recounted at the friendly meetings of the tribes, and these stories have in the same manner passed across the continent, changed and magnified with each new relation, until on reaching the coast tribes of the south, the crocodile became a nondescript animal of most terrible form, frightening the blacks and puzzling the whites under the name of the Bunyip.

In Dongola, at the present day, the crocodile is caught for the sake of its flesh, which is regarded as a delicacy. The flesh and fat are eaten by the

Berbers, who consider them excellent. Both parts, however, have a smell of musk so strong that few strangers can eat crocodiles' flesh without violent sickness following.

The Rev. Mr. Haensel, in his *Letters on the Nicobar Islands*, tells us that 'part of the flesh of the crocodile, or cayman, is good and wholesome when well cooked. It tastes somewhat like pork, for which I took it, and ate it with much relish, when I first came to Nancauwery, till, on inquiry, finding it to be the flesh of a beast so disgusting and horrible in its appearance and habits, I felt a loathing, which I could never overcome; but it is eaten by both natives and Europeans.' The aboriginal natives of Trinidad considered a broiled slice of alligator as a dainty morsel; and Mr. Joseph, the historian, records having tasted it, and found it very palatable. Tastes in this, as in other matters, differ.

Mr. Henry Koster, in his *Travels in Brazil*, says—'I have been much blamed by my friends for not having eaten of the flesh of the alligator, and, indeed, I felt a little ashamed of my squeamishness when I was shown by one friend a passage in a French writer, whose name I forget, in which he speaks favourably of this flesh. However, if the advocate for experimental eating had seen an alligator cut into slices, he would, I think, have turned from the sight as quickly as I did.' The Indians of South America eat these creatures, but none of the negroes will touch them.

Dr. Madden, in his *Travels in Egypt*, appears to have experimentalized on the saurians as food—

'I got' (he says) 'a small portion of a young crocodile, six feet long, broiled, to ascertain its taste. The flavour a good deal resembles that of a lobster, and, though somewhat tough, it might certainly be considered very excellent food.'

The spectacled cayman (*Alligator sclerops*) is known under the name of yacaré, or jacquare, in South America. Azara, the naturalist, tells us that the eggs of this animal are white, rough, and as large as those of a goose; they are deposited, to the number of sixty, in the sand, and covered with dried grass. The Indians of Paraguay, and other districts, esteem them as food, and also relish the white and savoury flesh of this alligator, although it is dry and coarse. Cayman is the Spanish word for alligator, and, according to Walker, alligator is the name chiefly used for the crocodile in America.

Mr. Wallace thus describes an alligator hunt, as pursued on the lakes in Mexiana, an island lying off the mouth of the Amazon:—'A number of negroes went into the water with long poles, driving the animals to the side, where others awaited them with harpoons and lassos. Sometimes, the lasso was at once thrown over their heads, or, if first harpooned, a lasso was then secured to them, either over the head or the tail, and they were easily dragged to the shore by the united force of ten or twelve men. Another lasso was fixed, if necessary, so as to fasten them at both ends; and, on being pulled out of the water, a negro cautiously approached with an axe, and cut a deep gash across the root of the tail, rendering this formidable weapon useless; another blow across the neck disabled the head; and the animal was then left, and pursuit of another commenced, which was speedily reduced to the same condition.

'Sometimes the cord would break, or the harpoon get loose, and the negroes had often to wade into the water among the ferocious animals in a very hazardous manner. They were from ten to eighteen feet long, sometimes even twenty, with enormous mis-shapen heads and fearful rows of long, sharp teeth. When a number were out on the land, dead or dying, they were cut open, and the fat, which accumulates in considerable quantities about the intestines, was taken out, and made up into packets in the skins of the smaller ones, taken off for the purpose. After killing twelve or fifteen, the overseer and his party went off to another lake at a short distance, where the alligators were more plentiful, and by night had killed nearly fifty. The next day they killed twenty or thirty more, and got out the fat from the others. In some of these lakes 100 alligators have been killed in a few days; in the Amazon or Para rivers it would be difficult to kill as many in a year. The fat is boiled down into oil and burned in lamps. It has rather a disagreeable smell, but not worse than train-oil.'

The flesh of the land alligator, as it is termed by the Malays (the *Hydrosaurus salvator*), which occasionally attains the length of five or six feet, makes, it is said, good eating, and is much esteemed by the natives for its supposed restorative and invigorating properties. At Manila, these creatures are regularly sold in the markets, and fetch a good price; the dried skin is readily bought by the Chinese, who use it in some of their indescribable messes of gelatinous soup.

Another species eaten is the *Hydrosaurus giganteus*. Like that of the *Iguanæ* of the New World, the flesh of these saurians is delicate eating, and has been compared to that of a very young sucking pig.

The eggs of all the different kinds of alligators, and there are three or four distinct species abounding in the Amazon and its tributary streams, are eaten by the natives, though they have a very strong musky odour. The largest species of alligator (*Jacare nigra*), reaches a length of 15 or rarely 20 feet.

Mr. Wallace, in his *Travels*, records, that on one occasion, the Indians on the Rio Negro supped off a young alligator they had caught in a brook near, 'but the musty odour was so strong that I could not stomach it, and after getting down a bit of the tail, finished my supper with mingau, or gruel of mandioc.'

Alligators are killed in great numbers in parts of the river Amazon, for their fat, which is made into oil.

Hernandez states, that the flesh of the Axolotl, an aquatic reptile, is very agreeable and wholesome. It is the *Siren pisciformis* of Shaw; the *Menobranchus pisciformis*, Harl. It is commonly sold in the markets of Mexico. When dressed after the manner of stewed eels, and served up, with a stimulating sauce, it is esteemed a great luxury. The flesh of the sauve-garde or common Teguixin of Brazil (*Teguixin monitor* of Gray, *Teius Teguixin*) is eaten, and is said to be excellent.

The flesh of the common ada of Mr. Gray is accounted excellent by the natives of Guiana, who compare it to a fowl; its eggs are also in great request. It is the *Thorictes dracæna*, Bibron; *La grande dragonne*, Cuvier, and attains the length of four to six feet.

Some species of lizards are used as food in Burmah. One of these especially, called pada, is stated not to be inferior to a fowl, — this is probably the iguana. Nearly every species of serpent is eaten there, after the head has been cut off. All have a fishy taste. Some few kinds, however, although the teeth are carefully removed, cannot be used, as the flesh appears to be poisonous.

The flesh of snakes is eaten by many in Dominica, particularly by the French, some of whom are very fond of it; but it is reckoned unwholesome, and to occasion the leprosy.

A snake called, by the natives of Western Australia wango, is particularly liked by them as food.

There is a very venomous yellow-bellied snake, from five to six feet long, called locally dubyt, which is much dreaded; but that is also eaten by them.

The formidable lance-headed viper, of the Leeward Islands (*Trigonocephalus lanceolatus*), feeds chiefly on birds, lizards, and rats. After swallowing their prey, these snakes exhale a disgusting odour; this does not prevent the negroes from eating their flesh, which they find, it is said, free from any unpleasant flavour.

Mr. Buckland, in his interesting volume, *Curiosities of Natural History*, says, he once had the opportunity of tasting a boa-constrictor, that had been killed by an accident, and came into his possession.

'I tried the experiment,' he observes, 'and cooked a bit of him; it tasted very like veal, the flesh being exceedingly white and firm. If I had had nothing else, and could have forgotten what I was eating, I could easily have made a dinner of it.'

The flesh of serpents was held in high repute by the ancients, medicinally; and, when properly prepared, seems to have made a very agreeable article of diet, corresponding with the turtle soup of the present day. Even now, in the French tariff, vipers are subject to a duty of 4s. the cwt.

In Guatemala, there is a popular belief, that lizards eaten alive cure the cancer. The Indians are said to have made this important discovery; and in 1780, the subject was investigated by European physicians. I do not find the remedy in the modern pharmacopœias, nevertheless, the inhabitants of Amatitlan, the town where the discovery was first made, still adhere to their belief in its efficacy. The man who first eat a live oyster or clam, was certainly a venturous fellow, but the eccentric individual who allowed a live lizard to run down his throat, was infinitely more so. There is no accounting for taste.

Probably some of our learned physiologists and medical men may be able to explain the therapeutic effects.

Some of the tribes of Southern Guinea, eat the boa-constrictor, or python, and consider it delicate food. The more informed among them, however, regard the practice as peculiarly heathenish. In Ceylon, the flesh of the anaconda, which is said to devour travellers, is much esteemed as food by some of the natives.

Who shall determine what is good eating? When we have gone over so many delicacies, we must not be surprised at men's eating rattlesnakes, and pronouncing them capital food. An English writer, who has recently published a work entitled *A Ride over the Rocky Mountains to Oregon and California*, in describing the journey across the great desert, says:—

'12th July.—Shot two prairie dogs. Jem killed a hare and rattlesnake. They were all capital eating, not excepting the snake, which the parson cooked, and thought it as good as eel!'

The Australian aborigines, and some of the Kafir tribes, commonly eat snakes roasted in the fire—and stewed snakes may, for aught I know, be as good as stewed eels.

The Italians regale themselves with a jelly made of stewed vipers.

The Bushman of Africa catches serpents, not only as an article of food, but to procure poison for his arrows.

Various reliable accounts before me prove that rattlesnakes are not unfit for food, and may be placed among the multifarious articles regarded by man as delicacies of the table. The negroes eat the flesh of the rattlesnake, as well as that of other serpents. When the skin and intestines are removed, no bad odour remains. A correspondent of the *Penny Magazine* thus describes his experience of fried rattlesnakes, at a tavern in Kaskaskia, a small town on the Mississippi. He finds there a party of four or five travellers, who had been on an exploring expedition: —

'After a brief interview, they politely invited me to partake of the supper they had already bespoken, informing me, at the same time, that they considered themselves peculiarly fortunate in having procured an excellent dish, — in fact, a great delicacy — in a place where they expected to meet with but indifferent fare. What this great delicacy was, they did not attempt to explain; and, having without hesitation accepted of their invitation, I felt no inclination to make any farther inquiries.

'When the hour of supper arrived, the principal dish — and, indeed, almost the only one upon the table — appeared to me to be a dish of good-sized eels fried. I being the guest of my new acquaintances, had the honor of being the first served with a plate of what the person who presided called 'Musical Jack.' 'Musical Jack,' thought I, is some species of eel peculiar to the Mississippi and its tributary waters; and taking it for granted that it was all right, I forthwith began to ply my knife and fork. 'Stop,' said the individual that occupied the bottom of the table, before I had swallowed two mouthfuls. 'You, sir, have no idea, I presume, what you are eating; and since you are our guest for the time being, I think it but right that you should have no cause hereafter to think yourself imposed upon. The dish before you, which we familiarly call 'Musical Jack,' is composed of rattlesnakes, which the hunter who accompanies us in our tour of exploration was so fortunate to procure for us this afternoon. It is far from the first time that we have fared thus; and, although our own hunter skinned, decapitated, and dressed the creatures, it was only through dint of coaxing that our hostess was prevailed upon to lend her frying-pan for so vile a purpose.'

'Although curiosity had on many occasions prompted me to taste strange and unsavoury dishes, I must confess that never before did I feel such a loathing and disgust as I did towards the victuals before me. I was scarcely able to listen to the conclusion of this short address, ere I found it prudent to hurry out of the room; nor did I return till supper was over, and 'Musical Jack' had either been devoured or dismissed their presence.

'As far as I recollect the circumstance, there was nothing peculiar or disagreeable in the flavour of the small quantity I ate; and when the subject was calmly discussed on the following day, one of the party assured me he was really partial to the meat of the rattlesnake, although some of the other members of his party had not been fully able to conquer their early-conceived antipathies towards this snake; but that during their long journey they had been occasionally prevailed upon to make trial of a small quantity of the flesh, and were willing to own that had they, been ignorant of its nature, they should have pronounced it of a quality passably good.

'Ever afterwards in my visits to Kaskaskia, I narrowly examined every dish of a dubious character that was placed before me, in order to satisfy myself that it was not 'Musical Jack."

Dr. Lang, in one of his works, gives us an account of snake cooking in Australia:—

'One of the black fellows took the snake, and placing it on the branch of a tree, and striking it on the back of the head repeatedly with a piece of wood, threw it into the fire. The animal was not quite dead, for it wriggled for a minute or two in the fire, and then became very stiff and swollen, apparently from the expansion of the gases imprisoned in its body. The black fellow then drew it out of the fire, and with a knife cut through the skin longitudinally on both sides of the animal, from the head to the tail. He then coiled it up as a sailor does a rope, and laid it again upon the fire, turning it over again and again with a stick till he thought it sufficiently done on all sides, and superintending the process of cooking with all the interest imaginable. When he thought it sufficiently roasted, he thrust a stick into the coil, and laid it on the grass to cool, and when cool enough to admit of handling, he took it up again, wrung off its head and tail, which he threw away, and then broke the rest of the animal by the joints of the vertebræ into several pieces, one of which he threw to the other black fellow, and another he began eating himself with much apparent relish. Neither Mr. Wade nor myself having ever previously had the good fortune to witness the dressing of a snake for dinner by the black natives, we were much interested with the whole operation; and as the steam from the roasting snake was by no means unsavoury, and the flesh delicately white, we were each induced to try a bit of it. It was not unpalatable by any means, although rather fibrous and stringy like ling-fish. Mr. Wade observed, that it reminded him of the taste of eels; but as there was a strong prejudice against the use of eels as an article of food in the west of Scotland, in my boyhood, I had never tasted an eel, and was therefore unable to testify to the correctness of this observation. There was doubtless an equally strong prejudice to get over in the case of a snake, and for an hour or two after I had partaken of it, my stomach was ever and anon on the point of insurrection at the very idea of the thing; but, thinking it unmanly to yield to such a feeling, I managed to keep it down.'

In a paper which I published in the *Journal of the Society of Arts*, in October 1856, (vol. 4, p. 872,) I entered very fully into a description of the various snakes which are met with in different countries, poisonous or harmless, and to that paper I would refer those who wish to obtain descriptive details—scientific or general—not bearing on the subject of food, at present under our consideration.

The consumption of frogs is not, as is very often supposed, confined to the French. It is now also indulged in, to a considerable extent, by Americans; and frogs appear to command a high price in the New York market. An enthusiastic writer tries to convince us, that the only objection to frogs as an article of diet is a mere prejudice on the part of those who have never eaten them. 'In what respect are they worse than eels? The frog who swallows young birds and ducklings is surely as clean a feeder as the snake-like creature that dines on dead dogs, and makes the celebrity of the ait at Twickenham. Or is a frog less savoury than a rat? And yet what a price was paid for rats at the siege of Kars! If the garrison could only have been supplied with lots of frogs—literal or metaphorical—the Russians would never have taken the place. Again, does a snail—the large escargot, which people are so fond of in Paris—appear more tempting than a frog? Or that animal picked out of its shell with a pin, and called, in vulgar parlance, a winkle. 'Away, then,' as indignant orators say, 'away, then, with this cant of false delicacy and squeamishness, and the very first opportunity you have, *O lector fastidioso!* order *A Dish of Frogs*. They are quite as good as whitebait, when assisted by a flask of Rhenish.'

The *Athenæum*, also, recently came out in favour of frogs. 'There is no reason,' it remarks, 'why we should eschew frogs and relish turtle; still less is there for our eating one or two of the numerous edible funguses, which our island produces, and condemning all the rest.'

The green or edible frog (*Rana esculenta*) is a native of Europe, some parts of Asia, and also of Northern Africa. It is in high request on the Continent for its flesh, the meat of the hind quarters, which is alone used, being delicate and well tasted. In Vienna, where the consumption of these frogs is very considerable, they are preserved alive, and fattened in froggeries (grenouillières) constructed for the express purpose.

In America, the flesh of the huge bull-frog (*R. pipiens*, Harl.; *R. mugiens*, Catesby,) is tender, white, and affords excellent eating. Some bull-frogs weigh as much as half-a-pound, but the hind legs are the only parts used as food. They make excellent bait for the larger cat-fish.

In the Antilles, another huge bull-frog is reared in a state of domestication for the table. It is the *Rana ocellata*, Linn; *R. gigas* of Spix; *Cystignathus ocellatus*, Wagler.

Toads seem also to be eaten by the French, though unwittingly. Professor Dumeril used to relate, in his lectures at the Jardin des Plantes, that the frogs brought to the markets in Paris are caught in the stagnant waters round Montmorenci, in the Bois de Vincennes, Bois de Boulogne, &c. The people employed in this traffic separate the hind quarters and legs of the frogs from the body, denude them of their skin, arrange them on skewers, as larks are done in this country, and then bring them in that state to market. In seeking for frogs, these dealers often meet with toads, which they do not reject, but prepare them in the same way as they would frogs; and, as it is impossible to determine whether the hind quarters of these creatures, after the skin is stripped off, belong to frogs or toads, it continually happen that great numbers of the supposed frogs sold in Paris for food are actually toads.[18]

This account of the mode of bringing the frogs to market, in Paris, does not tally with that given by my friend, Mr. F. T. Buckland, in his *Curiosities of Natural History*; he says:—

'In France, frogs are considered a luxury, as any *bon vivant* ordering a dish of them at the *Trois Frères*, at Paris, may, by the long price, speedily ascertain. Not wishing to try such an expensive experiment in gastronomy, I went to the large market in the Faubourg St. Germain, and enquired for frogs. I was referred to a stately-looking dame at a fish-stall, who produced a box nearly full of them, huddling and crawling about, and occasionally croaking as though aware of the fate to which they were destined. The price fixed was two a penny, and having ordered a dish to be prepared, the *Dame de la Halle* dived her hand in among them, and having secured her victim by the hind legs, she severed him in twain with a sharp knife; the legs, minus skin, still struggling, were placed on a dish; and the head, with the fore-legs affixed, retained life and motion, and performed such motions that the operation became painful to look at. These legs were afterwards cooked at the *restaurateur's*, being served up fried in bread crumbs, as larks are in England; and most excellent eating they were, tasting more like the delicate flesh of the rabbit than anything else I can think of. I afterwards tried a dish of the common English frog, but his flesh is not so white nor so tender as that of his French brother.'

The Chinese seem also to appreciate frogs, for Mr. Fortune, in describing a Chinese market, says—

'Frogs seemed much in demand. They are brought to market in tubs and baskets, and the vender employs himself in skinning them as he sits making sales. He is extremely expert at this part of his business. He takes up the frog in his left hand, and with a knife, which he holds in his right, chops off the fore part of its head. The skin is then drawn back over the body and down to the feet, which are chopped off and thrown away. The poor frog, still alive, but headless, skinless, and feetless, is then thrown into another tub, and the operation is repeated on the rest in the same way. Every now and then the artist lays down his knife, and takes up his scales to weigh these animals for his customers, and make his sales. Everything in this civilised country, whether it be gold or silver, geese or frogs, is sold by weight.'

According to Seba and Madame Merian, the negroes eat the flesh of the Surinam toad (*Pipa Surinamensis*).

Frogs or toads of an enormous size (*Crapaux*) are very numerous in Dominica, and much esteemed as an article of food; the flesh, when fricasseed, being preferred by the English, as well as French, to chickens; and, when made into soup, recommended for the sick, especially in consumptive cases.

Wallace, in his *Travels on the Amazon*, tells us, 'his Indians went several times early in the morning to the gapo to catch frogs, which they obtained in great numbers, stringing them on a sipo, and boiling them entire, entrails and all, and devoured them with much gusto. The frogs are mottled of various colours, have dilated toes, and are called jui.'

The eating of frogs seems to be indulged in in the Philippines, for a traveller tells us that—

'After the rains there may generally be procured, by those who like them, frogs, which are taken from the ditch round the walls in great numbers, and are then fat and in good condition for eating, making a very favourite curry of some of the Europeans, their flesh being very tender.'[19]

FISH

More than two-thirds of our globe being covered by the waters of the ocean, and of the remaining third a great part being washed by extensive rivers, or occupied by lakes, ponds, or marshes, these watery realms, teeming with life, furnish man with a great variety of food. Some of these have already passed under consideration in the reptilia, and others in the great class mammalia, as seals, morses, and manatees, which can remain at no great distance from the sea, together with whales, which never leave it, though constantly obliged, by the nature of their respiration, to seek its surface.

Mollusca, crustacea, annelides, and zoophytes are almost peculiar to this element, having but few scattered representatives on earth; but, amidst all its varied inhabitants, there are none more exclusively confined to its realms, none that rule them with such absolute sway, none more remarkable for number, variety of form, beauty of colour, and, above all, for the infinite advantages which they yield to man, than the great class of fishes. In fact, their evident superiority has caused their name to pass as a general appellation to all the inhabitants of the deep. Whales are called fish, crabs are called shell-fish, and the same term is used to denote oysters; though the first are mammalia, the second articulata, and the third mollusca.

Milton has well described the abundance of fish—

——'Each creek and bay,

With fry innumerable swarm and shoals

Of fish, that with their fins and shining scales,

Glide under the green waves; * * *

* * * part single, or with mate

Graze the sea-weed, their pasture, and through groves

Of coral stray; or sporting, with quick glance,

Show to the sun their way'd coats dropp'd with gold.'

The modes of preserving fish are various; they are salted and dried, smoked and potted, baked or marinated, preserved in oil, and pounded in a dry mass.

Several savage nations possess the art of preparing fish in a great variety of ways, even as a kind of flour, bread, &c.

Dr. Davy, commenting upon the remarkable facts respecting the exemption of fish-eating persons from certain diseases, suggests that there is undoubtedly something in the composition of fish which is not common to other articles of food, whether vegetable or animal. He believes this consists of iodine. He says, that in all instances in which he sought for this substance in *sea fish* he has found it; and also traces of it in migratory fish, but not in *fresh-water fish*.

The trials he made were limited to red gurnard, mackerel, haddock, common cod, whiting, sole, ling, herring, pilchard, salmon, sea-trout, smelt, and trout.

The experiment was as follows.—He dried and charred, lixiviated, reduced to ashes, and again washed from a quarter of a pound to a pound of fish.

A good deal of limy matter was afforded from the washings of the charcoal of the sea fish.

The saline matter was principally common salt, had a pretty strong alkaline reaction, and by the blue hue produced by starch and *aqua regia*, afforded a clear proof of the presence of iodine. Only a slight trace was detected in the fresh-water salmon, sea-trout, and smelt. In the spent salmon descending to the sea, only just a perceptible trace was observable, and no trace in either parr or trout.

Dr. Davy states further, that he has detected it in an unmistakable manner in the common shrimp; also in the cockle, mussel, oyster, crab, &c.; nor is this remarkable, considering that it enters into the greater part of the food of fishes.

He observes, also, that cod liver oil is well established as an alterative or cure of pulmonary consumption, and as this oil contains iodine, the inference is, that sea fish, generally, may be alike beneficial. The practical application of this inquiry is obvious. A suggestion is also made as to the efficacy of drying fish, even without salt, the drying being complete to the exclusion of even hydroscopic water, for the use of the explorer and traveller.

The inference as to the salutary effects of fish depending on the presence of iodine, in the prevention of tubercular disease, might be extended to *goitre*, which it is known has already yielded to iodine. This formidable complaint appears to be completely unknown to the inhabitants of sea-ports and sea-coasts. Respecting another and concluding question, viz., the different parts of fish, it is to be remarked that, so far as experiments have gone, the effects will not be the same from all parts of the fish, because the inorganic elements are not the same. The examples chosen are the liver, muscle, roe, or melt. In the ash of the liver and muscle of sea-fish, Dr. Davy always found a large proportion of saline matter, common salt, abounding, with a minute portion of iodine, rather more in the liver than the muscle, and free alkali, or alkali in a state to occasion an alkaline reaction, as denoted by test-paper; whilst in the roe or melt there has been detected very little saline matter, no trace of iodine, nor of free alkali; on the contrary, a free acid, viz., phosphorus, analogous to what occurs in the yolk of an egg, and in consequence of which it is very difficult to digest either the roe or melt of a fish, or the yolk of an egg. The same conclusion on the same ground is applicable to fresh-water fish, viz., the absence of iodine.

A very common North American dish is chowder, which is thus prepared:—

Fry brown several slices of pork; cut each fish into five or six pieces; flour, and place a layer of them in your pork fat; sprinkle on a little pepper and salt; add cloves, mace, and sliced onions; if liked, lay on bits of the fried pork, and crackers soaked in cold water. Repeat this till you put in all the fish; turn on water just sufficient to cover them, and put on a heated bake pan lid. After stewing about 20 minutes, take up the fish, and mix two teaspoonfuls of flour with a little water, and stir it into the gravy, adding a little pepper and butter. A tumbler of wine, catsup, and spices will improve it. Cod and bass make the best chowder. In making clam chowder, the hard part of the clam should be cut off and rejected.

Fish glue consists almost wholly of gelatine; 100 grains of good dry isinglass, containing rather more than 98 of matter soluble in water.

Isinglass may be obtained from many fish. Jackson states, that the sounds of cod afford it; and that the lakes of America abound with fish, from which the very finest isinglass may be obtained. This substance is best prepared in summer, as frost impairs the colour, and deprives it of weight and of gelatinous principle.

It is made into jellies and blanc-manger, by the cook and confectioner, and with some sort of balsam, spread on silk, forms the court-plaister of the shops.

Fish maws are the dried stomachs of fishes, like our cod's sounds, which being considered a great luxury by the Chinese, and as possessing strengthening and aphrodisiac properties, are brought over in the junks from the Indian islands.

Crawford states, that they often fetch upwards of £14 per cwt. in the Canton market. The exports of fish maws from Bombay average from 1500 to 2500 cwts. per annum; from Madras, about 50 cwts.; and from Bengal about 4,000 lbs.

Caviar is the common name for a preparation of the dried spawn, or salted roe of fish. The black caviar is made from the roe of sturgeon, and a single large fish will sometimes yield as much as 120 lbs. of roe. A cheaper and less prized red kind is obtained from the roe of the gray mullet, and some of the carp species, which are common in the rivers, and on the shores of the Black Sea. Caviar is principally consumed in Russia, Germany, and Italy, by the Greeks, during their long fasts, and also in small quantities in England. Inferior caviar is made into small, dry cakes. One thousand cwt. of caviar has been shipped from Odessa in a single season, and from Astracan, about 30,000 barrels. The produce of caviar from the Caspian sea, some years ago, was as much as a million and a half of pounds.

A preparation called botargo is made on the coasts of the Mediterranean from the spawn of a kind of fine mullet of a red color. The best is said to be made at Tunis, but it is also common in Sicily.

The dried roe of an enormous species of shad, which frequents the great river of Siak in Sumatra, constitutes an article of commerce in the East. According to Dr. Richardson, very good bread may be made from the roe of the pollack, an ocean fish (*Gadus pollachius*), found on both sides of the Atlantic, and in the Indian seas: on the British coasts it is often termed the cod-fish; and when young, the whiting pollack. In North America, this fish is so plentiful that it is salted and sold by the quintal like cod or ling.

The Chinook Indians of the Columbia rivers are very fond of herrings' roes, which they collect in the following manner:—They sink cedar branches to the bottom of the river, in shallow places, by placing upon them a few heavy stones, taking care not to cover the green foliage, as the fish prefer spawning on anything green, and they literally cover all the branches by next morning with spawn. The Indians wash this off in their water-proof baskets, to the bottom of which it sinks; this is squeezed by the hand into little balls and then dried, and is very palatable.

The large roe of the Callipeva fish, already alluded to, is considered a delicacy in the West Indies. The mode of curing it differs widely from that in which the roe of the sturgeon and the sterlet is prepared.

The following is the account given by Goldsmith, in his *History of the Earth and Animated Nature*, of the way in which the latter is manufactured:—

'They take the spawn, and freeing it from the small membranes that connect it together, they wash it with vinegar, and afterwards spread it to dry upon a table; they then put it into a vessel with salt, breaking the spawn with their hands, and not with a pestle. This done, they put it into a canvas bag, letting the liquor drain from it. Lastly, they put it into a tub with holes at the bottom, so that if there be any moisture still remaining, it may run out; then it is pressed down and covered up for use.'

Very different is the manner adopted by the Spaniards in Central America in curing the roe of the callipeva. They do it in this wise:—First, they rub the roe well with salt and a little nitre, then they put a number of them one upon another, and compress them by means of a heavy weight. After this, they make an altar of green boughs, covering the top also with green branches traversing each other. The inside being filled with straw and fresh leaves, which are ignited, they place the roes on the top and cover them well up likewise with green boughs. They are allowed to remain there six or seven days, during which time the fire keeps smouldering and sending up a thick smoke which is concentrated upon the roes by the upper layer of branches. This they call barbecuing. The membraneous covering of the roe is not taken off, consequently it will keep for a long time, the air being entirely excluded from it. When the roe is eaten, it should be cut in very thin slices. The outer coating should not be taken off, but rubbed clean with a dry napkin.

In New Caledonia, the natives are said to eat the roe of the *Salmo scouleri* mixed with rancid oil, which, in their estimation, gives the savoury morsel additional flavour. The smell alone is said by a traveller to be so nauseous as to prevent any but a native from partaking of it, unless severely pressed with hunger.

Dr. Richardson tells us that, when well bruised and mixed with a little flour, the roe of the methy (*Lotha maculosa*) can be baked into very good biscuits, which are used in the fur countries as tea-bread.

Among the Anglo-Saxons and in the middle ages, fish of almost every kind were eaten, including many now thought unwholesome. Whales, when accidentally taken on our coasts, appear in those early times to have been also salted for food; an allowance is entered, amongst the other expenses of John de Lee, Sheriff of Essex and Herts, for guarding a whale taken off Mersey Island; for emptying of casks to put it in; for salt to salt it; and for carrying it to the court of Stamford.

Brand states porpoises to have been sold for food in the Newcastle market as late as 1575. Sturgeon, and in the northern nations, whales, were early reserved as royalties; and in England, whales and great sturgeons taken in the sea were, by the Act 17 Edward II., to be the king's, except in certain privileged places. In the dinner bills of the Goldsmiths' Company, besides the ordinary fish, we find blote-fish, jowls and middles of sturgeons, salt lampreys, congers, pike, bream, bass, tench, and chub, a seal, and porpoise mentioned.

The red herring is included in an inquisition 28 Henry III.; and the Act of Parliament 31 Edward III., called the *Statute of Herrings*, shows the great request in which this most useful article of food was then held by the English.

Herrings by the *last*, or 10,000, were sent from Hull to London, and from Yarmouth to Hull, as also red herrings, in the time of Edward I.

The tariff of prices of fish, fixed by the same king, acquaints us with the rates at which the various kinds were sold. It limits the best soles to 3*d*. per dozen; the best turbot to 6*d*.; the best mackerel in Lent to 1*d*. each; the best pickled herrings to twenty the penny; fresh oysters to 2*d*. per gallon; a quarter of a hundred of the best eels to 2*d*.; and other fish in proportion. 'Congers, lampreys, and sea-hogs,' are enumerated. Mackerel are first mentioned in 1247, as allowed to certain religions on the third day of the Rogation, and are noticed as a metropolitan cry in the ballad of *London Lickpenny*;[20] and 'stokfish, salt fische, whyt herring, réde herring, salt salmon, salt sturgeon, salt eels, &c.,' are mentioned as common provisions in the Earl of Northumberland's household, in the reign of Henry VII.; and then formed part of every meal. Thus, 'for my Lord and Ladie's table,' is to be bought, 'ij pecys of salt fische, vj pecys of salt fische, vj becormed herryng, iiij white herryng, or a dish of sproots.' And these breakfasts of salt fish extended through the household, whose separate departments, and the way they were to be served with this article, both in and out of Lent, are particularized, and afford a curious picture of the style of living in the ancient Catholic periods, and of the amazing use and consumption of salt-fish. In short, it formed part of the allowances of the King and the Nobility, of monastic establishments, and of all ranks of society.

The fish ordinaries still kept up at the taverns at Billingsgate, where all kinds of fish in season may be partaken of for a moderate charge at fixed hours, are but a continuation of a very old practice, although the locality is removed; for Stow tells us that Knightrider street, was famous *'for fish and fish dinners;'* and he derives the name of Friday-street from fishmongers dwelling there and serving the *Friday* markets.

Philip II. of Spain, the consort of Queen Mary gave a whimsical reason for not eating fish. 'They are,' said he, 'nothing but element congealed, or a jelly of water.'

The broth or jelly of fish, which is usually thrown away, will be found one of the most nourishing animal jellies that can be obtained. It is a pity that those who find it difficult to obtain a sufficiency of nourishing food should not be aware of this, as they might thereby make a second meal of what otherwise yields but one. Supposing a poor family to buy a dinner of plaice, which is a cheap fish—the plaice would be boiled and the meat of the fish eaten, and the liquor and bones of the fish thrown away. Now, let the good housewife put the remains of the fish into the liquor and boil for a couple of hours, and she will find she has something in her pot, which, when strained off, will be as good to her as much of that which is sold in the shops as 'gelatine.' This she may use as a simple broth, or she may thicken it with rice, and flavor it with onion and pepper, and have a nourishing and satisfying meal; or, should she have an invalid in her family, one-third of milk added and warmed with it, would be nourishing and restoring.

Dr. Davy, in his *Angler and his Friend*, tells us, 'There is much nourishment in fish, little less than in butcher's meat, weight for weight; and in effect it may be more nourishing, considering how, from its softer fibre, fish is more easily digested. Moreover, there is, I find, in fish—sea-fish—a substance which does not exist in the flesh of land-animals, viz., iodine—a substance which may have a beneficial effect on the health, and tend to prevent scrofulous and tubercular disease, the latter in the form of pulmonary consumption, one of the most cruel and fatal with which civilized society, and the highly educated and refined are afflicted. Comparative trials prove that, in the majority of fish, the proportion of solid matter—that is, the matter which remains after perfect desiccation, or the expulsion of the aqueous part—is little inferior to that of the several kinds of butcher's meat, game or poultry. And, if we give our attention to classes of people—classed as to quality of food they principally subsist on—we find that the ichthyophagous class are especially strong, healthy, and prolific. In no class than that of fishers do we see larger families, handsomer women, or more robust and active men, or greater exemption from maladies just alluded to.'

In the pastry cooks' shops of Russia, the tempting morsel offered to Russian appetites is the *piroga*, an oily fish-cake. Little benches are ranged round tables, on which the favourite dainty is placed, covered over with an oily canvass, for it must be eaten hot. A large pot of green oil and a stand of salt are in readiness, and, as soon as a purchaser demands a piroga, it is withdrawn from its cover, plunged into the oil, sprinkled with salt, and presented dripping to the delighted Muscovite.

'In some countries, fish, when tainted or even putrid is preferred to that which is fresh. The inhabitants of the banks of the Senegal and Orange rivers pound some small fish of the size of sprats in a wooden mortar, as they are taken from the stream, and afterwards make them up into conical lumps, like our sugar-loaves, which they dry in the sun. In this state, they soon become slightly decomposed, and give out a most unpleasant odour;

notwithstanding which, these people consider them a luxury, and eat them dissolved in water, mixed with their kouskoussoo, or dough. Fish, prepared in a somewhat similar manner, is eaten by the Indians on the banks of the Orinoco.[21]'

In Beloochistan, the inhabitants feed almost entirely on fish; and their cattle are also fed on dried fish and dates mixed together.

No one who has observed a boiled fish upon the table can have passed unremarked the spinal column with its upward and downward processes, and the four transverse strips of flesh, adjusted alternately in different directions with strong semi-transparent tendons between. The spinous processes, proceeding from the vertebræ upward, support the dorsal fins, whilst the transverse processes downward, with curved bones, encircle partially the bulk of the body. Without being ribs, these latter resemble ribs. Those placed far forward represent the proper thoracic ribs of fishes, but have no direct connexion with the spine. There are other rib-like bones behind. These are abdominal appendages; very numerous in some fishes, such as the herrings, and very few,—and those few conveniently large,—in others, such as the perches and labruses. They are wanting in several of the osseous tribes, such as the Diodons and Tetradons, and are altogether non-existent in the cartilaginous fishes. It is from this fact—that so many of the West Indian fishes belong to the Percoid and Labroid families—that persons are so seldom troubled with what are called by the cook, 'bony fishes.'—Hence, very little annoyance is experienced from the bones in the fish dishes there.

Very serious consequences have often arisen from eating fish or molluscs, which are poisonous or in an unhealthy state. All Ostraceans, Diodons, and Tetradons, are deleterious, and are to be treated as objectionable, if not absolutely dangerous fishes.

Every one acquainted with the bad reputation of the common mussel (*Mytilus edulis*) knows also the symptoms produced by the hurtful qualities of it, even when cooked—for it is not generally, like the oyster, eaten raw.

The mussels would seem to owe this injurious quality to feeding on the spawn of the star-fish (*Asteria*).

There are many persons who break out with irritative eruptions after eating certain descriptions of shell-fish, though they injure no other idiosyncrasies—others again are subject to diarrhœa from fish-diet, though the same food be harmless to other persons.

Almost all fishes are unwholesome at certain seasons, and hence the regulations laid down for the vend of oysters, lobsters, salmon, &c., only in prescribed periods. Science, in searching to determine the reason why this is the case, encounters certain wholesale occurrences which are due to some general, but at the same time, very specific causes. Mackerel sold in the New York market occasionally produce poisonous effects; and London is sometimes supplied with unwholesome salmon in large quantities.

Dr. Burroughs, in a paper on *Poisonous Fishes*, published last year in a Jamaica journal, remarks:

'There are five obvious circumstances to be taken into consideration in the incidents of fish-poison.

'1st. The existence of a *sanies*, from some disorder indicated in the living tissues of the animal.

'2ndly. A natural deleteriousness in the flesh, without reference to a state of disease.

'3rdly. The adventitious presence of something deleterious in the fish, from the food recently eaten.

'4thly. The injury resulting from cooking fish with such large organs as the liver unextracted,—the liver being at all times dangerous as food in some particular fishes.

'5thly. The poisonous putrefaction known to prevail in some fishes after 24 hours keeping. Morbid action set up in the healthy animal body that receives the putrefactive poison being indicated by oppression, nausea, giddiness, and general prostration.'

We might add a 6th,—the known existence of an irritating fluid,— issuing from the surface of some fishes of peculiar structure.

We know that fish liver contains an enormous quantity of oil; that fish oil is an important article of commerce, and fish liver oil is a valuable medicine; but we know beside, that these oils, in a corrupt state, are active poisons. Hence, we may infer that the liver is a great operator in the injury done by the deleterious fishes, and if we but knew all the genera in which the gall bladder is wanting, we might arrive at some rule for estimating the possible development of those prejudicial fluids that mingle from the liver with fish-flesh in cooking.

We must not overlook, when speaking of fish-liver, the adventure of Tobias and the Angel at the River Tigris, in chap. vi. of the Apocryphal Tobit. The heart and liver of the fish they took were a charm against evil spirits, and the gall was a salve for blind eyes; the one was used successfully in the nuptial chamber of Sarah, the daughter of Ragual, and the other as an ointment in restoring the sight of the blind Tobit. The two incidents are thus related. Ch. viii.—'Tobias took the ashes of the perfumes, and put the heart and the liver of the fish thereupon, and made a smoke therewith—the which smell when the evil spirit had smelled, he fled into the utmost parts of Egypt, and the angel bound him.' Ch. xi.—'Tobit stumbled, and his Son Tobias ran unto him, and strake of the gall on his Father's eyes, and when his eyes began to smart, he rubbed them, and the whiteness pilled away from the corners of his eyes.'

There are but few natural orders of fishes—and they divide themselves for the purposes of our enquiry chiefly into the *Acanthopterygii*, or those that possess bony skeletons, with prickly, spinous processes on the dorsal fins, such as the perch, the mullet, and the gurnard; the *Malacopterygii*, or soft-finned fishes, including the carp, the salmon, &c.; and the *Chondropterygii*, with cartilaginous spines and bones, embracing such fish as the sturgeon, shark, and skate. Instead of describing or specifying them in consecutive order, it will perhaps be better to take a glance at the fishes of different seas, at least, as far as they are held in any repute as food. Many of the most common must, however, be passed over without notice.

It is strange how little attention, (comparatively speaking,) is paid even to our coast fisheries, and especially those of our colonies. Fisheries have been called the agriculture of the sea. Raleigh attributes the wealth and power of Holland, not to its commerce or carrying trade, but to its fisheries. Mirabeau was of the like opinion; De Witt held the same; and Franklin seemed to prefer the fisheries of America to agriculture itself. A great nursery of the marine is by this means best supported, from whence a constant supply of men, inured to the perils of the sea and the inclemency of the weather, is always ready for the maritime service of their country. Fishing has been celebrated from the earliest times, as being the prelude, and if I may be allowed the expression, the apprenticeship of navigation; offering, from the line to the harpoon, more amusement with less fatigue than perhaps any other species of pursuit, and occupying the smallest boat up to ships of great burthen; thus drawing forth the means of subsistence and profit to an infinite number of persons.

The ocean fish are generally very dry eating.

In eating the flesh of the bonito, it is necessary to lard it well, as its flesh is very dry.

The flesh of the tunny of the Atlantic is something like veal, but dryer and more firm.

That of the dolphin was formerly held in great esteem. It is also, however, very dry and insipid; the best parts are those near the head. It is seldom eaten now at sea, except when the fish caught happens to be young and tender.

In the Maldive Islands, the bonito is preserved in the following manner:—

The back bone is taken out, the fish laid in the shade, and occasionally sprinkled with sea water. After a certain period has elapsed, the fish is wrapped up in cocoa-nut leaves, and buried in sand, where it becomes hard. Fish thus prepared is known in Ceylon, and perhaps over all India, by the name of *cummelmums*. The pieces of this fish brought to the market have a horny hardness. It is rasped upon rice to render it savoury.

The Havana is, I believe, the only place where the flesh of the shark is exposed for sale in the markets, although it is often tasted at sea by the curious.

The shark, judging by an European palate, is not good eating; the flesh is dry and of an acid taste. The fins and tail are, however, very glutinous, and are the portions most relished by the seamen; and dried, they form an article of commerce to China, where they are used in soups, and considered an excellent aphrodisiac.

'How thankful we ought to be to a bountiful Providence, who has created all things for us richly to enjoy,' observed an alderman at the last great city dinner, whilst sumptuously regaling on turtle soup, crimped cod, with oyster sauce, and other delicacies. 'The beasts of the earth, the fowls of the air, and the fishes of the sea,' he continued, 'were all created for the use of man.'

'Very true,' replied his next friend, 'but if you had witnessed the hair-breadth escape which I experienced of being devoured alive by a shark, when in the West Indies, you would have been satisfied that the horrible monster entertained just the opposite opinion. He believed that man was created for him!'

Sharks, which are very numerous there, form a common article of food with the Gold Coast negroes, and hippopotami and alligators are occasionally eaten.

Mr. George Bennett informs us, that 'the shark is eaten eagerly by the natives of the Polynesian Islands; and I have often seen them feasting on it in a raw state, when they gorge themselves to such an excess as to occasion vomiting.'

It is not an unfrequent source of illness among these islanders, and they suffer so much in consequence, as to lead them to suppose that their dissolution is nigh: but they cannot be persuaded that the eating of raw fish is the cause. An emetic soon removes the symptoms by removing the cause, and the sufferer considers the cure as almost miraculous. Sharks are caught on the New Zealand shores in great numbers, during the months of November, December, and January, by the natives, who use them as an article of food.

Shark hunting is most exciting sport.

He who has hooked the fish holds tight—like grim Death on his victim; and if you watch his face you will see powerful indication of excitement, mental and muscular; his teeth are set, his colour is heightened, the perspiration starts on his brow, while something like an oath slips through his lips as the cord, strained to the utmost, cuts into the skin of his empurpled fingers: he invokes aid, and with his feet jammed against stretcher, thwart, or gunwale, gradually shortens his hold. Meanwhile, the others, seizing lance and gaff-hook, stand by to assist the overtasked line, as the monster, darting hither and thither in silvery lightnings beneath the translucent wave, is drawn nearer and nearer the surface. 'My eyes, he's a whopper!' cries the excited young boatman. 'He's off!' shouts another, as the shark makes a desperate plunge under the boat, and the line, dragged through the hands of the holder, is again suddenly slackened. 'He's all right, never fear—belay your line a bit, sir, and look here,' says the old fisherman. And sure enough there is the huge fish clearly visible, about ten feet under the keel of the boat, and from stem to stern about the same length as herself. 'Now, sir, let's have him up.' And the instant the line is taut, the shark shoots upwards, his broad snout showing above the surface, close to the boat. Then comes a scene of activity and animation indeed. The fish, executing a series of summersaults, and spinning, gets the line into a hundred twists, and if once he succeed in bringing it across his jaws above the chain links—adieu to both fish and tackle. But, in the midst of a shower-bath, splashed up by the broad tail of the shark, both lance and gaff are hard at work. He is speared through and through, his giant struggles throwing waves of bloody water over the gunwales of the little boat; the gaffs are hooked through his tough skin, or within his jaws—for he has no gills to lay hold on; a shower of blows from axe, stretcher, or tiller, falls on his devoted head, and, if not considered too large, heavy, or dangerous, he is lugged manfully into the centre of the boat, and, threshing right and left with his tail to the last, is soon dispatched. A smart blow a few inches above the snout is more instantly fatal than the deepest stab. The school-shark is dealt with as above. But if the 'grey-nurse,' or old solitary shark be hooked, the cable is cut, or the grapnel hauled on board, and he is allowed to tow the boat as he darts away with the line. The tables, however, are soon turned upon him; and after being played (as this cruel operation in fishing is blandly styled) for a while, until some portion of his vast strength is exhausted, the line is drawn over a roller in the stern of the boat, the oars are set to work, and, towed instead of towing, the shark is drawn into some shallow cove near the shore, where his bodily powers avail him less than in deeper water; and after a fierce resistance, and some little risk to his assailants, he falls a victim to their attack. Man has as innate an horror of a shark as he has of a snake, and he who has frequented tropical climates, felt the absolute necessity of bathing, had his diurnal plunge embittered by the haunting idea of the vicinity of one of these sea-pests, and has occasionally been harrowed by accidents arising from their voracity—feels this antipathy with double force. There is, therefore, a species of delightful fury, a savage excitement, experienced by the shark-hunter, that has no affinity with the philosophy of Old Isaak's gentle art. He revels in the animated indulgence of that cruelty which is inherent in the child of wrath; and the stings of conscience are blunted by the conviction that it is an act of justice, of retribution, of duty, he is engaged in, not one of wanton barbarity. These were precisely my own sensations when, drenched to the skin with showers of salt water, scorched to blisters by the burning sun, excoriated as to my hands, covered with blood, and oil, and dirt, and breathless with exertion, I contemplated the corpse of my first shark. Tiger-hunting is a more princely pastime; boar-hunting in Bengal Proper the finest sport in the world; fox-hunting an Englishman's birthright; the chase of the moose is excellent for young men strong enough to drag a pair of snow shoes five feet long upon their toes; and Mr. Gordon Cumming tells you how man may follow the bent of his organ of destructiveness on the gigantic beasts of South Africa: shark-fishing is merely the best sport to be had in New South Wales; and affords a wholesome stimulation to the torpid action of life in Sydney. The humane or utilitarian reader will be glad to hear that the shark is not utterly useless after death. The professional fishermen extract a considerable quantity of excellent oil from the liver; and the fins cut off, cured, and packed, become an article of trade with China—whose people, for reasons best known to themselves, delight in gelatinous food. The most hideous to behold of the shark tribe is the wobegong, or woe-begone as the fishermen call it. Tiger-shark is another of the names of this fish. His broad back is spotted over with leopard-like marks; the belly is of a yellowish white; but to describe minutely so frightful a monster would be a difficult and ungracious task. Fancy a bloated toad, elongated to the extent of six or seven feet, and weighing some 20 stone; then cut off his legs, and you have a flattering likeness of the wobegong—two of which we killed this day. A heavy sluggish fish, he lies in wait for his prey at the edge of some reef of rocks, or bank of sea-weed; swallows the bait indolently; appears but little sensible to the titillation of the barbed hook, and is lugged hand over hand to the slaughter without much trouble or resistance. Neither lance nor gaff will penetrate his tough hide, but a blow on the head with an axe proves instantly fatal.'

The schnapper affords a long and strong pull at the line; and is considered by the colonists as one of their best table fish. 'We killed one to-day,' writes a correspondent, 'weighing 21 lbs. The flat-head is half buried in the sand at the bottom, but bites freely; and is, in my mind, a much better fish than the former. Our fishing-basket of this day comprised nine sharks, four schnappers, and about 40 flat-heads.'

The picked shark (*Galeus acanthias*) is very common about the coasts of Scotland, where it is taken in order to be prepared for sale, by splitting and drying; and is then much used as food among the poorer classes.

In some parts of Scotland the large spotted dog-fish constitute no inconsiderable part of the food of the poor. In North America, they are principally caught for their oil. If very large, the liver will yield a barrel of oil, or about thirty gallons. In Nova Scotia, the dried bodies are sold at 2s. 6d. the hundred, for feeding pigs. During the winter, from November till May, two fish, boiled or roasted, are given per day to a good sized store pig.

In 1842, in consequence of the great havoc committed by the swarms of sharks on the fishing banks on the coast of Finmark, eight vessels were fitted out at Hammerfest, expressly for the purpose of shark fishing, and no less than 20,000 of these rapacious fish were taken, without any apparent diminution in their numbers. The shark oil obtained from them was about 1,000 barrels.

There are shark fisheries on the eastern coast of Africa, and in several parts of the Indian Ocean, for the sake of the fins, which are exported to China. About 7,000 cwt. were imported into Canton, in 1850, chiefly from India and the Eastern Archipelago. From 7,000 to 10,000 cwt. of sharks' fins are shipped annually from Bombay, and about 1,400 cwt. from the Madras territories, to China. Sumatra, Manila, Malacca, Arracan, and the Tenasserim Provinces, also send large quantities.

Dr. Buist, of Bombay, in a communication to the Zoological Society, in 1851, stated, 'that there are thirteen large boats, with twelve men in each, constantly employed in the shark fishery at Kurrachee; the value of the fins sent to market varying from 15,000 to 18,000 rupees (£1500 to £1800), or 1000 to 1200 rupees for each boat, after allowing the Banian or factor his profit. One boat will sometimes capture at a draught as many as 100 sharks of different sizes. The average capture of each boat probably amounts to about 3000, so as to give the whole sharks captured at not less than 40,000 a year.

The great basking shark, or mhor, is always harpooned: it is found floating or asleep near the surface of the water.

'The fish, once struck, is allowed to run till tired; it is then pulled in, and beaten with clubs till stunned. A large hook is now hooked into its eyes or nostrils, or wherever it can be got most easily attached, and by this the shark is towed on shore; several boats are requisite for towing. The mhor is often 40, sometimes 60, feet in length; the mouth is occasionally 4 feet wide. All other varieties of shark are caught in nets, in somewhat like the way in which herrings are caught at home. The net is made of strong English whip-cord; the meshes about 6 inches; they are generally 6 feet wide, and from 600 to 800 fathoms, or from three-quarters to nearly a mile, in length. On the one side are floats of wood about 4 feet in length, at intervals of 6 feet; on the other, pieces of stone. The nets are sunk in deep water, from 80 to 150 feet, well out at sea.

'They are put in one day and taken out the next; so that they are down two or three times a week, according to the state of the weather, and success of the fishing. The lesser sharks are commonly found dead, the larger ones much exhausted. On being taken home, the back fins, the only ones used, are cut off, and dried on the sands in the sun: the flesh is cut off in long strips, and salted for food; the liver is taken out and boiled down for oil; the head, bones, and intestines left on the shore to rot, or thrown into the sea, where numberless little sharks are generally on the watch to eat up the remains of their kindred. The fishermen themselves are only concerned in the capture of the sharks. So soon as they are landed they are purchased up by Banians, on whose account all the other operations are performed. The Banians collect them in quantities, and transmit them to agents in Bombay, by whom they are sold for shipment to China.'

At the Bonin Islands, the colonists have trained their dogs to catch fish; and Dr. Ruschenburger, who visited the islands in the United States' ship *Peacock*, tells us, 'that two of these dogs would plunge into the water and seize a shark, one on each side, by the fin, and bring it ashore in spite of resistance.'

Blumenbach states, 'that the white shark weighs sometimes as much as 10,000 lbs.; and even a whole horse has been found in its stomach.' I may cite a few statements which have come under my notice in the course of newspaper reading:—

The *New Orleans Picayune* tells the following:—'We have read many fish stories, and they are generally of that tenour that the very name inclines one to disbelieve them. We have one to tell now, and, as we know the person who was the main actor in the incident, we can vouch for its being true, particularly as there is ocular evidence of the matter. Some days ago, the captain of a ship at anchor outside the Pass, threw overboard a shark hook baited, not expecting in the least, as the captain himself says, to catch anything of the fish tribe. There was hooked, however, a shark of the spotted kind, and, as it afterwards proved, a regular 'man-eater.' He had to be harpooned before his capture could be effected. His size and weight may be imagined from the fact, that it took 11 men to hoist him in, with a double lift on the main yard. The monster measured 17 feet 11 inches in length, from tail to snout, and 9 feet in circumference. He had seven rows of teeth, three of the rows being almost hidden in the upper gums. His liver exactly filled up a beef barrel. In his paunch was found the body of a man in a half decomposed state. So far as could be judged, the corpse was that of a well-dressed man, of medium-size—shirt white, with pearl buttons, coarse silk under-shirt, cotton socks, and shoes nearly new, of the Congress gaiter kind. The shark had also in his stomach several pieces of old canvas, such as are used by vessels on their rigging. The jawbone of this sea pirate has been brought up to the city. It is large enough to take in a sugar barrel.'

A shark was caught a year or two ago, by the boats of one of the East-end whaling establishments at Bermuda, which measured 18 feet in length. Its liver yielded 72 gallons of oil. The jaws, when detached from the body and extended to their full width, afforded space sufficient for three persons—the tallest at least 5 feet 10 inches—to stand erect within them. It had two-and-a-half rows of teeth.

The basking shark, or sun-fish (*Squalus maximus*), is the largest of the genus. The average size is about 25 feet long, by 18 in circumference, in the largest part. It often lies on the surface of the water, apparently sunning itself, and very frequently may be seen steadily swimming with its dorsal fin above the water. This species is viviparous, and possesses nothing of the fierceness and voracity so peculiar to the shark family.

A large one, caught not long ago in the Mersey river, Van Diemen's Land, 14 feet long, upon hoisting it upon deck, gave birth to 23 young ones, each about 18 inches long.

'Some 25 years since, the capture of this valuable fish was prosecuted very successfully from Innis Boffin and the vicinity of Westport, at which town, as well as Newport, there were works erected for trying out the oil. About that date, as much as five pipes of oil of 120 gallons were received by one Dublin house alone per season. It has much decreased of late years, which is attributable rather to the decline of the means of pursuit than to the absence of the fish, as it is seen every year in large numbers on the distant banks, and occasionally close to the shore in packs of 25 or 30, in very fine weather. There were four taken at Galway this year, and many were seen in the vicinity of the Arran Islands. The liver has hitherto been considered the only valuable part, averaging 30 cwts., and containing about 180 gallons of fine oil, second only to sperm, and selling from 4s. to 5s. per gallon. The carcase, which may be estimated at from four to five tons, is of a gelatinous character, consequently of great value; *it is now thrown away as useless*. Neither skill nor courage is required in the capture; it being of a sluggish nature, and literally presenting its most vulnerable part to the harpoon.'[22]

A correspondent of the *New York Tribune*, writing from Stone Bridge House, Tiverton, Rhode Island, says:—'A party of ladies and gentlemen, on the evening of the 4th, caught and hauled about 20 of these monsters (sharks) upon the bridge, measuring from 3 to 5 feet. The sport is generally continued from twelve until nine o'clock in the evening, and as each new-comer is laid at his scaly length up the stone causeway, the 'head-ache stick,' as Uncle Ned quaintly calls it, is applied to his hard sconce, until all propensity for biting off swimmers' legs has disappeared. One Deacon Smith caught, on the same evening, an enormous shark, which on being beached, measured over 7 feet across the fins. But the crowning sport was reserved for the next day, when Mr. R. W. Potter, of Pawtucket, went off with a party, among whom were several ladies, and fastened to a huge shark, of the mackerel species. The monster, on taking the bait and finding himself hooked, went off with the line, like a harpooned whale, despite all efforts to hold him. Having a small tow-boat at hand, Mr. P. took to that, and paid out, the shark towing him rapidly a long distance into the bay, when, getting tired, returned, and came toward the little boat with expanded jaws, and made desperate fight to extricate himself, snapping at the line to bite it off, and then throwing up his tail, would again shoot off rapidly, carrying the boat after him, spinning through the water. Hauling him cautiously back, however, he was at last mastered by repeated vigorous blows with the end of the oar, which was finally run down the rascal's throat, in which condition he was towed ashore. It required the united strength of six men, with a stout rope, to haul the creature upon the beach, and he measured, from the tip of his nose, over the fin, to the end of his tail, 3 feet 9 inches.'

A shark, 28 feet long, and measuring 18 feet round the body, was caught in a weir, by John Horan, at Rice's Island, between Eastport and Lubec. His liver, it is said, filled three barrels, and yielded a large quantity of valuable oil.

The *Rangoon Chronicle* of 3rd March, 1854, reported the capture of a shark of enormous size. The animal, it seems, got stranded on the shoal or bar at Yangeensiah, from which it could not extricate itself. About 40 boatmen plunged into the water with dahs and spears, and commenced a furious attack on the monster, who inflicted very serious wounds on six of the party, stripping the flesh entirely from the thigh of one and leaving the bone bare. After a hard fight, the shark fell a victim, dyeing the water with his blood. The creature measured 35 feet, and afforded by very imperfect cutting 365 lbs. of solid flesh, which the men dried and brought to Rangoon for food.

The Barotse of Central Africa eat alligators. The meat has a strong, musky odour, not at all inviting for any one except the very hungry. After crossing the Kasai, Livingstone saw that he was in a land where no hope could be entertained of getting supplies of animal food, for one of the guides caught a light blue coloured mole and two mice for his supper. The care with which he wrapped them up in a leaf and slung them on his spear, told the Doctor that he would have but little chance of enjoying larger game. At Cabango, in Western Londa, a large amount of beer and beef was consumed at a funeral; yet when the leg of a cow was offered to Bango, a Londa chief, he said that neither he nor his people ever partook of beef, as they looked upon cattle as human, and living at home like men. There are several other tribes who refuse to keep cattle, though not to eat them when offered by others, 'Because,' say they, 'oxen bring enemies and war;' but this is the first instance met with by Livingstone in which they have been refused as food. The fact of these people killing pallahs for food shows that their objection does not extend to meat in general. Near the Tanba, (W. Londa,) Dr. Livingstone saw some women carefully tending little lap dogs, which were to be eaten. The Mambari, while in the Borotse valley, showed their habits in their own country, (S.E. of Angola,) digging up and eating, even there, where large game abounds, the mice and moles which infest the country.

The flesh of the sturgeon has been esteemed in all ages; but modern nations do not consider it so great a luxury as the ancients; and, although deemed a royal fish, it often hangs on hand in Billingsgate market, and is retailed at a low price by the pound. This fish was in high repute among the Greeks and Romans.

The flesh is white, delicate, and firm, and when roasted resembles veal; it is generally eaten pickled, and what we receive in that form comes from the Russian rivers or from North America. There are several varieties of sturgeon, the flesh of most of which is nutritious, wholesome, and of an agreeable flavour. The fat may be used as a substitute for butter or oil.

The flesh of the sharp-nosed sturgeon of North America (*Acipenser oxyrinchus*) is like coarse beef, quite firm and compact, but very rank and unsavoury. The Indians of New Brunswick cut it up in large pieces and salt it for winter use. It is only eaten by those who can obtain no better fare. The flesh of a young fish is much more delicate than that of an old one; when stewed with rich gravy, its flavour is not unlike that of veal.

Mr. Wingrove Cooke, in his account of a select Chinese dinner, says:— 'The next dish was sturgeon skull-cap—rare and gelatinous, but I think not so peculiar in its flavour as to excuse the death of several royal fish. This fish, being taken from its brazen, lamp-heated stand, was succeeded by a stew of shark fins and pork. The shark fins were boiled to so soft a consistency that they might have been turbot fins. The Chinaman must have smiled at the unreasonable prejudices of the occidentals when he saw some of us tasting the pork but fighting shy of the shark. He probably, however, did not know that the same occidentals would eat with relish of a fish which they themselves enticed to their angle by a worm or a maggot. Next in order came a soup composed of balls of crab. I have tasted this better prepared at Macao. It assumes there the form of a very capital salad, made of crab and cooked vegetables.'

The fondness of the Chinese for all gelatinous substances is well known, and has been described by all those who have visited that country and partaken of their banquets. In addition to employing animals and parts of animals which are rejected in other countries, as articles of diet, they import various substances which can be valuable only as yielding gelatine of different degrees of purity; of these we have examples in tripang, birdsnests, sharks' fins, fish maws, and agar-agar, a fucus.

The fresh water lamprey (*Petromyzon fluviatilis*) was formerly of great importance as a delicacy, and also largely used as bait by fishermen. In Germany another species (*P. Planeri*) are taken in large quantities, fried, packed in barrels by layers, with bay leaves and spices, sprinkled with vinegar, and thus exported to other countries.

The sea lamprey (*P. marinus*) is held in high estimation by epicures in the United States and elsewhere, but is not eaten in the British American Provinces. It is a formidable enemy to the royal sturgeon, fastening upon its belly and eating into the flesh; and not unfrequently a sturgeon has leaped into a canoe, in its efforts to disengage itself from several of these troublesome parasites.

Lampreys, well known to have given a fatal surfeit to Henry I., when made into pies, were anciently esteemed a 'pretty present.'

Eels appear to have been early favourites, particularly in the monasteries. The cellaress of Barking Abbey, Essex, in the ancient times of that foundation, was amongst other eatables 'to provide russ aulx in Lenton, and to bake with *elys* on Shere Tuesday:' and at Shrovetide she was to have ready 'twelve *stubbe eles* and nine *schaft eles.*' The regulation and management for the sale of eels seems to have formed a prominent feature in the old ordinances of the Fishmongers' Company. There were artificial receptacles made for eels in our rivers, called *Anguilonea*, constructed with rows of poles that they might be more easily taken. The cruel custom of salting eels alive is mentioned by some old writers.

The flesh of the eel (*Anguilla vulgaris*), being highly nutritious, is excellent as food, but is sometimes found too oily for weak stomachs.

Eel pies and stewed eels cause a large demand in this metropolis, and some 70 or 80 cargoes, or about 700 tons a year, are brought over from Holland. The total consumption of this fish in England is estimated at 4,300 tons per annum. Eels are very prolific. They are found in almost all parts of the world.

An abundance of large eels of fine quality are caught in the rivers and harbours of New Brunswick.

If a market should be found for this description of fish from North America, they could be furnished to an unlimited extent. My friend and correspondent, Mr. Perley, says, 'In the calm and dark nights during August and September, the largest eels are taken in great numbers by the Micmac Indians and Acadian French, in the estuaries and lagoons, by torch-light, with the Indian spear. This mode of taking eels requires great quickness and dexterity, and a sharp eye. It is pursued with much spirit, as, besides the value of the eel, the mode of fishing is very exciting.

'In winter, eels bury themselves in the muddy parts of rivers, and their haunts, which are generally well known, are called eel grounds. The mud is thoroughly probed with a five pronged iron spear, affixed to a long handle, and used through a hole in the ice. When the eels are all taken out of that part within reach of the spear, a fresh hole is cut, and the fishing goes on again upon new ground.'

It was by a mistake that the Jews abstained from eating eels. The prohibition is as follows:—'All that have not fins and scales, &c., ye shall have in abomination.'—Lev. xi., 10, 11. The *Siluridæ*, which have no scales, were held in abomination by the Egyptians. In describing one of them (the Schall) which he had found in the Nile, M. Sonnini, says—'A fish without scales, with soft flesh, and living at the bottom of a muddy river, could not have been admitted into the dietetic system of the ancient Egyptians, whose priests were so scrupulously rigid in proscribing every aliment of unwholesome quality. Accordingly, all the different species of *Siluri* found in the Nile were forbidden.' This then was probably one of the forbidden kinds, and this fact supports the opinion before ventured as to the origin of the custom. The rest of the prohibition was probably levelled against aquatic reptiles, which were generally looked upon as possessing poisonous qualities.

It has been well observed by a recent popular writer, that any Cockney, with two shillings and sixpence in his pocket, may regale himself at Billingsgate, at Blackwall, or Richmond, on delicacies to which the senate and people of Rome were utter strangers. Indeed, it is no inconsiderable set off against the disadvantages of living so far from the sun, that the supplies of northern fish markets are incontestably and greatly superior to those of any Italian or Sicilian pascheria: superior, 1st, because in those kinds which are common to our great ocean, and their 'great sea,' our own are better flavoured; because, 2ndly, even the finer sorts, which belong exclusively to the Mediterranean, are for the most part poor; and 3rdly, and above all, because there is an almost total want in its waters of species which we consider, and advisedly, as our best. Were superiority to be determined by mere beauty and variety of colouring, the market of Billingsgate could not enter into competition for a moment with the smallest fishing town in the south, where the fish are for the most part coasters, and derive their gorgeous hues from the same buccina and coquillage whence the Tyrians got their superb dyes. But as the gayest plumage is by no means indicative of the bird best adapted for the table, so brilliancy of scales affords no criterion by which to judge of the culinary excellence of fish, the beauty of whose skin, in this instance, contrasts singularly with the quality of the fish, which is generally poor and insipid, and sometimes unwholesome and even deleterious. The Mediterranean pelagians (or open sea-fish) have neither brilliancy of colour nor delicacy of flesh to atone for the want of it; so that no Englishman will repine to leave tunny beef to the Sicilian ichthyophagist, whilst he has the genuine pasture-fed article at home in place of it. Nor though, to such coarse feeders as the ancient Greeks, sword-fish might be held equal to veal, will his better instructed palate assent to such a libel upon wholesome butcher's meat. Mullet must indeed be admitted on all hands to be good fish; but one good thing only in a hundred does not satisfy omnivorous man, and *toujours Triglia* is not better than *toujours Perdrix*, as every one who has passed a winter at Naples knows to his cost. Sardines are only palatable in oil; *au naturel* they are exceedingly poor and dry: and for that other small clupean, the anchovy (the latent virtues of which are only elicited by the process which metamorphoses the fish into sauce), British whitebait is far more than an equivalent.—But if the Mediterranean has but few *alumni* to be proud of, the poverty of its waters is certainly more conspicuous in its deficiencies than in its supplies; indeed, the instinct of all first-rate fish seems to be to turn their tails upon this sea. Thus among the

Salmonidæ, salmon and smelt are alike unknown; of the Gadian family, all the finest species, as cod, haddock, whiting, ling, and coal fish are wanting; and to quote but one other example—

'Whilst migrant herrings steer their myriad bands
From seas of ice to visit warmer strands,'

as we read in the Apocrypha of Dr. Darwin, not one ever entered the Bay of Naples, unless salted in a barrel from England.[23]

The Finnon, Buckie, and Bervie smoked haddock is largely vended in London and other large towns, being esteemed an excellent relish. They are split, cleaned, and steeped in strong pickle about three hours, and then smoked for fifteen or sixteen hours. After a kiln full is smoked and cooled, the fish are packed in dry barrels the same as pickled mackerel, excepting that every two tiers are packed face to face, so that the back of one fish does not come in contact with the split side of another fish. The increase in the timber trade of late years, and the establishment of saw-mills, have rendered sawdust abundant, and the Scotch fisherwives have made the discovery that haddocks can be smoked with sawdust to look nearly as well as when smoked with peat; while they have not the wisdom to anticipate the loss of custom which must unavoidably ensue as soon as the deficiency of flavour is discovered.

Fresh herrings come in in enormous quantities to our metropolitan markets, and, from the consumption of several millions of them, must be esteemed a dainty by some. Pickled or cured herrings,—of which 580,814 barrels were salted in 1857, at the British Fisheries,—are chiefly consumed abroad; the shipments to the Continent last year having been 219,000 barrels, and 58,534 barrels went to Ireland. In 1855, out of a cure of 766,703 barrels, the Continental export reached 344,029 barrels. Last year (1857), 128,600 barrels went to Stettin.

Scotch herrings go to Russia quite as much as St. Petersburgh tallow comes to London, 60,000 or 70,000 barrels passing the Sound, or going *via* Konigsberg and Dantzic. One great inducement to the Russian population to purchase the herrings is, it is said, the quantity of undissolved salt the barrels are found to contain.

It is in the form of red-herrings and bloaters that the largest consumption of this fish takes place in the metropolis. The sale of bloaters at Billingsgate is about 265,000 baskets of 160 each annually, and about 50,000,000 of red-herrings.

There was a pleasant tradition current in Yarmouth not many years since, that the 'red' herring was the result of accident. According to the story, a fisherman had hung up some salted herrings in his hut and forgotten them. They hung where they were exposed to the smoke from the wood fire of the hut; and, some days afterwards, his attention was attracted to them, when, being struck by their appearance, he determined to see how one of them tasted. The result was so satisfactory that he hastened to King John, who was then lying near Norwich, to make a present of the remainder; when the herrings were esteemed such a delicacy by the monarch that he then and there expressed his determination to grant a charter of incorporation to the town from which they were brought. The only certain portion of this story is, that the first charter of Yarmouth was granted by King John.

There is a curious item in this town charter of Yarmouth, long famous for its herring fair. The burgesses are obliged to send to the sheriffs of Norwich 100 herrings, to be made into 24 pies; and these pies are to be delivered to the Lord of the manor of East Carleton, who is to convey them to the king.

The receipt for making herring pie would be a curious, though perhaps not a valuable, addition to our modern cookery books. It is probably lost, unless Her Majesty continues to receive these once prized patties.[24]

The stromming, or herring of the North seas, is only about the size of a sprat, but a much more delicate fish; when salted and mixed with potatoes it is the staple food of the people, being washed down with a bowl of milk, or a glass of corn-brandy.

The conger is found in the seas of Europe, of Northern Asia, and in those of America, as far as the Antilles. It is very abundant on the coasts of England and France, in the Mediterranean Sea, where it was much sought after by the ancients, and in the Propontis, where it was not long ago in considerable estimation. Those of Sicyon were more especially esteemed. The flesh of this fish is white and well flavoured; but as it is very fat, it does not agree with all stomachs. In many places the conger eels are dried for exportation. For this purpose, they are cut open in their under part, through their entire length, the intestines are removed, deep scarifications are made upon the back, the parts are kept separate by means of small sticks, and they are suspended by the tail to poles, on the branches of trees. When they are perfectly dry, they are collected in packets, each weighing about 200 lbs.

The voracious conger eel (*Conger vulgaris*, of Cuvier; the *Muræna conger*, of Linnæus,) although a coarse fish, forms a considerable article of commerce in Cornwall and Devonshire. I only notice it here from the fact, that it is sometimes dried and shipped to Spain and other Catholic countries, where fish of any kind is acceptable. When dried in a particular manner, the flesh used formerly to be ground or grated to powder, and in this state was employed to thicken soup.

The *Murænæ conger*, were carefully reared in vivaria by the Romans. As early as the time of Cæsar, the multiplication of the domestic *Murænæ* was so great, that on the occasion of one of his triumphs, that great general presented 6000 of them to his friends; Licinius Crassus reared them so as to be obedient to his voice, and to come and receive their food from his hands; while the celebrated orator, Quintus Hortensius, wept over the loss of those of which death had deprived him.

Such is the testimony to the quality and estimation of the conger eel, which Griffiths has collected in his *Supplement to Malacopterygii apodes in Cuvier's Animal Kingdom*. Its flesh does not agree with all stomachs; but it is yet a matter of dispute what renders it so frequently deadly. The condition of the liver of the fish in most cases has a great deal to do with danger attending fish-poisons.

The sand eel (*Ammodytes tobianus*) and the sandlaunce (*A. lancea*), though of small size, are very delicate eating, and vast numbers are consumed in summer by the natives of the Hebrides. They are also much sought after by the fishermen for bait.

The smelt or spirling (*Osmerus eperlanus*), found abundantly on the British coasts, is a very delicate fish. It is generally taken in greatest plenty at the mouths of large rivers, or in estuaries, such as the Thames and Medway, from August to May, as well as on sandy shores, in small nets; and always commands a ready sale. It has a peculiar odour, whence its popular name, which has been compared to that of a cucumber or a violet. This is strongest when the fish is first taken, but it may be perceived by raising the gill covers, after the fish has been for some time out of the water.

A whitebait dinner, at Blackwall or Greenwich, is one of the epicurean celebrities of the metropolis; and the fishing for whitebait, which commences about the beginning of April, and becomes abundant during the summer months till September, is productive of considerable benefit to those concerned. It was long supposed that these were the fry of a larger fish, but they are now identified as a particular species (*Clupea alba*), so named from the sides of the fish being uniformly of a white colour. It attains to the length of 6 inches. The whitebait are taken in long bag-nets, from vessels moored in the tide-way; and the fish are taken out by untying the end of the hose, and shaking it into the boat.

But there are small and delicate fish, which are substitutes for whitebait, in other quarters of the world.

Thus Mr. T. Atwood (*History of Dominica*) tells us, 'that the chief dainty among the fresh-water fish of that island is the young frey, with which the rivers there are filled twice or thrice every year, and which are called by the

French 'Tréz-tréz.' These consist of various kinds of sea-fish just spawned, and with which that element swarms for some miles distance from the shore, in numbers truly astonishing. These little creatures come into the rivers like a living stream, and in a short time swim two or three miles, to an amazing height up the country. This they perform in a wonderful manner, skimming over such rapid streams as repel their weak endeavours, from rock to rock, the surfaces of which are covered with them; or seeking the smoothly gliding stream at the sides of the banks, by degrees ascend the highest parts of the rivers.

'The first day of the appearance of these frey in the rivers, they are transparent and clear as crystal, so that every bone in them may be counted, and the movement of their vitals can be plainly discerned. The second day after they lose much of that transparency; and the third or fourth day, it is wholly lost by the nutriment which they feed on. They are caught in baskets, in which is put a tablecloth or sheet, and sinking the basket with stones, vast quantities are taken at a time. They are fried in a batter made of flour and milk, or stewed with herbs and spices, and are excellent food cooked either way.'

At Moutrah, a town situated in a deep bay, not far from Muscat, they dry and export large quantities of a diminutive fish, about two inches long, which are packed in bales. This species of fish literally fills the waters of Oman. Dr. Ruschenberger (*Voyage Round the World*, p. 121) says, 'They sometimes appeared in dense strata about the ship, so as completely to hide the cable from view, which was distinctly seen when they were not present.'

Don Pernety, in his *Journal of a Voyage to the Falkland Islands*, speaks of a small fish, called by the Spaniards pajes, and by the French *gras dos*, which was almost transparent, and of a most exquisite delicacy. It was found excellent when fried, and not inferior to the eel pout.

There is a small fish resembling a shrimp, not half-an-inch long, which makes its annual appearance in some of the rivers of Peru, in February, or in the beginning of March. It is called *chantisa*, and is really a great delicacy, when prepared by the natives. The numbers which ascend the rivers are so great, that on each side they appear to form a white path in the water, about two feet broad, and several miles in length. The women employ themselves in taking them, for which purpose they have a canoe; two of them hold a piece of flannel, three yards long, by the corners, and place it under the surface of the water, one end being a little elevated, to prevent the chantisa from passing; and when a considerable quantity are collected, the flannel is taken up and emptied into the canoe, after which the operation is repeated. Mr. Stephenson (*Travels in America*) says, he has frequently seen in the course of two hours, from six to eight bushels taken in this manner by these women. They are preserved by using as much salt as is necessary to season them; they are then put into baskets, lined with leaves, and a large stone is placed on the top, to press them into a solid mass, like a cheese. After standing a day or two, the baskets are placed on a frame made of canes, which is elevated about a yard from the ground; they are then covered with plantain leaves, and a small fire of green cedar, sandal, or other aromatic wood, is kindled underneath, for the purpose of smoking them. After remaining 10 or 12 hours, the cakes are taken out of the baskets, and again exposed to the smoke till it has penetrated through them, when they are laid up for use. A small portion of the smoked chantisa is generally added to the fish while cooking, to which it communicates a very delicate flavour.

At the mouth of the river Columbia, a very small fish, about the size of the sardine, is caught in immense numbers by the Chinooks. It is called by them *uhlekun*, and is much prized on account of its delicacy and extraordinary fatness. When dried, this fish will burn from one end to the other with a clear, steady light, like a candle. The uhlekuns are caught with astonishing rapidity by means of an instrument about seven feet long; the handle is about three feet, into which is fixed a curved wooden blade, about four feet, something the shape of a sabre, with the edge at the back. In this edge, at the distance of an inch and a half, are inserted sharp bone teeth, about an inch long. The Indian, standing in the canoe, draws this edgeways with both hands, holding it like a paddle, rapidly through the dense shoals of fish, which are so thick, that almost every tooth will strike a fish. One knock across the thwarts sharply deposits them in the bottom of the canoe. This is done with such rapidity, that they will not use nets for this description of fishing.[25]

The anchovy (*Engraulis encrasicolus*, Cuvier) is a small fish, much resembling the sprat, which is often sold for it, but may be readily distinguished from the sprat by the anal fin being remarkably short. It is common on the southern coasts of France and Spain, on the shores of Italy, Greece, and other parts of the Mediterranean, but those coming from Gorgona (an island in the gulf of Leghorn) are esteemed the best. Anchovies should be chosen small, fresh pickled, silver white on the outside, and red within. They must have a round back, for those which are flat or large, dark outside, with pale coloured flesh, and tapering much towards the tail, are often nothing but sardines. First quality anchovies are used as a condiment, and among epicures are esteemed a luxury. The trade in them with the Italian States is very considerable; about 150,000 lbs. being annually exported. The fishing is chiefly in the night time, when a light being placed on the stern, the anchovies flock around, and are caught in the nets. Mr. Couch, in his

Cornish Fauna, says, that he has seen it about the Cornish coast, of the length of seven inches and a half, which is nearly double the length it is met with in the Mediterranean. It abounds, he adds, towards the end of summer, and if attention were paid to the fishing, enough might be caught to supply the consumption of the British islands.

Frezier (*Voyage to the South Seas*) speaks of seeing a sort of anchovy on the west coast of America, in such great numbers, that whole baskets full of them were readily taken on the surface of the water.

The anchovy and tunny fisheries of Dalmatia are important, though not so much so as during the last century; at present they furnish employment to about 8,000 men.

Anchovies are imported in small kegs, weighing about 12 lbs. each. The consumption varies here, from 50 to 100 tons a year.

Sheridan used to relate an amusing story of an Irish officer, who once belonged to a regiment in Malta, who returned to England on leave of absence, and, according to the custom of travellers, was fond of relating the wonders he had seen. Among other things, he one day, in a public coffee-room, expatiated on the excellence of living in general among the military at Malta. But, said he, 'as for anchovies, by the powers, there is nothing to be seen like them in the known world;' and he added, 'I have seen the anchovies grow upon the trees with my own eyes many's the hundred times, and beautiful is the grove of them the governor has in his garden on the esplanade.' A gentleman present disputed the statement that anchovies grew on trees, which the Irishman with much warmth re-affirmed. The lie passed, a challenge was given, and the upshot of the matter is thus humorously related.

'The Englishman gave his address, and the next day the parties met, attended by their seconds; they fired, and O'Flanagan's shot took effect in the fleshy part of his opponent's thigh, which made the latter jump a foot from the ground, and fall flat upon his back, where he lay a few seconds in agony, kicking his heels. This being observed by the Irishman's second, he said:—'You have hit your man, O'Flanagan, that is certain, I think not dangerously, however, for see what capers he cuts.'

"Capers, capers!' exclaimed the Irishman. 'Oh! by the powers, what have I done? What have I done? What a dreadful mistake!' and running up to his wounded antagonist, he took his hand, and pressing it eagerly, thus addressed him:—'My dear friend, if you're kilt, I ax your pardon in this world and in the next, for I made a devil of a mistake: and it was capers that I saw growing upon the trees at Malta, and no anchovies at all.'

'The wounded man, smiling at his ludicrous explanation and apology, said,—'My good fellow, I wish you had thought of that a little sooner; I don't think you have quite killed me, but I hope you will remember the difference between anchovies and capers as long as you live."

That highly esteemed fish, the sardine (*Clupea sardina*), which is closely allied to the pilchard, though much smaller, is found chiefly in the Mediterranean. It is taken in considerable quantities on our shores, and is exceedingly plentiful on the coast of Algarva, in Portugal, Andalusia and Granada in Spain, and along the shores of Italy. The small sardines, caught on the coast of Provence, in France, are esteemed the best. The French frequently cure them in red brine, and when thus prepared, designate them anchovied sardines. Sardines constitute a considerable portion of the food of the lower orders in Lisbon. 6,269 cases of sardines were imported into San Francisco, in 1853.

In 1852, 576 millions of sardines were taken on the coast of Brittany, which extends about 200 miles. Half of these were sold fresh and the other half preserved in oil. 160 vessels manned by 3,500 sailors and fishermen are engaged in the trade. The preparation, transport, and sale of the fish employ 10,000 persons. 9,000 of these, of whom one half are females, are occupied all the winter in making and mending of nets. On shore, the preparation, conveyance, and sale of the fish give occupation to 4,500 persons, of whom 2,500 are women; and in the interior of the country 4,400 other persons are occupied in the sale.

The fishing lasts about 200 days, and yields a net profit to all concerned of three millions of francs. The sardines disappear in November and return in April. Where they go during these four months, why they go, or what they do while gone, has never yet been discovered. The fishermen say that the same individuals never come twice, that every successive arrival is composed of fish of smaller size than those that left last, and that they appear to be their young. At any rate, they count implicitly on their appearance, and no sardine was ever yet known to break an engagement thus tacitly entered into.

A very intelligent naturalist and correspondent of mine, Mr. R. Hill, has furnished me with some interesting information respecting the West Indian fishes. One of the best labroid fishes is the hog fish, both for its flesh, thick, white, and luscious, separating in large strata, and its exemption from small abdominal bones. It is one of the commonest and yet one of the best fishes taken in the harbour of Port Royal, either by the fish pot or the line, the only source for supplying the Kingston market in the deep waters there.

The hog fish has its scales red with yellow at the base of each. It feeds amongst rocks, attains 3 and 4 feet of length, though 2½ feet is usually the largest dimension in Jamaica. The flesh is most delicious, but its fullness and firmness make it good for drying and smoking, when too large for a one day's dish.

There are several *Lachnolaimes* ordinarily in the market, but only one properly called the hog fish (*Suillus*). The villous membrane that covers part of the pharyngeals and palate gives it its scientific name, 'woolly throat.'

The most beautiful is the *aigula*, the aigrette of the Windward Islands. They are all sought after for the excellence of their flesh, '*la bonté de leur chair*,' but one, the *caninus*, is occasionally poisonous.

The yellow tail snapper (*Mesoprion cynodon*) and other species of the genus, attain a large size, and are much esteemed in the East and West Indies as an article of food.

The flesh of the Queen mullet (*Upeneus martinicus*) of the Indian and American seas is very delicious, and resembles in some respects the true mullet (*Mullus surmuletus*).

The paracuta (*Sphyræna Barracuda*), the pike of the ocean, has a firm and palatable flesh, and is esteemed by many people. It proves, however, sometimes poisonous when caught in certain localities.

The callipeva (*Mugil liza*) is an esteemed river fish of the West Indian seas, which seldom extends further than the embouchures of streams or into the ponds and marshes. Chief Justice Temple, of Honduras, characterizes it as the salmon of the tropics; and indeed, it very much resembles that prince of the finny tribe in its size, shape, habits, and flavour. The flesh, however, is not red, neither is it so firm as that of the salmon, but it is quite as fat and infinitely more juicy and delicate. When cut in slices, folded in tissue paper, and lightly fried — which is the only way in my opinion of dressing a fish, the flavour of which is so volatile, so smooth, so ethereal, that it more resembles an odour, or the rich fragrance of a thousand different flowers mixed and mellowed by distance, than an actual taste on the palate — nothing can surpass it; — to subject it unprotected to the fumiginous influence of an iron pan, would be the act of a Hottentot or a Tartar. Dressed in the manner I have mentioned, it would not have disgraced Olympus, nor offended the critical taste of the Apicii, the last of whom would have refrained from hanging himself whilst a single callipeva remained in his fish pond. The callipeva is very excellent when cured, and it is often brought in that state to the Belize market in large quantities. The roe of this fish is very superior and almost equals caviare. This is dried and sold separately. I may incidentally mention that the large strong brilliant scales of this fish now enter into commerce for the manufacture of those pretty fish-scale ornaments, brooches, bracelets, &c., sold at the Crystal Palace and elsewhere.

The *Mugil curema*, another species, is taken about Port Royal harbour, Jamaica, and when large, passed off in the Kingston market for callipeva. The true callipeva or calipever, as it is indifferently spelt, is the 'white salmon' of Jamaica, and weighs from 6 to 18 lbs. It is caught in the brackish waters of the Ferry on the road to Spanish Town.

Mullet of various kinds, the salt water species being white, and the mountain or river species red, are one of the three delicacies of Jamaica.

Then, there is the delicate smook, either fresh or salt water, weighing from 10 to 16 lbs.; the stone bass, of the river or sea, much esteemed, from 2 to 4 lbs.; the delicate black snapper, weighing 4 or 5 lbs.; the chuck, a delicate fresh-water fish, of about 6 lbs.; and the cutlass, a good flat frying fish: which will suffice to show that there need be no lack of a dish of good fish for the West Indian epicure.

The anchovy or silver fish (*Engraulis edentatus* of Cuvier and Val) abounds on the palisade shallows of Port Royal harbour. They are a most exquisite fry, cooked, strung together on a palm straw through the eye by half-dozens, and served up as they serve whitebait.

King fish are only occasionally taken within the harbour, at Port Royal Bank. They are very delicate eating and weigh from 10 to 20 lbs. The king fish mackerel (*Cymbium regale*) is taken at the head of the harbour by being gently towed for with a line. The pine fish, in great estimation with the Jews, which ranges from four to thirty pounds, are frequently harpooned from Port Royal dock yard, six feet long.

The sun fish, or lucannany of Demerara, is excellent food, being firm, fat, and with few bones; owing to its extreme lusciousness, it is difficult to salt or dry. It is about two feet in length and attains to 7 or 8 lbs. in weight.

The arawan is another Guiana fish, particularly fine as food, but like the last named, very fat and luscious.

The pacou are caught in large numbers by means of weirs or dams, and weigh on an average 7 lbs. each. They are split, salted, and dried, and when cured, highly prized. The morocoto, or osibu, is also a most delicious fish, in taste nearer resembling flesh than fish, and eagerly sought after by the epicure.

If the gourami, which the French have introduced to the tanks and ponds of Cayenne and their West Indian Islands, was entitled to no more than half the praise Commerson bestows upon it, it must be considered a fish worth some trouble and expense to possess. 'Nihil inter pisces,' he says, 'tum marinos, tum fluviatiles, exquisitius unquam degustavi.' If neither the fishes of the sea nor those of fresh water streams, to Commerson, who had described so many fishes, and tasted as many as he had described, were found to exceed the deliciousness of the gourami, — the *Osphromenus olfax*, — it should be imported into every West Indian colony. The Dutch at Batavia, in Java, have long bred it in large earthen vases, changing the water daily, and feeding it on herbs of rivers and ponds, particularly on the *Pistia natans*. In the Mauritius, they have become a common river fish, and are esteemed the most delicate of the dishes brought to table.

Capt. Philibut carried the specimens of the gourami from Mauritius to Cayenne. Out of 100 taken on board he lost 23 on the passage. The French colonists feed and breed it in ponds, much as the Barbadians do the caffum (*Megalops Atlanticus*). The caffum is allied to the herring, and weighs 12 or 15 lbs.; and though an important stand-by for a dinner in Barbados, it is an inferior fish.

Twenty years ago, I well remember that Mr. Richard Hill called attention in Jamaica to the gourami, which was first then being introduced as a tank fish into Martinique and Guadaloupe. His communication appeared in Dr. Paul's *Physical Journal*, published at Kingston.

It is supposed that this valuable fresh-water fish was procured originally from China, but not a single author gives intimation of it in the natural history of the Chinese empire. So interesting a species, among people so attentive to the breeding and cultivating whatever can be added to their food supplies, must have been brought under their notice. The Dutch have it only artificially bred in Java, but neither Renard, Valentine, Russell, nor Buchanan, who have all written largely on the fishes of India and of the Indian Islands, are acquainted with any such river-fish as the gourami. In India they give the name *gouragi* or *koragi* to a fish known to naturalists as the *Ophicephalus*, and the probability is that Commerson, who first noticed the *Osphromenus olfax*, had corruptly applied that word and made *gourami* of it.

This delicious fish, so easily bred and fed, from its food being the duck weed of the ponds, has a contour plump, round, and massy like the carp of Europe. The colour is a burnished brown, somewhat golden tinted, faintly ruddy, particularly on the head and fins. Vertical bands of bronze stretch obliquely from the back to the belly;—and the ventral fin in its first spine is lengthened into a long thread as long as the entire fish from head to tail. It belongs to a very curious family distinguished as *labyrinthan-pharyngeals*. The structure of fishes of this family is peculiar:—it consists of the upper surface of the pharyngeal bones being divided into leaves, which form cavities and ledges, more or less complicated, for the retention of water, very much like the web of cells in the paunch of the camel. This apparatus lies immediately under the opercula. It is closely shut in, and pours out a ceaseless stream to moisten the gills and keep them from drying up when the fish quits the water and betakes itself to the grass, either to feed on herbs or to change its domicile when the ponds grow muddy and stagnant.

The ancient writers on Natural History were familiar with the character of these curious *pharyngeals*. Theophrastus, in his Treatise, speaks of certain of the fishes of India that come forth from the rivers at times, and then return to them again: and he mentions that they resemble mullets. The strange habit of the *Anabas*, which has received this name from its climbing predilections, (anabaino, ascendo,) is well authenticated. M. Daldorf, a Lieutenant in the service of the Dutch East India Company, in an article in the *Linnæan Transactions for 1797*, mentions that, in the month of November 1791, he took one of these anabas fishes from the cleft foot-stalk of a palm tree, growing near a pond. The fish was five feet above the water, and was endeavouring to ascend still higher. Another observer, M. John, tells a similar story. The fish, he says, usually remains in the muddy bottom of ponds and lakes; but it will take to creeping on dry ground for several hours, by the inflexion of its body; and by the assistance of its serrated opercula, and the spines of its fins, it will climb on the palm-trees which are in the neighbourhood of ponds, along which drops the water that the rains have accumulated at their tops. — (Griffith's *Supplement to Cuvier's Animal Kingdom. Fishes*, p. 361.)

Though the gourami belongs to the family of fishes, having a reservoir for water to moisten the gills when they quit their ponds, it does not climb trees as the anabas, but only traverses the grass. This fish would be a most desirable acquisition to our colonies. It could be readily procured from Guadaloupe. It is as remarkable for its size as its flavour. It becomes as large as a turbot, and is equally delicious. It would be soon naturalized in our streams. The female hollows a little fosse in the edge of the reservoir in which it is kept, and there deposits its eggs.

The pirarucu (*Sudis gigas*) is a splendid fish 5 or 6 feet long, with large scales of more than an inch in diameter, and beautifully marked and spotted with red.

The lakes in Brazil contain great quantities of them, and they are salted and dried for the Para market. It is a very fine flavoured fish, the belly in particular being so fat and rich that it cannot be cured, and is therefore generally eaten fresh. 'This fish' (remarks Mr. Wallace) 'with farinha and some coffee made us an excellent supper; and the alligator's tails which I now tasted for the first time, was by no means to be despised. A smaller kind is that eaten, the flesh being more delicate than in the larger species.'

The sheep's head, or, in more scientific language, the *Sargus ovis*, is a favourite fish in North America, where it visits the coasts in large shoals during the summer and autumn. The principal fishery is off the coasts of New York, and thousands are occasionally taken at a single cast of the large nets used at some places. The fish, immediately on their capture, are packed in ice, and sent to the New York market, where they have been known to sell as high as £7 for one of large size, although the usual price for one is only about a dollar. This fish is pretty generally considered throughout the States, both by epicures and others, as an almost *sans-pareil*; and Dr. Mitchell, who has written much on American ichthyology, is of the same opinion.[26]

The green cavalla (*Caranx Bartholomæi*) is very good eating, and much in demand. They are caught by the Barbados fishermen, sometimes in nets and in large numbers. Another species, the Jack 'or John and Goggle-eye,' as it is locally termed (*C. Plumieri*), is in some seasons of the year very poisonous. When they are suspected of being so, an experiment is tried upon a duck, by giving her one of them to swallow, and if at that season it is poisonous, the duck dies in about two hours.

The flounder or plaice (*Rhombus ocellatus*), a fish which belongs to the turbots, is a very delicate fish.

The common flying-fish (*Exocœtus Roberti*) is so abundant in some seasons of the year about Barbados, that they constitute an important article of food, and during the season, a large number of small boats are occupied in fishing. They are very delicate and tender. Some experiments have been made to preserve them, by salting and smoking, and with perseverance this would probably be successful, and a new dainty be added to European tables. Such large numbers are occasionally caught that they meet with no sale, and are thrown away, or used as manure.[27]

Sprats are a cheap delicacy with the lower classes in this country, and are pretty plentiful at times, but they are also greatly esteemed in the West India Islands. A species, called the 'yellow-tailed sprat,' proves unfortunately poisonous at certain periods of the year, chiefly among the Leeward and Virgin Islands.

The cuckold or horned coney fish (*Monacanthus tomentosus*) is much used as food, and, when stuffed and baked, considered a delicacy.

Under the general name of the Spanish mackerel, several species of *Cymbium*, *C. Caballa*, *C. regale*, and *C. immaculata*, are caught in the West Indian seas. They are a coarse, dry fish, and not much esteemed, except when *coveeched*. To coveech a fish, it must be cut into junks, fried with onions and oil, and afterwards potted with vinegar, a little pepper or cloves, fried onions, and some oil. It becomes an article of trade in that manner, and a considerable quantity, according to Sir Robert Schomburgk, is sent from the Leeward Islands and Barbados to Guiana.

The young king-fish, termed *Coramour* in the West Indies, kept in a fish pond or craal for some time, is esteemed a great delicacy.

The mud-fish (*Eleotris gyrinus*), found in the water courses of Antigua, is also considered a dainty. This fish is common in the streamlets and creeks of the other West Indian Islands, and is considered a most delicious fish when in full perfection. It resembles the smelt in appearance, and is easy of digestion.

The common cod of Newfoundland (*Morrhua vulgaris*) is well known as an article of food the wide world over. It is always a thick, well-fed fish, and often attains a great weight, sometimes 70 or 80 lbs., and even more.

There is another variety, slightly, though permanently distinct, the American cod, fine specimens of which may be seen in the fish market of Halifax, Nova Scotia, during the season; their quality is admirable.

Dried cod for the Brazils are packed in large flat tubs, called drums, into which they are pressed by a powerful screw. Each drum contains exactly 128 lbs. of dry fish, that being the Portuguese quintal; and the drums are shaped to suit the convenience of the Brazilians, who transport them into the interior of South America slung in pairs upon mules. For the Mediterranean markets, the fish are stowed in the holds of the vessels in bulk, and seldom receive damage, such is the excellent manner in which they are cured and stowed. The best and whitest of the cod are required for the Neapolitan market, for even the Lazzaroni of Naples are very particular as to the quality of their fish.

On the coast of Norway, cod are caught in nets, and it is stated by Mr. Laing, in his journal of a residence in that country, that these nets are becoming more in use every season. For this fishery, every boat is provided with six or eight nets, each twenty fathoms in length, and thirty meshes deep. The mesh of the cod net is six inches from knot to knot, and is made of three-ply hemp thread. The back ropes and ground ropes of each net are fastened to the net, and the whole are set like Scotch herring nets, only with longer buoy-ropes. The cod nets are set at night, in 60 to 80 fathoms water, and are taken up in the morning. The introduction of nets in the cod fishery is said to have improved very considerably the condition of the inhabitants of the coast of Norway, as by means of nets, the quantity of fish caught has been nearly doubled. It is not at all unlikely, that cod nets might be used with advantage on the Gulf-coast of New Brunswick, especially in the early part of each season, when the cod come close to the shore in pursuit of herring, capelin, and gaspereaux.

'Some of the purely national dishes of Sweden, as lut-fisk on Christmas-eve, are most extraordinary things, lut-fisk being the stock fish steeped in a solution of potash until in fact decomposition takes place. On Christmas-eve, the great evening of Sweden, this thing is boiled and eaten with oil sauce; and this, together with grot, which is simply boiled rice, form the Christmas dishes of Sweden, just as roast beef and plum pudding do of England. The smell of the lut-fisk is terrific, but a true Swede clings to his national dish on Julaften as much as any beef-eating Englishman does to his. The poor often substitute boiled corn for rice; and at all times rye porridge made with milk, not water, is their common food; the number of meals might seem to make amends for their quality. Fish is almost the staple of food; quantities are salted in the autumn, and even in winter. They are taken in a most ingenious manner from under ice. You see holes cut in certain distances, and a man seated on a stool at the furthest end on each side. The man you are looking at appears to be sitting idly on the ice, but suddenly he puts his hand into the small opening cut in it, and pulls up a bright coloured little fish, and then another and another, throwing them on the frozen lake, where they jump about, displaying their colours, poor things, to advantage, and suffering cruelly.'[28]

Much more attention is now paid to the prosecution of the fisheries, and the preparation of the fish for export, in our North American colonies. Last season, an enterprising firm in Carleton, New Brunswick, sent to the Gulf of St. Lawrence a vessel of 30 tons, fitted with the necessary apparatus and well supplied, for the preparation of spiced salmon; which vessel, after an absence of two months and a half, returned with a full fare of the estimated value of £1,750, or yielding a profit of about 700 per cent. on the outlay, with all expenses defrayed!

A large New Brunswick vessel recently brought to Liverpool 100 boxes, containing 1,200 tons of preserved lobsters, of the presumed value of £300, also the result of colonial enterprise.

The flesh of the sea-perch or cunner (*Ctenolabrus cæruleus*), sometimes called, on account of its prevailing colour, the blue perch, is sweet and palatable. They are skinned before being dressed. The fish is taken by myriads, on the coasts of Maine and Massachusetts.

The striped bass (*Labrax lineatus*) is a very fine salt-water fish, and so is the diminutive white bass, better known by its popular name 'white perch.' They are a very fine fish for the table when in season. Their ordinary weight is from four to six ounces in September; they are often taken above half-a-pound in weight; the largest seen weighed above a pound.

A schull of the striped bass, 500 or 600 in number, weighing from 4 to 8 lbs. each, have often been taken at one haul of the net, in New Brunswick. They ascend fresh-water streams for shelter during the winter, and were formerly taken in large quantities in the Richibucto and Miramichi rivers. The fish gathered in large shoals, lying in a dull, torpid state under the ice, and holes being cut, they were taken in nets in immense numbers, corded up stiff on the ice, like fire-wood, and sent off in sled-loads to Fredericton and St. John.

The chub is usually considered a coarse fish, but those of large size, eaten fresh, are very palatable. Mr. Yarrell says, 'that boiling chub with the scales on is the best mode of preparing it for table.'

'The brook-trout of America' (*Salmo fontinalis*), says Mr. Herbert, 'is one of the most beautiful creatures in form, colour, and motion that can be imagined. There is no sportsman, actuated by the true animus of the pursuit, who would not prefer basketing a few brace of good trout, to taking a cart-load of the coarser and less game denizens of the water. His wariness, his timidity, his extreme cunning, the impossibility of taking him in clear and much fished waters, except with the slenderest and most delicate tackle—his boldness and vigour after being hooked, and his excellence on the table, place him without dispute next to the salmon alone, as the first of fresh-water fishes. The pursuit of him leads into the loveliest scenery of the land, and the season at which he is fished for is the most delightful portion of the year.'

The sea-trout of the basin of Bonaventura are of large size, 3 lbs. and upwards, brilliantly white, in fine condition, very fine and well flavoured.

The summer gaspereaux, or alewives, (*Alosa tyrãñnus*) are an exceedingly fat fish, and well flavoured; the only objection to them is their oily richness. Besides their being fatter, they are smaller and more yellow in colour than the spring fish.

To the epicure, a fresh caught salmon-trout of the Gulf of St. Lawrence, especially early in the season, will always afford a rich treat. The flesh is of a brilliant pink colour, and most excellent: its exceeding fatness early in the season, when it first enters the mixed water of the estuaries, is such that it can be preserved fresh but a very short time. The sportsman will find it a thoroughly game fish; rising well at a brilliant fly of scarlet ibis and gold, and affording sport second only to salmon fishing. In some parts of the Gulf they have been caught weighing 5 to 7 lbs.

That beautiful and savoury fish, the smelt, is a great table delicacy with us; but on the Gulf coasts of New Brunswick, large quantities are used every season merely for manure.

As food, the skate is held in very different degrees of estimation in different places. In London, large quantities are consumed, and crimped skate is considered delicate and well flavoured; but on some parts of the English coast, although caught in considerable numbers, the flesh is seldom eaten, and is only used for baiting lobster pots. The French are great consumers of the skate; and its flesh is used extensively both at New York and Boston. By many it is deemed a great delicacy. After the fish is skinned, the fleshy part of the huge pectoral fins, which is beautifully white, is cut into long thin slips, about an inch wide; these are rolled like ribbon, and dressed in that form.

The capelan (*Mallotus villosus*), the smallest species of the salmon family, possesses like the smelt the cucumber smell, but it differs from the smelt in never entering fresh-water streams. As an article of bait for cod, and other fish of that class, the capelan is a fish of much importance; whenever abundant, the cod-fishing is excellent. It has been found as far north in the arctic region as man has yet penetrated; and it forms so important an article of food in Greenland, that it has been termed the daily bread of the natives. In Newfoundland, it is dried in large quantities, and exported to London, where it is sold principally in the oyster shops.

The large, flat-fish known as the halibut (*Hippoglossus vulgaris*), which sometimes attains the weight of 300 lbs, is often taken by the cod-fishers in the Gulf of St. Lawrence. These fish are cut in slices, and pickled in barrels, in which state they sell at half the price of the best herrings. The flesh, though white and firm, is dry, and the muscular fibres coarse. The fins and flaps are however esteemed delicacies.

The mackerel of the British North American coasts is of a much finer flavour than those caught on the shores of Europe.

The salmon are also noted for their very fine flavour.

If there are no turbot, brill, or sole, in the St. Lawrence, there are other delicacies. A species of eel is exceedingly abundant and frequently of large size. One of these, a sea-eel, split, salted, and smoked, without the head, was 30 inches in length, and 15 inches in diameter, breadth as split, nearly the size of an ordinary smoked salmon and quite as thick. 300 barrels of large eels, taken with the spear in the Buctouche river, are usually salted-down for winter use. They are generally excessively fat, the flesh very white and exceedingly well flavoured. Packages of eels have been lately imported into

London from Prince Edward's Island. Smoked eels are very delicious, and they have even begun to preserve these fish thus at Port Phillip.

The fisheries of the North American lakes and rivers are not prosecuted as they might be, but are beginning to receive more attention. The white-fish (*Corregonus albus*) is found in all the deep lakes west of the Mississippi, and indeed from Lake Erie to the Polar Sea. That which is taken in Leech Lake is said by amateurs to be more highly flavoured than even that of Lake Superior. There is another species of this fish, called by the Indians tuliby or ottuniby (*Corregonus artidi*), which resembles it, but is much less esteemed. Both species furnish a wholesome and palatable food.

The French Canadians call this fish *Poisson Pointu*, and the English term them 'gizzard fish.' The origin of the latter name appears to be, that the fish feeds largely on fresh-water shell fish and shelly molluscs; and its stomach thereby gains an extraordinary thickness, and resembles the gizzard of a fowl. The stomach, when cleaned and boiled, is a favourite morsel with the Canadian voyageurs.

The white-fish of the bays and lakes of Canada is represented to be the finest fish in the world by the Canadians. The flavour of it is incomparable, especially when split open and fried with eggs and crumbs of bread. They weigh on the average about 2 lbs. each when cleaned — 100 of them filling a good sized barrel. Those caught in Lake Huron are more highly prized than any others.

Several Indian tribes mainly subsist upon this fish, and it forms the principal food at many of the fur posts for eight or nine months of the year, the supply of other articles of diet being scanty and casual. Its usual weight in the northern regions is from 2 to 3 lbs., but it has been taken in the clear, deep, and cold waters of Lake Huron, of the weight of 13 lbs. The largest seen in the vicinity of Hudson's Bay weighed between 4 and 5 lbs., and measured 20 inches in length, and 4 in depth. One of 7 lbs. weight, caught in Lake Huron, was 27 inches long.

Among other species of fish that inhabit these great inland seas are the mashkinonge, or mashkilonge, the pike or jack, the pickerel or gilt carp, the perch, and a species of trout called by the Chippeways, namogus.

A huge mashkilonge, so ravenous is its propensities, is often caught from the stern of a steamer in full speed, by throwing out a strong line with a small tin fish attached. A marked peculiarity of most of the Lake fish is the quantity of fat, resembling that of quadrupeds, which they contain, entirely different from the salt-water fish — while their flavor differs from that of the latter, being much more delicate and white than that of river fish.

Lake Superior abounds with fish, particularly trout, sturgeon, and white-fish, which are caught at all seasons and in large quantities. Of these the trout, weighing from 12 to 50 lbs., and the white-fish, weighing often over 20 lbs., are perhaps the most important.

The salmon trout are equally large, weighing from 10 to 70 lbs.

Lake Champlain also abounds with fish, among which are salmon, lake-shad, pike, and other fish.

The reciprocity treaty has given a new field to the fisheries on the Canada side of Lake Huron. Some 200 American fishermen are now engaged within fifty miles each side of Goderich in the business. This has greatly stimulated the Cannucks, and it is estimated 400 of them are now engaged in the same business. About 100 miles of the Lake shore is lined with gill nets and seines. Every boat that comes in has a large number of salmon-trout from 30 to 50 lbs. weight. White-fish are very large. The fish caught at Collingwood terminus of the northern railway, from Toronto, are packed in ice, and go to Oswego, Rome, Utica, Albany, and New York. Great quantities taken at Goderich go in ice from thence to Cleveland and Cincinnati.

The Toronto and Oswego markets are supplied with fish from Collingwood, and a well organized company, with nets, ice-houses, &c., might do a fine business by supplying the New York, Boston, and other American markets, daily with trout, bass, and white-fish from the waters of Georgian Bay.

Fishing with the scoop net is the most laborious of all modes of fishing. It was found in practice at the Sault St. Marie by the Baron De Hortan, when he penetrated to that point in 1684. It has been practised ever since, because it is the only mode by which the white-fish can be taken. They go there to feed and not to spawn; the bottom of the river is a rocky broken ground, and the current runs at the rate of 12 miles per hour; the eddy in which the fish are found is of small circuit, and only one canoe at a time can enter it. The canoe is forced into it by setting poles. The man in the bow has a scoop net, the handle to which is about 15 feet in length. He has only time to make one stroke with the scoop, the next instant the canoe is whirled away by the current far below the point where the stroke was made.

The plunge of the scoop may be successful or not according to chance; one fish or half-a-dozen may be taken, or very frequently none. As soon as one canoe is thus swept away, another one supplies its place, and in this manner some eight or ten canoes in rapid succession take their turn. Canoes are used because, being lighter, they can be forced up where it would not be possible to put a boat. Even though the white-fish would take the hook, still in such rapid water it could not be used.

Again, the character of nearly the whole of the coasts of Lakes Huron and Superior forbids any other mode of fishing than by gill nets.

Gill nets are often set in 60 feet of water, and the fish cannot be taken at such localities in any other mode, except at some seasons of the year when they will take the hook.

Again, there are localities along Lake Superior, where fish such as the rock sturgeon and mashkilonge can only be taken with the spear, and that in 30 feet water; the bottom is so disturbed, distorted, upheaved, and broken by volcanic action, that gill nets cannot be used, and the fish can only be reached in the hollows, crevices, and chasms of the rock where they lie, by means of a spear, which is thrown and has a line attached to the extremity.

The *Lake Superior Journal* says:—'Angling through the ice to a depth of 30 fathoms of water is a novel mode of fishing somewhat peculiar to this peculiar region of the world. It is carrying the war into fishdom with a vengeance, and is denounced, no doubt, in the communities on the bottoms of these northern lakes as a scaly piece of warfare. The large and splendid salmon-trout of these waters have no peace; in the summer they are enticed into the deceitful meshes of the gill-net, and in the winter, when they hide themselves in the deep caverns of the lakes, with fifty fathoms of water above their heads, and a defence of ice two or three feet in thickness on the top of that, they are tempted to destruction by the fatal hook. Large numbers of these trout are caught every winter in this way on Lake Superior. The Indian, always skilled in the fishing business, knows exactly where to find them and how to kill them. The whites make excursions out on the Lake in pleasant weather to enjoy this sport. There is a favourite resort for both fish and fishermen near Gros Cap, at the entrance of Lake Superior, through the rocky gateway between Gros Cap and Point Iroquois, about 18 miles above the Sault, and many a large trout at this point is pulled up from its warm bed at the bottom of the Lake in winter, and made to bite the cold ice in this upper world. To see one of these fine fish, four or five feet in length, and weighing half as much as a man, floundering on the snow and ice, weltering and freezing to death in its own blood, oftentimes moves the heart of the fisherman to expressions of pity. The *modus operandi* in this kind of great trout fishing is novel in the extreme, and could a stranger to the business overlook at a distance a party engaged in the sport, he would certainly think they were mad, or each one making foot-races against time. A hole is made through the ice, smooth and round, and the fisherman drops down his large hook, baited with a small herring, pork, or other meat, and when he ascertains the right depth, he waits—with fisherman's luck—some time for a bite, which in this case is a pull altogether, for the fisherman throws the line over his shoulders and walks from the hole at the top of his speed till the fish bounds out on the ice. I have known of as many as fifty of these splendid trout caught in this way by a single fisherman in a single day; it is thus a great source of pleasure and a valuable resource of food, especially in Lent; and the most scrupulous anti-pork believers might here 'down pork and up fish' without any offence to conscience.'

The Cleveland *Plain-dealer* has a lengthy account of the trade of the house of J. M. Craw and Son, of that city. It says:—'At the warehouse, 133, River street, in this city, is a grand depôt of its receipts. From this place large supplies of salt provisions, fisherman's tackle, seines, lines, and everything needed on the coasts of the upper lakes, are forwarded. At Washington Harbour, in Green Bay, engagements are made with the fishermen of 118 boats, each of which has a head fisherman, who has his crew engaged in fishing. Over 300 men are constantly engaged, spring and fall, in that locality in catching, packing, and forwarding fish. Similar settlements of fishermen are scattered all along the coasts of Lakes Michigan, Superior, Huron, and Erie. The number of varieties of Lake fish fit for packing is large, including white-fish, siskawit, trout, pickerel, cat-fish, bass, herring, perch, shad, and bayfish. The amount of fish received by Craw and Son, in 1856, exceeded 14,000 barrels, and as their receipts this year from Lake Michigan will be about 6,000 barrels, an increased aggregate is anticipated. This large amount is so much added to the food of the country, and constitutes an important addition to its wealth. From the details of this single house we may learn something of the extent of the entire trade.'

In the Baikal Lake, Siberia, there is a fish (*Callyonimus Baicalensis*) from four to six inches long, so very fat, that it melts before the fire like butter. It yields an oil sold to great advantage to the Chinese.

The *Lake Superior Journal*, of October 27, notices the arrival of a 100 barrels of the famous siskawit from Isle Royale, and learns from one of the fishermen that there have been caught this season between 300 and 400 barrels of this fish, together with a few trout and white fish. They fish on that island for this fish principally, as the siskawit are worth as much again as whitefish and mackinac trout in the lake markets.—The siskawit is said to be the fattest fish that swims, either in fresh or salt water. The fishermen assert, that one of these fish, when hung up by the tail in the hot sun of a summer day, will melt and entirely disappear, except the bones. In putting up about 50 barrels this season, one of the fishermen made two and a half barrels of oil from the heads and 'leaf fat' alone, without the least injury to the marketableness of the fish. Besides this leaf fat, the fat or oil is disseminated 'in a layer of fat and a layer of lean' throughout the fish. They are too fat to be eaten fresh, and are put up for market like whitefish and trout.

'Fish being here very scarce,' (Falls of the Uaupés,) 'we were obliged,' says Mr. Wallace, 'to live almost entirely on fowls, which, though very nice when well roasted, and with the accompaniment of ham and gravy, are rather tasteless, simply boiled or stewed, with no variation in the cookery, and without vegetables.

'I had now got so thoroughly into the life of this part of the country, that like everybody else here, I preferred fish to every other article of food. One never tires, and I must again repeat, that I believe there are fish here superior to any in the world.

'Our fowls cost us about a penny each, paid in fish-hooks or salt, so that they are not such expensive food as they would be at home. In fact, if a person buys his hooks, salt, and other things in Para, where they are about half the price they are in Barra, the price of a fowl will not exceed a halfpenny; and fish, pacovas, and other eatables that this country produces, in the same proportion.

'Many of the fish of the Rio Negro are of a most excellent flavour, surpassing anything I have tasted in England, either from the fresh or the salt waters; and many species have real fat, which renders the water they are boiled in a rich and agreeable broth. Not a drop of this is wasted, but with a little pepper and farinha is all consumed, with as much relish as if it were the most delicate soup.'[29]

Pirarucú, the dried fish, which with farinha forms the chief subsistence of the native population of Brazil, and in the interior is the only thing to be obtained, resembles in appearance nothing eatable, looking as much like a dry cow-hide, grated up into fibres, and dressed into cakes, as anything I can compare it with. When eaten, it is boiled or slightly roasted, pulled to pieces and mixed with vinegar, oil, pepper, onions, and farinha, and altogether forms a very savoury mess for a person with a good appetite and a strong stomach.

If we pass to the Pacific coasts of South America, we find the most esteemed fish are the robalo, the corvino, the lisa, and the king-fish.

The robalo (*Esox Chilensis, Hemiramphus Brazillensis* of Cuvier,) is nearly of a cylindrical form, and from two to three feet long. It is coated with angular scales of a golden colour upon the back, and silver on the belly; the fins are soft and without spines, the tail is truncated, and the back marked longitudinally with a blue stripe, bordered with yellow. The flesh is very white, almost transparent, light, and of a delicious taste. Those taken upon the Araucanian coast are the most in repute, where they are sometimes caught of eight pounds weight. The Indians of Chiloe smoke them, after having cleaned and soaked them for 24 hours in sea water, and, when sufficiently dry, pack them up in casks of 100 each, which are generally sold for about three dollars. The robalo prepared in this manner is said to be superior to any other kind of dried fish.

The corvino (*Sparus Chilensis*) is nearly of the same size as the robalo; it is sometimes, however, found of five or six feet in length. This fish has a small head, and a large oval body, covered with broad, rhomboidal scales, of a mother-of-pearl colour, marked with white. The tail is forked, and the body encircled obliquely, from the shoulders to the belly, with a number of brownish lines. The fins are armed with spiny rays, and the flesh is white, firm, and of a good taste, particularly when fried. It would probably be better still if it were prepared like that of the tunny.

The lisa (*Mugil Chilensis*) in its form, scales, and back is much like the common mullet, but is distinguished by the dorsal fin, which in the lisa is entire. There are two species of this fish, the sea and the river lisa, neither of which exceeds a foot in length; the first is a very good fish, but the latter is so exquisite, that it is preferred by many to the best of trout.

Another esteemed fresh-water fish of Chile is the bagre, or luvur (*Silenus Chilensis*, probably the *A. geneionis inermis*), which has a smooth skin, without scales, and is brown upon the sides, and whitish under the belly. In appearance, it is not very prepossessing, for in form it resembles a tadpole; the head being of a size disproportionate to the length of the body, which does not exceed eleven inches at the most. It has a blunt mouth, furnished like that of the barbel with barbs. It has a sharp spine on the back fins, like the tropical bagre, but its puncture is not venomous, as that is said to be. The flesh is yellow, and the most delicious of any esculent fish that is known. There is said to be another species of this fish inhabiting the sea, which is black—the same, probably, that Anson's sailors called, from its colour, the chimney-sweep.

While on the subject of fish common to this locality, I may mention that the Abbé Molina states, that 'the river Talten, which waters the Araucanian provinces, produces a small fish called *paye*, which, as I have been assured by those who have seen them, is so diaphanous, that if several are placed upon each other, any object beneath them may be distinctly seen. If this property is not greatly exaggerated, this fish might serve to discover the secret process of digestion and the motion of the fluids.'

Mr. Ruschenberger thus describes a Hawaiian restaurant:—'The earth floor of a straw hovel was covered by mats. Groups of men squatted in a circle, with gourd plates before them, supplied with raw fish and salt-water, and by their side was an enormous gourd, of the dimensions of a wash tub, filled with poë, a sort of paste made of taro. They ate of the raw fish, occasionally sopping the torn animal in the salt water as a sauce, then sucking it, with that peculiar smack which indicates the reception of a delicious morsel.'

The noble salmon, which honest Izaak Walton justly calls, 'the king of fresh-water fish,' is too well known as a choice article of food to need description. A jowl of fresh salmon was one of the requisites, in 1444, at the feast of the Goldsmiths' Company; and in 1473, three quarters of Colnbrook salmon are charged 6s. 4d.; and at a fish dinner of the same company in 1498, among large quantities of fish mentioned, are a fresh salmon 11s.; a great salmon £1; and two salmon-trout 2s. 8d. In 1518, for ij. fresh samon xvij^s j^d Item, a fresh samon xiij^s iiij^d; and in the eighth year of King Henry VIII. iiij. fresh samons are charged xl^s

In the great rush after gold, the fisheries of the Pacific coast, which have been famous for years past for their extent and value, have not received that attention which they merit. Now that the living tide has again set in strongly towards the North-West, the demand for food to feed the thousands will cause the fishery to be more largely developed. The whole coast is particularly rich in the more valuable species of the finny tribe.

A San Francisco paper states:—'The salmon of California and Oregon, with which our markets are supplied in the fresh and cured state, are nowhere surpassed in quality or flavour. Our rivers, bays, and estuaries are alive with these valuable fish, and the fishermen are busy in securing them during the present run. It is estimated that there are 400 boats on the Sacramento river alone, engaged in fisheries. The boats are valued at 60,000 dollars, the nets at 80,000 dollars, and seines at 6,000 dollars. The fishing season lasts from the 1st of February to the 1st of August, during which time the estimated average of each boat per day is 30 dollars, or an aggregate of 12,000 dollars. The hauling seines yield 100 dollars each per day, or 2,000 dollars in the aggregate. The fish thus caught supply the markets of San Francisco, Sacramento, Marysville, and the mining towns in the interior. Sometimes 2,000 lbs. are sent to one order. The amount shipped daily to San Francisco at present is from 5,000 to 6,000 lbs., which will be increased as the season advances.

'The fishing smacks outside the harbour in the vicinity of Drake's Bay, Punto de los Reyes, Tomales, and similar points, as well as other portions of the coast, are busily engaged in the trade.

'This business is becoming every year of greater interest, and the attention of our legislature has recently been drawn to its proper regulation and protection. A description of the fishes common to these waters, with an account of their habits, quality, and relative value, would be of great interest.

'In addition to salmon there are other varieties of fish deserving more than a passing notice. Much difficulty is experienced in classifying them under the proper heads, and recognizing the species under their various arbitrary names. The sturgeon, the rock cod, the mackerel—which, although it bears some resemblance to the Atlantic fish is inferior to it in flavour and fatness—the herring, the smelt, the sardine, and other varieties found in our markets, are all more or less valuable. Myriads of sardines abound along the whole southern coast. The Bay of Monterey has especially become famous for its abundance of this small but valuable fish. It is a matter of surprise that the taking and preparation of this fish, which enters so largely into the commerce of the world, has never been attended to as a source of revenue and profit in this region. The experiment certainly is worth testing. There are doubtless many persons here, familiar with the trade as practised on the coast of France, whose services might be secured in the business.'

Another Californian paper, the *Sacramento Union*, remarks:—'The fishing interest in the Sacramento at this point is increasing and expanding with astonishing rapidity, from year to year, and from month to month. The water of the river must be alive with salmon, or such numbers caught daily would sensibly reduce their numbers. But experienced fishermen inform us, while the run lasts, so countless is the number, that no matter how many are employed in the business, or how many are taken daily, no diminution can be perceived. Even the 'tules' between this and the Coast Range are reported to be filled with salmon. The run this year is said to be greater than ever before known at this season. The extraordinary run of the present time is only expected to continue for something like three weeks. They seem to run in immense schools, with some weeks intervening between the appearance of each school, during which the numbers taken are light, as compared with the quantity taken during a time like the present. No account is kept of the number engaged in fishing, or of the amount caught, and all statements relative thereto are made from estimates obtained from those who have experience in the business, and probably approximate correctness. These estimates give the number of men employed now in taking fish in the Sacramento at about 600—the number of fish taken daily, on an average, at 2,000—their average weight 17 lbs., making 34,000 lbs. per day. Two cents per lb., which is probably more than the present average price by the quantity, would give a daily income to those employed of 680 dollars, not very high pay. Either the number of men engaged in the business, we imagine, must be over estimated, or the number of fish caught under estimated. It requires two men to man a boat, which would give 300 boats for 600 men: 2,000 fish a day would give to each man a fraction over three as his share. We presume few are fishing who do not catch a good many more than that number. We saw a boat-load, the product of the previous night, consisting of 66 salmon, weighed yesterday morning. They averaged a fraction over 17 lbs., and gave 33 as the number caught by each man, instead of three, as estimated above. Say the 600 fishermen man, on an average, 200 boats a night; the average number caught by each boat put at 20, and the sum total would be 4,000 fish, instead of 2,000, as estimated. Our impression is that the latter comes nearer the mark than the former, as a good many of the fishermen send their fish directly to San Francisco; others take them to different points for salting. Large numbers are salted down daily, several firms and individuals being extensively engaged in this branch of the trade. The fish are put down in hogsheads, which average, when filled, about 800 lbs. From 1,000 to 3,000 lbs. are put down daily by those engaged in salting. An acquaintance has filled 65 hogsheads this season. The most of those engaged in salting live on the Washington side of the river, and salt their fish there. Including those engaged in salting, catching, and selling, probably the fish business furnishes employment for 1,000 men.'

The salmon is found in no other waters in such vast multitudes as are met in the rivers emptying into the Pacific. On the Atlantic side, the leading fish feature is the run of shad in the spring; on the Pacific side, salmon ascend the rivers at all seasons, in numbers beyond all computation. In California and Oregon, the rivers are alive with them; the great number taken by fishermen are but a drop from the bucket. Above this, on the coast side, tribes of Indians use no other food. As a table luxury, they are esteemed by most persons the finest fish caught. Unlike many fish, they contain but few bones, and the orange-coloured meat can be served in slices to suit customers. It is emphatically the meat for the million; it costs so little—not a quarter that of other meats—that rich and poor can feast upon salmon as often in the day as they choose to indulge in the luxury. In the course of a few years, salmon fishing will extend itself to all the prominent rivers in the North Pacific States. Catching and curing salmon will then have become a systematized business; the fish consumption will then have extended itself generally over those States, and more than likely become, in the meantime, an important article of export.

While upon the subject of these fisheries, it may be added, that a considerable portion of the Chinese population, both at San Francisco and at Sacramento, have engaged extensively in this business. In the vicinity of Mission Creek, near the former city, they have gone into the business upon a large scale. The average 'catch,' each day, is estimated at about 5,000 lbs., for which a ready market is found among the Chinese population, at five dollars per cwt. The process of catching, cleaning, and curing, presents a busy and curious scene.

Sir John Bowring remarks that, 'The multitudes of persons who live by the fisheries in China afford evidence not only that the land is cultivated to the greatest possible extent, but that it is insufficient to supply the necessities of the overflowing population; for agriculture is held in high honour in China, and the husbandman stands next in rank to the sage, or literary man, in the social hierarchy. It has been supposed that nearly a tenth of the population derive their means of support from fisheries. Hundreds and thousands of boats crowd the whole coasts of China—sometimes acting in communities, sometimes independent and isolated. There is no species of craft by which a fish can be inveigled which is not practised with success in China. Every variety of net, from vast seines, embracing miles, to the smallest hand-filet in the care of a child. Fishing by night and fishing by day—fishing in moonlight, by torchlight, and in utter darkness—fishing in boats of all sizes—fishing by those who are stationary on the rock by the seaside, and by those who are absent for weeks on the wildest of seas—fishing by cormorants—fishing by divers—fishing with lines, with baskets—by every imaginable decoy and device. There is no river which is not staked to assist the fisherman in his craft. There is no lake, no pond, which is not crowded with fish. A piece of water is nearly as valuable as a field of fertile land. At daybreak every city is crowded with sellers of live fish, who carry their commodity in buckets of water, saving all they do not sell to be returned to the pond or kept for another day's service.

The fishing grounds of Van Diemen's Land are periodically visited by a splendid fish named arbouka, a well-known piscatory visitant on the coast of New Zealand. Great numbers of these beautiful denizens of the deep have been caught, varying in weight from 60 lbs. to 100 lbs. each. The trumpeter is one of the most magnificent of Tasmanian fish; and is unrivalled in the quality of its flesh by any visitant in those waters. A demand has been created for them in Victoria; and before long, a stirring trade will be established between the two colonies in these beautiful fish.

The native cooking-oven of New Zealand, called the unu, is a very curious contrivance, and is thus described by Mr. S. C. Brees. It consists of a round hole, about two or three feet in diameter, and twelve inches deep, in which some wood is placed and lighted. Large pebble-stones are then thrown on the fire and heated, which remain at the bottom of the hole after the wood is consumed; the stones are next arranged, so as to present a level surface, and sprinkled with water; wild cabbage or other leaves are moistened and spread over them, upon which the food intended to be cooked is laid; the whole is then covered over with leaves and flax-baskets, and lastly, filled over with earth, which completes the operation. After allowing it to remain a certain time, according to circumstances, which the cook determines with the utmost precision, the oven is opened and the food removed. Eels and potatoes are delicious when cooked in this manner, and every other kind of provision.

The seer-fish (*Cybium guttatum*) is generally considered the finest flavoured of the finny race that swims in the Indian seas; it has a good deal the flavour of salmon.

There are several esteemed fish obtained round Ceylon. The Pomfret bull's eye (*Holocentrus ruber*) is found at certain seasons in abundance on the southern coast of Ceylon, in deep water. It is greatly esteemed by the natives as an article of food, and reaches a considerable size, frequently nearly two feet in length. The flesh is white and solid. For splendour and beauty, this fish is almost unsurpassed.

A fish called by the natives great-fire (*Scorpæna volitans*) is eaten by the native fishermen, the flesh being white, solid, and nutritive. Linnæus describes the flesh as delicious.

The pookoorowah (*Holocentrus argenteus*) is a very delicious fish, seldom exceeding twelve or thirteen inches in length. The gal-handah (*Chætodon araneus*), a singular and much admired fish, only about three inches in length, has a delicate and white flesh, and is greatly esteemed.

In Java and Sumatra, a preparation of small fish, with red-rice, having the appearance of anchovies, and the colour of red-cabbage, is esteemed a delicacy. So in India, the preparation called tamarind fish is much prized as a breakfast relish, where the acid of the tamarind is made use of for preserving the white pomfret-fish, cut in transverse slices. The mango-fish (*Polynemus longifilis*, Cuvier; *P. paradiscus* of Linnæus), about eight or nine inches long by two deep, is much esteemed in India. At Calcutta the *Lates nobilis*, different species of *Polynemus*, and the *Mugil Corsula*, daily cover the tables of Europeans, who will more readily recognize these fishes under the names of the *Begti* or *Cockup*, *Sudjeh*, *Tupsi*, and the Indian Mullet.

At the Sandheads may be found some of those delicious fishes, which are more familiar to the residents of Madras and Bombay, for instance, the Indian soles, the roll-fish, and above all, the black and white pomfrets, and the bummolah, which latter in a dried state is known by the name of the Bombay duck. The bummolah is a small glutinous transparent fish, about the size of smelt.

There are many excellent fish obtained from the sea round the Cape Colony, and about 2,500 tons are shipped annually to the Mauritius, forming nearly three fourths of the island consumption; the principal consumers being the coolie labourers or Indian population.

Geelbeck, or yellow mouth, sometimes called Cape salmon (*Otolithus æquidens*, Cuv. and Val.), is the finest as to quality; they are taken abundantly with the hook and line, or net, and weigh about 14 lbs. The cost of preparation ready for shipment is about £12. It forms an article of food for the poor and lazy. The Malays at the Cape cure a great deal in vinegar (for home consumption), the same as pickled salmon in England; and it is not a bad representative of it. For exportation they are opened down the back, the intestines taken out, head cut off, salted for a night, and dried in the sun.

Snook (*Thyrsites atua*), similar to the baraconta, is a long, slim, oily fish, taken with any shining bait; it is a perfect salt-water pike, very strong and ferocious, and is dispatched, after being pulled on board, by blows on the head with a kind of knob-kerrie. These are cured the same way as the geelbeck; the cost of production is about £16 per ton. They are highly prized by the colonists, and esteemed before any fish imported into Mauritius, fetching about £2 per ton more than cod. These fish are very fine eating when cured fresh. They are also much esteemed in Ceylon. The Malays cure them without salt by drying in the sun, with a little pepper and spice; they are then delicious.

Silver fish (*Dentex argyrozona*) are similar to the bream of England; each weighs from 6 to 8 lbs. They are got up for shipment the same as the others; the cost of production is about £10 per ton. They are the least esteemed of any at the Mauritius market, but when fresh they are very nice eating. The bastard silver fish (*D. rupestris*) is considered one of the very finest fishes in the colony. It is esteemed for foreign markets. Harders are a mullet, about eight inches long, which are principally cured in small casks in brine, for up-country use. The Cape farmers are very fond of them, but few are exported. They have also mackerel very large, very fat, which are better cured than fresh.

The Jacob Evertsen (*Sebastes capensis*), so called after a Dutch captain, remarkable for a red face and large projecting eyes, is a fish which, though common in Table Bay almost at all seasons, is highly prized for its flesh by most colonists. Another species, the sancord (*S. maculatus*), which is not so common, is a very delicious fish. The kabeljauw (*Sciæna hololepidota*) is a large fish from two to three feet long, common on the coast, being caught with the hook and the drag-net. It is one of the staple fishes in the Cape Town market; dried and salted like cod it is exported to the Mauritius and elsewhere. Its flesh when young is good, but firm and dry in adult individuals. The baardmannetje (*Umbrina capensis*, Pappe), another newly described fish of the same family, which is chiefly caught in False Bay during summer, measures from 2 to 2½ feet, and is reputed for its delicious flesh.

The hangberger (*Sargus Hottentotus*), a fish about 18 inches long, which is common in Table Bay from June to August, is much in request, particularly at the time when it is with roe. It is also cured and pickled for economical purposes. It feeds on shell fish, and is caught with the hook.

The Hottentot fish (*Sargus capensis*), from 12 to 14 inches long, which is mostly confined to Table Bay and the West Coast, may be caught at all seasons with the hook. It is not only a superior table fish, but forms when salted and dried an article of export.

The roode steen brassem of the Dutch (*Chrysophrys laticeps*, Cuvier) is a bulky fish, often exceeding 3½ feet in length and 14 inches in breadth. It is very voracious, and feeds generally on crabs and cuttle fish (*Sepia* and *Loligo*). As food it is much prized, and is also cured for exportation.

The Roman fish (*Chrysophrys cristiceps*) is one of the prettiest and most delicious fish met with in the Cape markets. It is generally acknowledged to be a superior dish.

The daggerath (*Pagrus laniarius*) is of a dark rose colour, about 12 inches long. It is highly prized in the colony for its delicious flesh. This handsome fish owes its surname, *laniarius* (butcher), both to its colour and to its sharp teeth and voracity.

The windtoy (*Cantharus Blochii*) is a delicious table fish, more commonly caught in winter, and often put up in bundles along with the Hottentot fish (*Sargus capensis*). The flesh of the dasje fish, another species (*Cantharus emarginatus*), is also highly esteemed as food.

There is a fish called by the colonists the bamboo fish (*Boops salpa*), from feeding on algæ and being caught principally in localities where there is an abundance of sea-weed. On account of its vegetable nourishment, it exhibits at times a particular smell when embowelled, and is for that reason called stink-fish by some of the fishermen. It is a rich and delicate fish, and though scarce in the Cape Town market, is common in Saldanha Bay, where it is dried and salted for home consumption.

The flesh of the bastard Jacob Evertsen (*Pimelepterus fuscus*) is well flavoured and very nice. This fish is of a uniform dusky brown colour. It feeds on shell-fish.

The galleon fish (*Dipterodon capensis*) is more plentiful in the western division of the Cape Colony; it is highly esteemed as food and always fetches a good price. It is, however, disliked by some on account of the many black veins traversing its flesh, and is at times rather unwholesome, from being too rich and requiring good digestive organs.

The elft-fish (*Temnodon saltator*) is uniformly lead coloured, shaded with dark green on its back. From leaping now and then out of the water it has obtained its name of *saltator* (jumper). It is held in great esteem as a table fish, and the younger individuals are truly deemed a dainty.

There are several species of mullet recorded as inhabitants of the bays and rivers of the Cape Colony. All of them are caught with the net. They make good table fish, but are more frequently salted or smoke-dried (under the name of bokkoms) like the herring, and thus preserved, form a very considerable article of home consumption as well as of export.

The klip-fish (*Blennius versicolor*, Pappe) is greatly reputed for its flesh, which is nice, well flavoured, and wholesome.

The flesh of the bagger (*Bagrus capensis*) is extremely delicate, and bears a greater resemblance to that of the eel than that of any other sea fish in the colony. Owing to its ugliness, this curious fish, which hides itself among stones in muddy water the better to entrap its unsuspecting prey, is from popular prejudice less prized than it deserves.

English writers on Ichthyology comment very unfavourably on the merits of the hake (*Gadus merluccius*) and call it 'a coarse fish, scarcely fit for the dinner table.' At the Cape its qualities are generally and fully appreciated; in fact, its flesh is highly delicate and little inferior to that of the haddock (*Gadus æglefinus*). At times it makes its appearance in large shoals. It is then abundantly caught, salted, and dried, for exportation. The cured or dried Cape stock-fish is an excellent dish, far superior to that insipid stuff introduced from Holland or other countries.

The rock-cod (*Serranus Cuvierii*) is highly esteemed as an article of food.

Sardines in myriads swarm round Table Bay, at one season of the year; klip-fish, king klip-fish, and soles (rather scarce), are considered a luxury.

It is hardly requisite to say much of that cosmopolitan fish, the sole, which is for its delicacy prized as well at the Cape as elsewhere.

Thousands of cray-fish are caught daily; four of the largest can be obtained for a penny; but it is not fashionable to eat them, although they are very good.

The quantity of fish throughout the whole extent of the coast, bordering on the Agulha's bank, is immense, and would be the richest fishery in the world. Exports of sardines in the French style, of potted cray-fish in the American, and the choicest fish preserved fresh in tins, might be made profitable.

I may add here that Dr. L. Pappe, of Cape Town, to whom I am indebted for my information on the Cape fishes, has published in the Colony an interesting synopsis of the edible fishes at the Cape of Good Hope, in which he furnishes much new and interesting descriptive scientific detail.

INSECTS

Insects furnish more food delicacies than is generally supposed. In the popular *Introduction to Entomology*, by Kirby and Spence, it is well remarked, that,

'If we could lay aside our English prejudices, there is no reason why some of the insects might not be eaten, for those used by various nations as food, generally speaking, live on vegetable substances, and are consequently much more select and cleanly in their diet than the pig or the duck, which form a favourite part of our food. They who would turn with disgust from a locust, or the grub of a beetle, feel no symptoms of nausea when a lobster, crab, or shrimp is set before them. The fact is, that habit has reconciled us to the eating of these last, which, viewed in themselves, with their threatening claws, and many feet, are really more disgusting than the former. Had the habit been reversed, we should have viewed the former with appetite, and the latter with abhorrence—as do the Arabs, who are as much astounded at our eating crabs, lobsters, and oysters, as we are at their eating locusts.'

Herrick, an old author, 200 years ago, in describing a feast given by Oberon to the fairy elves, alludes to the insects as amongst their choicest cates.

'Gladding his palate with some store
Of emmet's eggs: what would he more?
But beards of mice, a newt's stewed thigh,
A bloated earwig, and a fly.
With the red-capp'd worm that's shut
Within the concave of a nut,
Brown as his tooth;—a little moth,
Late fatten'd in a piece of cloth.'

Herrick's *Hesperides*, 1658.

COLEOPTERA

Many larvæ of insects, and especially of beetles, are eaten in different parts of the world.

The grub of the palm weevil (*Cordylia palmarum*), which is the size of the thumb, has long been in request in the East and West Indies. The natives of Surinam roast and eat them as something exquisite. In Jamaica, where it is known as the grou-grou worm, I have seen it eaten commonly. A grub named *Macauco* is also there in request at the principal tables. It is eaten both by whites and blacks, who empty, wash, and roast them, and find them delicious. A similar insect is dressed at Mauritius, and eaten by all classes.

An old writer—Brookes, *On the Properties and Uses of Insects*, 1772, says—'They are eaten by the French, in the West Indies, after they have been roasted before the fire, when a small wooden spit has been thrust through them. When they begin to be hot, they powder them with a crust of rasped bread, mixed with salt, and a little pepper and nutmeg. This powder keeps in the fat, or at least, sucks it up; and when they are done enough, they are served up with orange juice. They are highly esteemed by the French, as excellent eating.'

The larva, or grub, of one of the species of beetles which infest cocoa-nut trees, is called *Tucuma*, or *Grugou*, in British Guiana. It is about two or three inches long, and three-quarters of an inch in diameter, and the head is black. They are reckoned a great delicacy by wood-cutters and epicures of the country, and they are generally dressed by frying them in a pan. By some they are preferred in a raw state, and after seizing them by the black head, they are dipped in lime-juice, and forthwith swallowed.

The late Mr. J. C. Bidwell, a botanist, travelling in Australia, states—'I never before tasted one of the large grubs, which are a favourite food of the blacks. They are about four inches long, and about as thick as a finger. They inhabit the wood of the gum-trees. I had often tried to taste one, but could not manage it. Now, however, hunger overcame my nausea. It was very good, but not as I had expected to find it—rich; it was only sweet and milky.'

Sir Robert Schomburgk writes:—'The decaying woods of the West India islands, the Central and some of the southern portions of America, afford a delicacy to the Indian, which many colonists do not even refuse, in the larvæ of a large beetle, which is found in considerable numbers in the pith, when the trunk is near its decay. The larva, or grub, is frequently of the size of the little finger; and, after being boiled or roasted, resembles in its taste beef marrow. The Indians of Guiana frequently cut down the Mauritia palm, for the purpose of attracting the beetle to deposit its eggs in it, and when they collect a large quantity, they are roasted over a slow fire, to extract the fat, which is preserved in calabashes.

The Roman epicures fattened some of these larvæ, or grubs, on flour. Some naturalists think that the grubs of most of the beetles might be safely eaten; and that those of the cockchafer, which feeds upon the roots of grass, or the perfect insects themselves, which, if we may judge from the eagerness with which cats, and turkeys and other birds devour them, are no despicable morsel, might be added to our food delicacies. This would certainly be one means of keeping down the numbers of these occasionally destructive animals.

The Goliath beetles are said to be roasted and eaten by the natives of South America and Western Africa, and they often make a *bonne bouche* of splendid insects which would gratify many an entomologist. Although the large prices of £30, £40, or £50, which used to be asked for them, are now very much reduced, fine specimens of some of the species even now fetch five to six pounds for cabinet specimens.

The Australian aborigines are gourmands in their way, and able to appreciate the good things which surround them. Mr. Clement Hodgkinson in a work on Australia says:

'Bellenger Billy amused me very much by his curious method of diving to the bottom of the river in search of cobberra, the large white worms resembling boiled maccaroni, which abound in immersed wood. He swam to the centre of the river with a tomahawk in his hand, and then breathing hard that his lungs might be collapsed, he rendered his body and tomahawk specifically heavier than water, and sank feet foremost to the bottom. After groping about there for some moments, he emerged on the river's edge, with several dead pieces of wood, which he had detached from the mud. Although I had tasted from curiosity various kinds of snakes, lizards, guanas, grubs, and other animals which the blacks feed upon, I never could muster resolution enough to try one of these cobberra; although, when I have been engaged in the survey of salt-water creeks, and I felt hot and thirsty, I have often envied the extreme relish with which some accompanying black could stop and gorge himself with this moist, living marrow.'

The women of Turkey cook and eat a certain beetle (*Blaps sulcata*) in butter to fatten themselves.

ORTHOPTERA

In the next order of insects, the locust tribe, as they are the greatest destroyers of food, so, as some recompense, they furnish a considerable supply of it to numerous nations. They are recorded to have done this from the most remote antiquity, some Ethiopian tribes having been named from this circumstance locust-eaters. The generic name of the locusts, *Gryllus*, sounds like an invitation to cook them. Pliny relates that they were in high esteem as meat amongst the Parthians. When there is a scarcity of grain, as a substitute for flour the Arabs grind locusts in their hand-mills, or pound them in stone mortars. They mix this flour with water into a dough, and make thin cakes of it, which they bake like other bread. They also eat them in another way; they boil them first a good while in water, and afterwards stew with oil or butter into a kind of fricassée of no bad flavour.

The large kinds of locust are made use of in several quarters as food, and in the markets of the Levant fresh and salted locusts are vended. Hasselquist tells us, that when corn is scarce, the Arabians grind the locusts in hand-mills, or pound them in stone mortars, and bake them as bread; and that even when there is no scarcity of corn, the Arabs stew them with butter and make them into a kind of a fricassée, the flavour of which is by no means disagreeable. Why should land shrimp sauce not be equal to sea shrimp sauce?

Locusts, Cumming tells us, afford fattening and wholesome food to man, birds, and all sorts of beasts. The hungry dogs and hogs feed greedily on them,—so that there are plenty of enemies to prey in time upon these wholesale depredators. Young turkeys live almost entirely on them in some parts of America, and become very fat when they are plentiful. Hence, if so many animals thrive upon them, they must necessarily be dainty food.

It is not only by the inhabitants of the Great Desert that the locusts are hailed with joy. The Kafirs also give them a hearty welcome, and make many a good meal upon them too,—not only eating them in large quantities, but making a sort of coffee-colored soup of their eggs.

Locusts are cooked in various ways—roasted, boiled, and fried. They are also salted and smoked, and packed away against a time of scarcity. It is said, they taste very much like fish, and are particularly light, delicate, and wholesome food. They are carried into many of the towns of Africa by waggon-loads, as we bring poultry to market.

The Hottentots are highly rejoiced at the arrival of the locusts in their country, although they destroy all its verdure, eating them in such quantities as to get visibly fatter than before, and making of their eggs a brown or coffee-coloured soup.

In the Mahratta country in India, the common people salt and eat them. This was anciently the custom with many of the African nations, some of whom also smoked them.

Dishes of locusts are generally served up at the principal tables in Barbary, and esteemed a great delicacy. They are preferred by the Moors to pigeons; and a person may eat a plateful of 200 or 300 without feeling any ill effects. They usually boil them in water half-an-hour, having thrown away the head, wings, and legs, then sprinkle them with salt and pepper and fry them, adding a little vinegar.

Another traveller describes the way they are prepared for food in the desert of Zahara.—'In and about this valley were great flights of locusts. During the day, they are flying around very thickly in the atmosphere; but the copious dews and chilly air in the night render them unable to fly, and they settle down on the bushes. It was the constant employment of the natives in the night to gather these insects from the bushes, which they did in great quantities. My master's family, each with a small bag, went out the first night upon this employment, carrying a very large bag to bring home the fruits of their labor. My mistress, Fatima, however, and the two little children, remained in the tent. I declined this employment, and retired to rest under the large tent. The next day, the family returned loaded with locusts, and, judging by the eye of the quantity produced, there must have been about fifteen bushels. This may appear to be a large quantity to be gathered in so short a time, but it is scarcely worth mentioning when compared with the loads of them gathered, sometimes, in the more fertile part of the country over which they pass, leaving a track of desolation behind them. But as they were the first, in any considerable quantity, that I had seen, and the first I had seen cooked and eaten, I mention it in this place, hoping hereafter to give my readers more particular information concerning these wonderful and destructive insects, which, from the days of Moses to this time, have been considered, by Jews and Mahometans, as the most severe judgment which Heaven can inflict upon man. But, whatever the Egyptians might have thought in ancient days, or the Moors and Arabs in those of modern date, the Arabs who are compelled to inhabit the desert of Zahara, so far from considering a flight of locusts as a judgment upon them for their transgressions, welcome their approach as the means, sometimes, of saving them from famishing with hunger. The whole that were brought to the tent at this time were cooked while alive, as indeed they always are, for a dead locust is never cooked. The manner of cooking is by digging a deep hole in the ground, building a fire at the bottom, as before described, and filling it up with wood. After it is heated as hot as is possible, the coals and embers are taken out, and they prepare to fill the cavity with the locusts, confined in a large bag. A sufficient number of the natives hold the bag perpendicularly over the hole, the mouth of it being near the surface of the ground. A number stand round the hole with sticks. The mouth of the bag is then opened, and it is shaken with great force, the locusts falling into the hot pit, and the surrounding natives throwing sand upon them to prevent them from flying off. The mouth of the hole is then covered with sand, and another fire built upon the top of it. In this manner they cook all they have on hand, and dig a number of holes sufficient to accomplish it, each containing about five bushels. They remain in the hole until they become sufficiently cooled to be taken out with the hand. They are then picked out, and thrown upon tent-cloths or blankets, and remain in the sun to dry, where they must be watched with the utmost care to prevent the live locusts from devouring them, if a flight happens to be passing at the time. When they are perfectly dried, which is not done short of two or three days, they are slightly pounded, and pressed into bags or skins, ready for transportation. To prepare them to eat, they are pulverized in mortars, and mixed with water sufficient to make a kind of dry pudding. They are, however, sometimes eaten singly, without pulverizing, by breaking off the head, wings, and legs, and swallowing the remaining part. In whatever manner they are eaten, they are nourishing food.'

Captain Stockenstrom, in a paper in the *South African Journal* on these insects, observes, 'Not only the locust-bird, but every animal, domestic and wild, contributes to the destruction of the locust swarms; fowls, sheep, horses, dogs, antelopes, and almost every living thing, may be seen devouring them with equal greediness; whilst the half-starved Bushmen, and even some of the colonial Hottentots, consider them a great luxury, consuming great quantities fresh, and drying abundance for future emergencies. Great havoc is also committed among the locusts by their own kindred; for as soon as any one of them gets hurt, or meets with an accident which impedes his progress, his fellow travellers nearest to him immediately turn upon him, and devour him with great voracity.'

Mr. Moffat (*Missionary Labours in South Africa*) states—'The locusts for food are always caught at night, when they are at rest, and carried in sacks to the nearest encampment or village, to be prepared for keeping. A very small quantity of water is put into a pot, and the locusts, piled up to the very brim, are covered very closely, so that they are rather steamed than boiled. They are next carefully separated and laid out to dry, which the heat of an Arabian or African sun does thoroughly and speedily; after which they are winnowed to get rid of the wings and legs, when they are laid up in heaps, or packed in bags of skin for future use. Sometimes the dry locusts are beaten into a powder, of which, with water and a little salt, a kind of pottage is made.'

Mr. R. Gordon Cumming, in the course of his rambles in Africa, fell in with swarms of locusts, and gives interesting accounts respecting them. Here are some extracts from his work:—

'The next day, as we crossed a vast plain, a flight of locusts passed over our heads during upwards of half-an-hour, flying so thick as to darken the sun. They reached in dark clouds as far as we could see, and maintained an elevation of from 6 to 300 or 400 feet above the level of the plain. Woe to the vegetation of the country on which they alight! * *

'On the march we crossed a swarm of locusts, resting for the night on the grass and bushes. They lay so thick that the waggons could have been filled with them in a very short time, covering the large bushes just as a swarm of young bees covers the branch on which it pitches. Locusts afford fattening and wholesome food to man, birds, and all sorts of beasts; cows and horses, lions, jackals, hyænas, antelopes, elephants, &c., devour them. We met a party of Batlapis carrying heavy burdens of them on their backs. Our hungry dogs made a fine feast on them. The cold frosty night had rendered them unable to take wing until the sun should restore their powers. As it was difficult to obtain sufficient food for my dogs, I and Isaac took a large blanket, which we spread under a bush, whose branches were bent to the ground with the mass of locusts which covered it, and having shaken the branches, in an instant I had more locusts than I could carry on my back. These we roasted for ourselves and dogs. Soon after the sun was up, on looking behind me, I beheld the locusts stretching to the west in vast clouds, resembling smoke; but the wind soon after veering round, brought them back to us, and they flew over our heads, for some time actually darkening the sun. * * * * * * * *

'The dullness of the scene, however, was enlivened by a wondrous flight of locusts, the largest I had ever beheld. The prospect was obscured by them as far as we could see, resembling the smoke arising from a thousand giant bonfires; while those above our heads darkened our path with a double flight, the one next the ground flying north, while the upper clouds of them held a southerly course. The dogs, as usual, made a hearty meal of them. * * * *

'We crossed the Limpopo, and having followed it for five miles, we at length got into a country so densely covered with locusts that the spore was no longer visible. A large herd of elephants had, during several previous nights, however, been there feasting upon these insects.'

According to Niebuhr, the Arabians distinguish several kinds of locusts, to which they give separate names. They refer only to the delicacy of its flesh, and not to the nature of the insect. The red locust is termed *Merrken*, as it is esteemed by the epicures much fatter and more succulent than the light locust, which is called by them *Dubbe*, because it has a tendency to produce diarrhœa. The inhabitants of Arabia, Persia, Africa, and Syria, are accustomed to eat them. The Turks have an aversion to this kind of food; but if the Europeans express the same, the Arabians remind them of their fondness for crabs, &c. This kind of food, however, is supposed to thicken the blood, and produce melancholy.

The custom of feeding upon locusts seems more generally diffused than is supposed, and is not merely confined to Africa and Arabia. They are eaten by the Nanningetes in the Malay Peninsula.

Dampier states that, on islands near Timor, 'They make also a dish of locusts, which come at certain seasons to devour their potatoes. They take them with nets, and broil or bake them in an earthen pan. This dish,' he adds, 'eats well enough.'

And the author of *A Mission to Ava* speaks of them as a Burmese dainty.

'The most notable viand produced consisted of fried locusts. These were brought in, hot and hot, in successive saucers, and I was not sorry to have the opportunity of tasting a dish so famous. They were by no means bad, much like what we might suppose fried shrimps to be. The inside is removed, and the cavity stuffed with a little spiced meat.'

The Rev. R. Sheppard caused some of our large English grasshoppers, or field crickets, to be cooked in the way here recommended, only substituting butter for vinegar, and found them to be excellent food.

From these statements it will be seen, that the locusts which formed part of the sustenance of John the Baptist, and about which there has been much controversy among learned men, could be nothing else but the animal locust, so common a food in the East, and even in Africa, to the present day. They are eaten even by the North American Indians.

'Among the choice delicacies with which the California Digger Indians regale themselves during the summer season,' (says the *Empire County Argus*,) 'is the grasshopper roast. Having been an eye witness to the preparation and discussion of one of their feasts of grasshoppers, we can describe it truthfully. There are districts in California, as well as portions of the plains between Sierra Nevada and the Rocky Mountains, that literally swarm with grasshoppers, and in such astonishing numbers that a man cannot place his foot to the ground, while walking there, without crushing great numbers. To the Indian they are a delicacy, and are caught and cooked in the following manner:— A piece of ground is sought where they most abound, in the centre of which an excavation is made, large and deep enough to prevent the insect from hopping out when once in. The entire party of diggers, old and young, male and female, then surround as much of the adjoining grounds as they can, and each with a green bough in hand, whipping and thrashing on every side, gradually approach the centre, driving the insects before them in countless multitudes, till at last all, or nearly all, are secured in the pit. In the meantime, smaller excavations are made, answering the purpose of ovens, in which fires are kindled and kept up till the surrounding earth, for a short distance, becomes sufficiently heated, together with a flat stone, large enough to cover the oven. The grasshoppers are now taken in coarse bags, and after being thoroughly soaked in salt water for a few moments, are emptied into the oven and closed in. Ten or fifteen minutes suffice to roast them, when they are taken out and eaten without further preparation, and with much apparent relish, or as is sometimes the case, reduced to powder and made into soup. And having from curiosity tasted, not of the soup, but of the roast, really, if one could but divest himself of the idea of eating an insect, as we do an oyster or shrimp, without other preparation than simple roasting, they would not be considered very bad eating, even by more refined epicures than the Digger Indians.'

NEUROPTERA

Another order of insects contains the so-called white-ant tribe (*Termes*), which, in return for the mischief it does at certain times, affords an abundant supply of food to some of the African natives. The natives of Western Australia pull out the young from the nests at one season of the year and eat them. Ducks and fowls also feed greedily on them.

In many countries, the termites, or white-ants, serve for food. In some parts of the East Indies, the natives catch the winged insects, just before their period of emigration, in the following manner:—They make two holes, the one to the windward, the other to the leeward; at the leeward opening, they place the mouth of a pot, the inside of which has been previously rubbed with an aromatic herb, called bugera; on the windward side, they make a fire of stinking materials, which not only drives these insects, but frequently the hooded snakes also, into the pots, on which account they are obliged to be cautious in removing them. By this method, they catch great quantities, of which they make, with flour, a variety of pastry, which they can afford to sell very cheap to the poorer ranks of people. When this sort of food is used too abundantly, it produces, however, cholera, which kills in two or three hours. It also seems that, in some form or other, these insects are greedily eaten in other districts. Thus, when after swarming shoals of them fall into the rivers, the Africans skim them off the surface with calabashes, and, bringing them to their habitations, parch them in iron pots over a gentle fire, stirring them about as is usually done in roasting coffee; in that state, without sauce or any other addition, they consider them delicious food, putting them by handfuls into their mouths, as we do comfits.[30]

'I have,' says Smeathman, 'eaten them dressed in this way several times, and think them delicate, nourishing, and wholesome. They are something sweeter, though not so fat and clogging, as the caterpillar or maggot of the palm-tree snout-beetle (*Curculio palmarum*), which is served up at all the luxurious tables of the West Indian epicures, particularly of the French, as the greatest dainty of the western world.'

Ants are eaten in many countries. In Brazil, the yellow ant, called cupia, and a larger species under the name of tama-joura, are much esteemed, being eaten by the aborigines mixed with resin for sauce. In Africa, they are stewed with butter. Ants have really no unpleasant flavour, but are very agreeably acid. In some parts of Sweden, ants are distilled along with rye, to give a flavour to the inferior kinds of brandy.

The large saubas (red-ants) and white-ants are an occasional luxury to the Indians of the Rio Negro; and when nothing else is to be had in the wet season, they eat large earth-worms, which, when the lands in which they live are flooded, ascend trees, and take up their abode in the hollow leaves of a species of *Tillandsia*, where they are often found accumulated by thousands. Nor is it only hunger that makes them eat these worms, for they sometimes boil them with their fish to give it an extra relish.[31]

The cocoons of the wood ant (popularly and erroneously called ants' eggs) are collected on the Continent as food for nightingales and larks. A recent writer tells us, that in most of the towns in Germany one or more individuals make a living, during summer, by the business. He describes a visit to an old woman at Dottendorf, near Bonn, who had collected for fourteen years. She went to the woods in the morning, and collected in a bag the surfaces of a number of ant hills where the cocoons were deposited, taking ants and all home to her cottage, near which she had a tiled shed, covering a circular area, hollowed out in the centre, with a trench full of water around it. After covering the hollow in the centre with leafy boughs of walnut or hazel, she strewed the contents of her bag on the level part of the area within the trench, when the nurse-ants immediately seized the cocoons and carried them into the hollow under the boughs. The cocoons were thus brought into one place, and after being from time to time removed, and the black ones separated by a boy, who spread them out on a table and swept off what were bad with a strong feather, they were ready for market, being sold for about 4*d.* or 6*d.* a quart. Considerable quantities of these cocoons are dried for winter food for birds, and are sold in the shops.

Humboldt mentions that he saw insects' eggs sold in the markets of Mexico, and which are collected on the surface of lakes. Under the name of axayacat, these eggs, or those of some other species of fly, deposited on rush mats, are sold as a caviare in Mexico. Something similar, found in the pools of the desert of Fezzan, serves the Arabs for food, having the taste of caviare.

In the *Bulletin de la Société Impériale Zoologique d'Acclimation*, M. Guerin Méneville has published a very interesting paper on a sort of bread which the Mexicans make of the eggs of three species of hemipterous insects.

According to M. Craveri, by whom some of the Mexican bread, and of the insects yielding it, were brought to Europe, these insects and their eggs are very common in the fresh waters of the lagunes of Mexico. The natives cultivate, in the lagune of Chalco, a sort of carex called touté, on which the insects readily deposit their eggs. Numerous bundles of these plants are made, which are taken to a lagune, the Texcuco, where they float in great numbers in the water. The insects soon come and deposit their eggs on the plants, and in about a month the bundles are removed from the water, dried, and then beaten over a large cloth to separate the myriad of eggs with which the insects had covered them.

These eggs are then cleaned and sifted, put into sacks like flour, and sold to the people for making a sort of cake or biscuit called 'hautlé,' which forms a tolerably good food, but has a fishy taste, and is slightly acid. The bundles of carex are replaced in the lake, and afford a fresh supply of eggs, which process may be repeated for an indefinite number of times.

It appears that these insects have been used from an early period, for Thomas Gage, a religionist, who sailed to Mexico in 1625, says, in speaking of articles sold in the markets, that they had cakes made of a sort of scum collected from the lakes of Mexico, and that this was also sold in other towns.

Brantz Mayer, in his work on Mexico (*Mexico as it was and as it is*, 1844), says, —'On the lake of Texcuco I saw men occupied in collecting the eggs of flies from the surface of plants, and cloths arranged in long rows as places of resort for the insects. These eggs, called *agayacath'* (Qy. *axayacat*), 'formed a favourite food of the Indians long before the conquest: and when made into cakes, resembles the roe of a fish, having a similar taste and appearance. After the use of frogs in France, and birdsnests in China, I think these eggs may be considered a delicacy, and I found that they are not rejected from the tables of the fashionable inhabitants of the capital.'

The more recent observations of Messrs. Saussure, Sallé, Virlet D'Aoust, &c., have confirmed the facts already stated, at least, in the most essential particulars.

'The insects which principally produce this animal farinha of Mexico, are two species of the genus *Corixa* of Geoffroy, hemipterous insects of the family of water-bugs. One of the species has been described by M. Guerin Méneville as new, and has been named by him *Corixa fermorata*: the other, identified in 1831 by Thomas Say as one of those sold in the market at Mexico, bears the name of *Corixa mercenaria*. The eggs of these two species are attached in innumerable quantities to the triangular leaves of the carex forming the bundles which are deposited in the waters. They are of an oval form with a protuberance at one end and a pedicle at the other extremity, by means of which they are fixed to a small round disc, which the mother cements to the leaf. Among these eggs, which are grouped closely together, and sometimes fixed one over another, there are found others, which are larger, of a long and cylindrical form, and which are fixed to the same leaves. These belong to another larger insect, a species of *Notonecta*, which M. Guerin Méneville has named *Notonecta unifasciata*.'[32]

It appears from M. Virlet d'Aoust, that in October the lakes Chalco and Texcuco, which border on the city of Mexico, are haunted by millions of small flies, which, after dancing in the air, plunge down into the shallowest parts of the water, to the depth of several feet, and deposit their eggs at the bottom.

'The eggs of these insects are called hautle (haoutle), by the Mexican Indians, who collect them in great numbers, and with whom they appear to be a favourite article of food.

'They are prepared in various ways, but usually made into cakes, which are eaten with a sauce flavoured with chillies. To collect the eggs the Indians prepare bundles of rushes, which they place vertically in the lake at some distance from the shore. In about a fortnight, every rush in these bundles is completely covered with eggs. The bundles are then drawn out and dried in the sun upon a cloth for not more than an hour, when the eggs are easily detached. The bundles of rushes are then placed in the water again for another crop.'[33]

Mr. Ruschenberger, the surgeon to the American expedition to Siam, in describing a state feast given to the officers, states that the dinner was remarkable for the variety and exquisite flavour of the curries. Among them was one consisting of ants' eggs, a costly and much esteemed luxury of Siam. They are not larger than grains of sand, and to a palate unaccustomed to them, are not particularly savory. They are almost tasteless. Besides being curried, they are brought to the table rolled in green leaves, mingled with shreds or very fine slices of fat pork. Here was seen an ever-to-be-remembered luxury of the East.

HYMENOPTERA

It would hardly be suspected that bees serve for food in Ceylon and some other places,—an ungrateful return for their honey and wax.

The African Bushmen eat the caterpillars of the butterflies.

The Chinese, who waste nothing, after they have unwound the silk from the cocoons of the silk-worm, send the chrysalis to table. They also eat the larvæ of a hawk-moth, some of which tribe, Dr. Darwin tells us, are, in his opinion, very delicious. The natives of New Holland eat the caterpillars of a species of moth, and also a kind of butterfly, which they call *bugong*, which congregate in certain districts, at particular seasons, in countless myriads. On these occasions, the native blacks assemble from far and near to collect them; and after removing the wings and down, by stirring them on the ground, previously heated by a large fire, winnowing them, eat the bodies, or store them up for use, by pounding and smoking them. The bodies of these butterflies abound in an oil, with the taste of nuts; when first eaten, they produce violent vomitings and other debilitating effects; but these go off after a few days, and the natives then thrive and fatten exceedingly on this diet, for which they have to contend with a black crow, which is also attracted by the butterflies, and which they dispatch with their clubs, and use as food.

Two insects, a kind of butterfly, and a thick, white grub, found chiefly in dead timber, are much esteemed by the aborigines of Australia as articles of food. The former is eaten at certain seasons by whole tribes of natives in the northern districts. Their practice is to follow up the flight of the insects, and to light fires at night-fall beneath the trees in which they have roosted. The smoke brings the butterflies down, and their bodies are pounded together into a sort of fleshy loaf. Upon this delicacy the natives not only feed, but fatten. The white grub is swallowed whole in his living state, and is much sought for by sable epicures.

In India, and in South America, these grubs are also eaten as a dainty.

The trunk of the grass-tree, or black-boy (*Xanthorea arborea*), when beginning to decay, furnishes large quantities of marrow-like grubs, which are considered a delicacy by the aborigines in Western Australia. They have a fragrant, aromatic flavour, and form a favourite food among the natives, either raw or roasted. They call them *bardi*—and they are also found in the wattle tree, or mimosa. The presence of these grubs in a *xanthorea* is thus ascertained: if the top of one of these trees is observed to be dead, and it contain any bardi, a few sharp kicks given to it with the foot will cause it to crack and shake, when it is pushed over and the grub extracted, by breaking the tree to pieces with a hammer. The bardi of the *xanthorea* are small, and found together in great numbers; those of the wattle are cream coloured, as long and thick as a man's finger, and are found singly. The excrement of the latter oozes from under the bark, of the appearance and consistence of clear gum. The galls formed on several species of sage by gall flies, in the Levant, are highly prized for their aromatic and acid flavour, especially when prepared with sugar. They constitute, in fact, a considerable article of commerce from Scio to Constantinople, where they are regularly sold in the market. They are known as sage apples, and in Greece are made into a kind of conserve, which is highly esteemed.

HEMIPTERA

Coming to another order of insects, the cicada, or chirping flies, we find that these were eaten by the polished Greeks, and accounted very delicious. They were caught, strung, sold, and greedily devoured; and especially the females were relished on account of their white eggs. One species, a very long-lived one, which, if spared, lives to the age of 17 years, is still eaten by the Indians of America, who pluck off the wings and boil them. The aborigines of Australia eat them raw, after stripping off the wings.

The 17-year locusts, while in an underground grub state, are a favourite food of various species of animals. Immense numbers are destroyed by hogs before they emerge from the ground; they are also, when in their perfect state, eagerly devoured by chickens, squirrels, and many of the larger birds. The Indians likewise consider them a delicate food when fried; and in New Jersey they have been turned to a profitable account in making soap.

No insects are more numerous with us than caterpillars, and sad havoc they occasionally commit among our cabbages and cauliflowers. Now we generally make wry faces, when a stray one is served up with our greens, and the cook is severely taken to task; but these are reckoned among the chief delicacies of an African Bushman's meal.

The Hottentots eat them boiled and raw, and soon get into good condition on this food. They bring large calabashes full of them to their habitations, and parch them in iron pots over a gentle fire, stirring them about as is done in roasting coffee. In that state, without sauce or other addition, they serve them up as delicious food, and eat them by handfuls, as we do sugar-plums.

One traveller tells us he has eaten them dressed in this way several times, and thought them delicate, nourishing, and wholesome, being sweeter than the grub of the weevil of the palm, and resembling in taste sugared cream or sweet almond paste.

ARACHNIDA

What will be said to spiders as food? But these form an article in the list of the Bushman's dainties in South Africa, according to Sparrman; and the inhabitants of New Caledonia, Labillardiere tells us, seek for, and eat with avidity, large quantities of a spider nearly an inch long, which they roast over the fire. Even individuals amongst the more polished nations of Europe are recorded as having a similar taste; so that if you could rise above vulgar prejudices, you would in all probability find them a most delicate morsel. If you require precedents, Reaumur tells us of a young lady, who, when she walked in her grounds, never saw a spider that she did not take and crunch upon the spot. Another female, the celebrated Anna Maria Schurman, used to eat them like nuts, which she affirmed they much resembled in taste, excusing her propensity by saying that she was born under the sign *Scorpio*.

If you wish for the authority of the learned: Lalande, the celebrated French astronomer, was equally fond of these delicacies, according to Latreille. And if, not content with eating spiders seriatim, you should feel desirous of eating them by handfuls, you may shelter yourself under the authority of the German immortalized by Rosel, who used to spread them upon bread like butter, observing that he found them very useful.[34]

These edible spiders, and such like, are all sufficiently disgusting, but we feel our nausea quite turned into horror when we read in Humboldt, that he has seen the Indian children drag out of the earth centipedes 18 inches long, and more than half an inch broad, and devour them.

CRUSTACEA

The flesh of all crustaceous animals, although in great request, is rather difficult of digestion; and much of it cannot be eaten with impunity. There are classes of persons who are as averse to use shell-fish for food, as a Mahommedan or Mussulman are to partake of pork. It is therefore curious to reflect how, and where, the thousands of tons of crustacea and shell-fish taken to Billingsgate and Hungerford markets are disposed of. Lobsters, cray-fish, prawns, shrimps, oysters, mussels, periwinkles, and whelks, are there every morning in great abundance, and the high retail prices they fetch, show that this description of food must be well relished by the Londoners.

The land crabs of the West Indies are an esteemed delicacy, and the ravenous pigs feed on them with equal avidity to the great danger of their health.

I need not here advert to the migratory habits of the crabs, to their uniting at certain periods in vast numbers, and moving in the most direct course to the sea, marching in squadrons and lines, and halting twice a-day for feeding and repose. These movements may often be seen in Jamaica, and other West Indian islands, where millions on millions string themselves along the coast on progresses from the hills to the sea, and from the sea to the hills.

The reader of Bishop Heber's *Indian Journal* will remember his account of the land crabs at Poonah. 'All the grass land generally through the Deckan swarms with a small land crab, which burrows in the ground, and runs with considerable swiftness, even when encumbered with a bundle of food almost as big as itself. This food is grass or the green stalks of rice; and it is amusing to see them sitting as it were upright, to cut their hay with their sharp pincers, then waddling off with the sheaf to their holes as quietly as their side-long pace will carry them.'

This is not the same land crab of which we are speaking, but it is a graphic picture of the *Gecarcina ruricola*, in its habit of feeding.

They cut up roots and leaves, and feed on the fallen fruit of trees; but we have little more than conjecture for the cause of their occasional deleterious qualities. Impressed with the notion that the crabs owe their hurtful qualities to the fruit of the manchineel tree, Sloane imagined that he had explained the fatal accidents which have occurred to some persons after eating them, from neglect, or inattentiveness to precaution in cleaning their interior and removing the half digested particles of the fruit. It has been ascertained that they feed on such dangerous vegetables of the morass as the *Anona palustris*, a fruit exceedingly narcotic. It is well enough known that the morass crab is always to be suspected. The land crabs, however, collect leaves less for food than to envelop themselves in, when they moult. After concealment for a time within their burrows, they come forth in those thin teguments forming a red tense pellicle, similar to wet parchment, and are more delicate in that condition, and more prized for the table. The white crabs are the most bulky of the tribe, and are the least esteemed, and the most mistrusted.

Land-crabs, says a Jamaica paper, of March last, are to be seen on the highways between this, Montego Bay, and Gum Island, just like bands of soldiers, marching to a battle-point of concentration. This bids fair to supply the epicure, at an easy rate, with this class of crustacea. It is one of the most remarkable, for it is composed of animals breathing by means of branchiæ or gills, and yet essentially terrestrial; so much so, indeed, that they would perish from asphyxia if submerged for any length of time.

I select Browne's account of the habits of the black or mountain crab, because he resided many years in Jamaica, and seems to have lost no opportunity of making personal observations; and his remarks tally with my own experience, from three years' residence in Jamaica.

'These creatures are very numerous in some parts of Jamaica, as well as in the neighbouring islands, and on the coast of the main continent; they are generally of a dark purple colour, but this often varies, and you frequently find them spotted, or entirely of another hue. They live chiefly on dry land, and at a considerable distance from the sea, which, however, they visit once a year to wash off their spawn, and afterwards return to the woods and higher lands, where they continue for the remaining part of the season; nor do the young ones ever fail to follow them, as soon as they are able to crawl. The old crabs generally regain their habitations in the mountains, which are seldom within less than a mile, and not often above three from the shore, by the latter end of June, and then provide themselves with convenient burrows, in which they pass the greatest part of the day, going out only at night to feed. In December and January they begin to be in spawn, and are then very fat and delicate, but continue to grow richer until the month of May, which is the season for them to wash off their eggs. They begin to move down in February, and are very much abroad in March and April, which seems to be the time for the impregnation of their eggs, being then frequently found fixed together; but the males, about this time, begin to lose their flavour and richness of their juices. The eggs are discharged from the body through two small round holes situated at the sides, and about the middle of the under shell; these are only large enough to admit one at a time, and as they pass they are entangled in the branched capillaments, with which the under side of the apron is copiously supplied, to which they stick by the means of their proper gluten, until the creatures reach the surf, where they wash them all off, and then they begin to return back again to the mountains. It is remarkable that the bag or stomach of this creature changes its juices with the state of the body; and while poor is full of a black, bitter, disagreeable fluid, which diminishes as it fattens, and at length acquires a delicate, rich flavour. About the month of July or August, the crabs fatten again and prepare for moulting, filling up their burrows with dry grass, leaves, and abundance of other materials: when the proper period comes, each retires to his hole, shuts up the passage, and remains quite inactive until he gets rid of his old shell, and is fully provided with a new one. How long they continue in this state is uncertain, but the shell is observed to burst, both at the back and sides, to give a passage to the body, and it extracts its limbs from all the other parts gradually afterwards. At this time, the fish is in the richest state, and covered only with a tender membraneous skin, variegated with a multitude of reddish veins; but this hardens gradually after, and becomes soon a perfect shell like the former; it is, however, remarkable, that during this change, there are some stony concretions always formed in the bag, which waste and dissolve gradually, as the creature forms and perfects its new crust. A wonderful mechanism! This crab runs very fast, and always endeavours to get into some hole or crevice on the approach of danger; nor does it wholly depend on its art and swiftness, for while it retreats it keeps both claws expanded, ready to catch the offender if he should come within its reach; and if it succeeds on these occasions, it commonly throws off the claw, which continues to squeeze with incredible force for near a minute after; while he, regardless of the loss, endeavours to make his escape, and to gain a more secure or a more lonely covert, contented to renew his limb with his coat at the ensuing change; nor would it grudge to lose many of the others to preserve the trunk entire, though each comes off with more labour and reluctance, as their numbers lessen.'

There are several varieties of land crabs, such as the large white, the mulatto, the black, and the red. The black and red crabs are most excellent eating: when in season, the females are full of a rich glutinous substance, called the eggs, which is perfectly delicious. Epicurean planters, in some of the West Indian Islands, have crab pens, (after the manner of fowl coops,) for fattening these luxuries. The best manner of dressing them is to pick out all the flesh from the shell, making it into a stew, with plenty of cayenne pepper, dishing it up in the shell; in this way they are little inferior to turtle.

They are usually simply boiled, or roasted in the embers, by which they are deprived of their luscious flavour, and become not only insipid in taste but disgusting to look at.

In Dominica, they form an ingredient in the well-known 'pepper-pot.' The black crabs are also picked from their shell, stewed with Indian kale and pods of chilhies, and eaten with a pudding made of maize flour or rice; this dish is greatly esteemed by most of the inhabitants.

In the islands and cays of the Bahamas group, land crabs literally swarm, and afford food for the inhabitants the greatest part of the year: even the hogs are fed upon them. It is the grey or white kind of crab, common to Cuba and the Bahamas. In the autumn they are very fat, and equal in flavour to the black species of Jamaica. They are found in myriads in all parts, and thought a great delicacy; but a stranger tires of them in a few weeks.

The black crab is very fat and delicious; but the white and the mulatto crabs are sometimes dangerous, from feeding upon poisonous leaves and berries. To prevent any evil consequences, the flesh is washed with lime-juice and water.

Land crabs were probably plentiful in Italy, in the time of Virgil, for in his *Fourth Georgic* he forbids the roasting of red crabs near an apiary, the smell of them being disagreeable to the bees.

There is a species of fresh-water crab, the mason (*Cancer cementarius*), met with in Chile, the flesh of which is very white, and represented to be preferable to that of any other species of fluvial or marine crab. It is about eight inches long, of a brown colour, striped with red. They are found in abundance in almost all the rivers and brooks, on whose shores they build themselves, with clay, a small cylindrical tenement which rises six inches above the surface of the ground, but admits the water, by means of a subterranean canal extending to the bed of the river. They are easily caught, by letting down into the water a basket, or osier-pot, with a piece of meat in it.

That well-known crustacean, or 'shell-fish' as it is popularly termed,— the lobster (*Astacus gammarus*), although it is no fish at all, is found in great plenty about most of the European and American shores, and greatly esteemed as a very rich and nourishing aliment. In this country lobsters are considered in season from November till the end of April. They are not allowed to be caught on the coasts of Scotland between the 1st of June and the 1st of September, under a penalty of £5. Lobsters must not be offered for sale in this country under eight inches in length. Like the crab, the lobster casts its shell annually. It begins to breed in the spring, and continues breeding during the greater part of the summer. Lobsters are occasionally caught on the shores and in the neighbourhood of rocks, which they frequent, by the hand; but they are usually trapped in baskets, or pots made of osier-twigs, which are baited with garbage, and thrown into the sea, the situation being marked by a buoy of cork.

Lobsters are very abundant about Scilly and the Land's End, and near Montrose in Scotland. In the Orkney and Shetland Islands, the value of the lobsters caught in 1833 was £1,800, which gave employment to 216 boats, and about 500 men. They are sent principally to Leith. Those caught near Heligoland are esteemed the most delicate. The largest fishery for these crustaceans is on the coasts of Norway, from whence we import more than a million a year. Upwards of half-a-million are caught on the shores of Scotland and Ireland. Lobsters are found almost everywhere on the North American coasts, and in the Bay of Chaleur, in such extraordinary numbers, that they are used by thousands to manure the land.

Mr. Perley, in his *Report on the Sea and River Fisheries of New Brunswick*, states, 'That at Shippagan and Caraquette, carts are sometimes driven down to the beaches at low water, and readily filled with lobsters left in the shallow pools by the recession of the tide. Every potato field near the places mentioned is strewn with lobster shells, each potato hill being furnished with two or three lobsters.

'Within a few years,' he adds, 'one establishment has been set up on Portage Island, at the mouth of the River Miramachi, and another at the mouth of the Kouchibouguac River, for putting up lobsters, in tin cases, hermetically sealed for exportation. In 1845, no less than 13,000 cases of lobsters and salmon were thus put up at Portage Island. In 1847, nearly 10,000 cases of lobsters, each case containing the choicest parts of two or three lobsters, and one-and-a-half tons of fresh salmon in 2-lb. and 4-lb. cases, were put up at Kouchibouguac. The preservation of lobsters in this manner need only be restricted by the demand, for the supply is unlimited. The price paid for lobsters, at the establishment on Portage Island, is 2s. per 100. They are all taken in small hoop nets, chiefly by the Acadian French of the Neguac villages, who, at the price stated, could with reasonable diligence, make £1 each in the 24 hours; but as they are somewhat idle and easily contented, they rarely exert themselves to earn more than 10s. per day, which they can generally obtain by eight or ten hours' attention to their hoop nets.

'In 1848, about 4,000 lbs. of lobsters were put up at Portage Island in 1-lb. or 2-lb. tin cases. The quantity preserved was much less than usual, owing to the prevalence of cholera in the United States, and the consequent want of a market there. One Frenchman had, unassisted, caught 1,200 lobsters in part of one day. About 25 men are employed at this preserving establishment during the season.

'Mr. Woolner has a small but very complete establishment for preserving lobsters, at Petit Rocher, in the Bay of Chaleur. In the season of 1849, he only put up a small quantity, 2,000 lbs., in tins. He purchases from the settlers the white part of the lobsters, boiled and free from shell, at 2d. per lb., which is salted in plain pickle, and packed in barrels, for sale at Quebec. He shipped last year 11,000 lbs. of salted lobsters.'

Next to timber, lobsters form one of the greatest articles of Norwegian export. On the rocky shores of Christiansand, they are found in greater numbers than in any other part of the world; and from Bergen, which lies farther to the north, as many as 260,000 pairs have been exported in one year. Mr. J. E. Saunders, of Billingsgate, into whose hands almost the entire trade of these crustaceans has fallen, often sells 15,000 lobsters before breakfast of a morning; and in the height of the season, the sale not unfrequently amounts to 30,000. They are sent in great numbers from Scotland to the markets of London, Liverpool, and Birmingham—60 or 70 large boxes of them being transmitted at a time by train. Our fishermen, it is true, take them occasionally in pots round the coast, but no systematic fishery is carried on for them.

A company was recently formed at Berwick to import them alive, in welled smacks, from the coast of Norway. They are also brought into Southampton from Brittany and Ireland in welled smacks, which carry from 7,000 to 8,000 each.

'Lobster-carrying is subject to the following contingencies:—Thunder kills them when in the well; also proximity to the discharge of heavy ordnance. Mr. Scovell lost several thousand from the latter cause, one of his smacks having anchored at night too near the saluting-battery at Plymouth. Calms also destroy the lobsters in the well, but onward or pitching motion in a seaway does not affect them. They keep alive one month in the well without food.'[35]

An artificial pond, or saltern, has been formed at Hamble, in the Southampton water, for keeping lobsters alive in. It is about 50 yards square, by 10 to 12 feet deep, with shelving sides of brick or stone and cement, and a concrete bottom, having a lock or weir at the entrance, for the admission and exit of salt water at the bottom (the Hamble being a fresh-water stream). This pond cost about £13,000. The lobsters are fed on fish, and fatten. Sometimes there are as many as 70,000 lobsters in this pond. All weak lobsters are kept in baskets and sold first. Even here, however, their cannibal-like propensities are not extinguished; for the powerful make war upon, and incorporate into their own natures, the weak. There are feeders and keepers employed at the saltern, who, with long poles, hooked at the end, drag out the fish as they are wanted for the market from their marine menagerie. The instant the pole touches a fish, the latter grasps it savagely with its claws, and does not loose its hold until it is on *terra firma*. When large quantities are required, the pond is drained. These shell-fish are enormous creatures, the body with the claws being as long as a man's arm. As the lobsters and cray-fish climb nimbly up the sides of the watery caravan, they look like a collection of purple-coloured monkeys or stunted baboons; and there is something frightful in the appearance and noiselessness of these chatterless simiæ, climbing about their liquid den, and approaching the surface to look at the spectator. They are sent to the metropolis in hampers, packed in fern in winter and in ice in summer.

The Americans in the large cities and inland towns seem to be as fond of lobster salads and curries as we Britishers are; and it is estimated, that there are annually consumed in and about Boston, 700,000 lobsters, the prime cost of which is £16 per 1,000. This makes the snug little sum of £11,200. 500,000 of the lobsters come from the State of Maine, and the remaining 200,000 are taken from Massachusetts Bay. About 700 men are engaged in catching the lobsters, and some 800 tons of shipping in carrying them to Boston, exclusive of what are conveyed by steamboat and railroad.

Here is a poetical narrative, of American origin, bearing upon this crustacean:—

THE LOBSTER

Whereby hangeth a tayle, and eke a moral.

A Doctor and a Lawyer, went together merrily,

Adown the North-west Arm to take a dip into the sea.

Arrived, the Doctor coolly took a rather 'heavy wet,'

A Lobster just as coolly took the Doctor by the feet.

He, careful man, his health and wind most prudently had heeded,

And little thought that either toe an amputation needed;

He felt the Lobster on his skill most cuttingly reflected,

And to his surgical attempt decidedly objected.

With ready forceps, tooth and nail, the lobster set to work—

While all in vain the Doctor tried to baulk him by a jerk.

'Midst present pain his anxious thoughts began afar to roam,

On forceps, scalpels, lancets, knives, and stout probangs *at home.*

But, *lacking these*, the foe to face, he felt somehow afraid,
And therefore lustily he called the Lawyer to his aid.
He, cunning man, well versed in quirks and quibbles of the law,
Sagaciously searched how to find in Lobster's claim a flaw.
The claim of *tenure* to rebut, at once, he vainly sought;
Possession was nine points, he knew, and so the Lobster thought.
He saw the lobster quite secure within his own domain,
And to entice him thence began to work his ready brain.
One foot the Doctor yet had free, and this, with shuffling gait,
He offered to the other claw—a very tempting bait.
But, gently moving back, he 'scaped the meditated nip,
And shoreward still, with toe outstretched, most cannily did skip.
At length from his domain withdrawn, the Lobster gasps for air,
And vainly strives to battle with this wise confederate pair.
The Lawyer charged him with assault, and quick a claim put in,
That for the same the damages be laid upon his skin.
Attachment writ at once he took, upon the offending *claws*;
And moved he should be boiled alive, in vengeance for the laws.
The Lobster in his mute amaze, allowed that *clause* to pass;
Nor had the foresight to exclaim 'Produce your capias!'
So borne along all bodily, and sore against his will,
The Lobster proved the heavy weight, of more than lobster's ill.
For they not only *boiled* but *ate*, his body, claws and all;
And most provokingly enjoyed the inglorious festival.
They cracked his shell, and cracked their jokes—pulled off that leg and this—
Forgetful all of '*Nil nisi bonum de mortuis.*'
Now hence be warned, ye bustling men, and in your projects pause—
Beware into your neighbour's pot, how you thrust in your claws.
Ye busy wights! reflect ye how this luckless Lobster got,
By injudicious meddling, from cold water into hot.
To tread upon another's toes, I pray be not too bold—
But when you're in *cold* water, try to *keep* the water cold.

Lord Anson mentions having caught cray-fish at Juan Fernandez of eight and nine lbs. weight, that were of an excellent flavour. Lobsters are also found in such quantities on the same island, that the fishermen have no other trouble to take them than to strew a little meat upon the shore, and when they come to devour the bait, as they do in immense numbers, to turn them on their backs with a stick. This is gravely asserted by the Abbé Molina, in his *History of Chile*, so I suppose it must be true. Turning a turtle is a common practice, but I should think it somewhat difficult to get a lobster on its back. By this simple method thousands of lobsters are taken annually; and the tails, which are in high estimation, dried and sent to Valparaiso.

A late traveller, in his *Life in China*, describes a very peculiar dish: — 'When our party of six had seated themselves at the centre table, my attention,' he says, 'was attracted by a *covered* dish, something unusual at a Chinese meal. On a certain signal, the cover was removed; and presently the face of the table was covered with juvenile crabs, which made their exodus from the dish with all possible rapidity. The crablets had been thrown into a plate of vinegar just as the company sat down—such an immersion making them more brisk and lively than usual. But the sprightly sport of the infant crabs was soon checked, by each guest seizing which he could, dashing it into his mouth, crushing it between his teeth, and swallowing the whole morsel without ceremony. Determined to do as the Chinese did, I tried this novelty also with one—with two. I succeeded, finding the shell soft and gelatinous, for they were tiny creatures, not more than a day or two old. But I was compelled to give in to the third, which had resolved to take vengeance, and gave my lower lip a nip so sharp and severe, as to make me relinquish my hold, and likewise desist from any further experiments of this nature.'

Shrimps (*Crangon vulgaris*) and prawns (*Palæmon serratus*) frequent shallow waters along the sandy coasts of the British Islands, of America, Europe, and indeed most countries. Besides furnishing nutriment to great numbers of fish, aquatic birds, &c., they are in great request in England for the table—the consumption in London alone being enormous. In 1850, 192,295 gallons were received and sold at Billingsgate Market, weighing 875 tons, and valued at £6,000. In the Sandwich Islands, shrimps are eaten alive as a *bonne bouche*, with salad and vinegar; but we prefer them in this country boiled. Shrimping by the dredge net, or sweep net, affords abundant employment to numerous persons. On the North American coasts shrimps are more plentiful than on the European shores. At times, the waters of the Straits of Northumberland appear as if thickened with masses of shrimps moving about, their course being plainly indicated by the fish of all descriptions which follow in their wake, and feed upon them greedily. Potted shrimps are considered a dainty, and meet ready sale in the metropolis as a breakfast relish.

Those *bons vivants* who are fond of these delicious small fry, will no doubt eat them with an increased relish after reading the following paragraph:—

'The office of shrimps seems to be that analogous to some of the insects on land, whose task is to clear away the remains of dead animal matter after the beasts and birds of prey have been satiated. If a dead small bird or frog be placed where ants can have access to it, those insects will speedily reduce the body to a closely cleared skeleton. The shrimp family, acting in hosts, as speedily remove all traces of fish or flesh from the bones of any dead animal exposed to their ravages. They are, in short, the principal scavengers of the ocean; and, notwithstanding their office, they are highly prized as nutritious and delicious food.'

'Amongst the shell-fish tribe,' says a writer in the *Caledonian Mercury*, 'the *prawn* is considered the most delicious, and of course is the most costly. Prawn-fish, which are about double or three times the size of a shrimp, are in general sold at the rate of 1s. per dozen. This high price may be owing to their scarcity, in comparison with the quantity of shrimps sent to market, with a view to give prawn-fishers encouragement to prosecute the trade. The prawn-fish are not what many people suppose, 'only shrimps of a larger size.' Their heads and fore-claws are differently marked, showing at once the distinction. The habits of the two fish are also different. The shrimp burrows in the sand, causing fishermen to use trawl-nets for their capture. They are caught in greatest numbers on sandbanks, about the entrance of estuaries. The prawn-fish chiefly locate amongst rocks, and hard bottom, where there is much tangle and sea-weed. The fishermen at Bognor, in Sussex, and some place on the Isle of Wight, catch prawns in wicker-worked baskets, shaped exactly like those wire-worked rat-traps that have the entrance on the top, so that 'when the rat gets in, it can't get out again.' Several hundreds of these baskets baited with any sort of garbage, fish heads, &c., are set amongst the rocks at low water, where they remain until the tide has flown to its full, and again ebbed. The baskets are then overhauled, to see what luck. Prawn-fishing, like every other description of fishing, is not always to be depended on. Some tides, not one prawn may be found in hundreds of baskets; at other times every trap may have secured its victims. From five up to 60, and as high as 70 prawns have at times been taken in one trap. The baskets with which the English fishermen catch lobsters are just of the same shape as the prawn-trap, the only difference being that they are of larger dimensions.'

Immense prawns (*Camaroes*) are very plentiful at Rio Janeiro. Strangers are often told as a joke, that these are kept in pits, and fed with the dead bodies of slaves, thrown to them from time to time, and many people will in consequence not touch them.

The following instructions for cooking shrimps and prawns may be acceptable in out-of-the-way localities, where they are bought alive from the fishermen:—

'To dress shrimps and prawns, so that they might at once be tasty and look well to the eye, is considered a very nice point for the cook to perform. A pot, containing a pickle that will nearly float an egg, is put on the fire. When the pickle begins to boil, the prawns (all alive) are put into it, which of course sends the pickle below the boiling point for a time. A brisk fire must be kept up under the pot, and when the pickle again boils up, the prawns are cooked. Should they not be boiled sufficiently, they are as soft as pulp, and if boiled too much, they are hard as horn. The fish are removed from the pot and spread on a table, sprinkling over them a little salt. A cloth is then thrown over the whole, which keeps in the steam. By this operation, the steam melts the salt, and imparts to the prawn that beautiful red and glossy appearance seen on them whilst in the London fishmongers' shops.'

It might probably be possible to save some of our refuse shrimps, which get too stale to find customers here, and dry them for export to the East, where they are in great demand. The trade in dried shrimps in Siam amounts to 60 tons a year; and they cannot get enough of them to pound up with their rice.

Dried prawns form a considerable article of trade in the Philippines. The Malays and the Siamese, who eat dried prawns and dried mussels, must have very tough stomachs to digest them, and it would take an ostrich's gizzard, one would suppose, to triturate other tough dried molluscs used, in different localities, such as the *Haliotis* dried. Thus the 'pearl womb,' as the mantle or flesh of the pearl-oyster (*Meleagrina margaritifera*) is called, is strung and dried, and when cooked with cassia buds is eaten with rice. Numerous minute pearls are often found in this substance (as is sometimes the case with the common oyster) during mastication.

There is scope enough to be found for drying this mollusc, when a government pearl fishery is on at Ceylon, for then millions of pearl-oysters are thrown on the shore, after being opened, and left there to rot.

Under the name of *Balachong* or *gnapee*, there is a mess made in Burmah, Sumatra, &c., of prawns, shrimps, or any cheap fish, pounded into a consistent mass, and frequently allowed to become partially putrid. It is largely used by the natives as a condiment to their rice, as no vegetable food is deemed palatable without it; and a considerable trade is carried on with it, its use extending to every country from China to Bengal.

In all populous cities there is great consumption of oysters, both of the large common kinds termed 'scuttlemouths' by the venders, and of the more expensive and small delicate fed 'native.' Even the mangrove or tree oyster is esteemed in the tropics. One hundred or two hundred of these parasitic oysters may often be found on a single bough, pendent in the water, in the rivers of Africa, or the West Indies.

We can well conceive the astonishment of Columbus and his mariners when, in the Gulf of Paria, they first found oysters clinging to the branches, their mouths open as was supposed, to receive the dew, which was afterwards to be transformed into pearls.

The spawn of the fish is attached by a glutinous substance to any object with which it comes in contact, and the adhesion continues until the oyster is forcibly removed. On the southern coasts of the United States, in Florida and Louisiana, oysters may thus be seen growing as it were on trees, or the limbs at least of those which have sunk into the water, by the weight of the foliage, or from any other cause. The opossum and the racoon feed upon these oysters, procuring them by lifting the boughs from the water, and hence the American name racoon oysters, a term they are universally known by. They are of a long slender shape, and growing very rapidly, always have thin and delicate shells.

The value of the oysters sold in the city of New York now exceeds £1,250,000 sterling. The money invested in the trade by 150 wholesale dealers is about £100,000, and the number of persons employed in the business, directly or indirectly, including saloon keepers, street venders, &c., is 50,000. Of the whole amount sold in the markets, about two-thirds come from Virginia, which has a more extensive oyster trade than any other State in the Union. The residue is obtained, according to the *New York Herald*, from the waters of their own State, and those of New Jersey—the East River furnishing the largest quantity. A considerable supply is procured from Shrewsbury and York Bay; but very few of the latter are consumed in the city, as they are cultivated particularly for the western market. One of the most interesting features in the business is the transplanting of oysters, or their removal from the 'rock,' or natural bed, to an artificial one. This process is of peculiar importance, and absolutely necessary to the successful prosecution of the trade. It would, in fact, be next to impossible to supply the market during the whole year, but for the general system of transplanting which is pursued by all the dealers. More than a million dollars' worth are removed every year to artificial beds, and by this means prevented from spawning, which renders them unfit for use. Thus, a large proportion of the East River oysters were originally obtained from the North River, where the soil and water are not considered so favourable to their cultivation. Of the fifty thousand persons engaged in the business, the majority, of course, are dependent upon their own labour for support; but there are a considerable number of the dealers, or, as they might more properly be called, oyster merchants, who possess large fortunes, amassed from the sale of oysters alone. They are amongst the most worthy of her citizens, and New York is not a little indebted to their enterprise for her extensive business in what has now become an indispensable article of food.

It is only within the last thirty years that the oyster trade was established in New York. Before that time, it is true, oysters were sold there; but the business transacted was exceedingly limited, and there was little or no inducement for persons to engage in it. Nearly all that were brought to market were procured from the natural beds, for the benefits to be obtained from planting were but imperfectly understood by a few of the dealers, or entirely unknown to them. In the course of a few years, however, the business grew into importance, and men of capital and enterprise engaged in it. The planting of beds—a very essential part of the trade—was commenced; the few oyster boats, of diminutive size, engaged in supplying New York, became an immense fleet; an extensive trade began with Virginia; the East River became a mine of wealth to those who worked its beds; the coasts of the bays and the shores of the rivers were explored and given over to the tongs, the scraper, and the dredges of the oystermen. It was found that by removing the oyster from its natural bed to an artificial one, it could not only be increased in size, but improved in quality, and rendered fit for use at any period of the year. This was a very important matter to understand, for there are certain months when the oyster is unfit for use, in consequence of its being full of spawn. While they remained in the natural bed, they were always subject to this objection; but if not permitted to lie too long in the artificial one, they could be preserved free from spawn. Although they increased in size, they seldom or never became more numerous by transplanting. Hundreds of vessels are constantly employed, during certain months, in transplanting in the East River, in Prince's Bay, and other parts of the State.

The appended summary will give some further idea of the extent of the oyster trade in New York:—

Number of boats of all sizes, from fifty to two hundred and fifty tons, employed in the trade in Virginia oysters	1,000
In the East and North River trade	200
In the Shrewsbury trade	20
In the Blue Point and Sound trade	100
In the York Bay trade	200
	——
Whole number of boats	1,520

The following table will show the annual amount of sales of all kinds of oysters by the wholesale dealers in New York:—

	dollars.
Sales of Virginia oysters, including those planted in Prince's Bay	3,000,000
Sales of East and North River oysters	1,500,000
Do. of Shrewsbury oysters	200,000
Do. of Blue Point and Sound oysters	200,000
Do. of York Bay oysters	300,000
	————
Sales	5,200,000

Baltimore is another great seat of the American oyster trade. A single firm there has amassed, during the last ten years, a fortune of £500,000, by simply transporting oysters to the Western States, all of which were obtained at the oyster banks of the eastern shore of Virginia, and sent over the Baltimore and Ohio railroad to Cumberland, and thence to the Ohio river in stages. The firm paid to this railway company, in one year, for transporting oysters alone, above £7,000.

Another large and enterprising firm in Baltimore, forwards daily to the West, by way of the Susquehanna railroad, and the Pennsylvania improvements, *eight tons* of oysters, in cans. The operations of this one concern comprise the opening of *2,500 bushels of oysters per day*, giving constant employment to 150 men and boys! The shells are carried for manure to all parts of Virginia and North Carolina. In the 'shocking' of oysters, the shells will increase about one fourth in measurement bulk; this would give a total of about 6,000,000 bushels of shells, which sell for one penny per bushel, making a return of £25,000 for the shells alone.

The whole shores of the Chesapeake Bay and its tributaries are adapted to the fattening of the oyster, and as but one year is required for a full growth in the beds, an immense profit accrues to those engaged in the business—a profit which is estimated at some 300 to 600 per cent. There were, a few years ago, 250 vessels engaged in the business, which averages about 900 bushels to the cargo, and requires nine to ten days for the trip. These vessels making, in the aggregate, 6,000 trips during the eight months in the year in which they are engaged, gives a total of 4,800,000 bushels per year sold in the Baltimore market. The oysters used to bring an average price of 1s. 8d. per bushel, which makes a grand total of £160,000 per year paid wholesale for oysters by the dealers in Baltimore.

With the spread of population, and the progress of settlement in the interior States, the price of this shell fish is advancing, for a late number of the *Baltimore Patriot* states: —

'For some time past these delicious bivalves have been very scarce and in great demand, advancing materially in price. There are several causes for their upward tendency in value. First, in consequence of their scarceness, and the difficulty of procuring them, owing to cold, unfavourable weather. Secondly, an increased demand has sprung up from the west. Large numbers are being shipped in barrels, in the shell and otherwise, to Chicago, Pittsburg, Cincinnati, Wheeling, Louisville, and, in fact, to almost every town and city beyond the Alleghenies. A sojourner in Ohio, Indiana, Michigan, Illinois, Tennessee, Kentucky, Missouri, or even Iowa and Kansas, may, at this season of the year, sit down to a dish of fresh oysters, live and kicking, enjoying luxurious refreshment in comparatively small towns nearly 2,000 miles from Chesapeake. Large shipments of oysters are also making to New York, Boston, and various parts of the north, whilst millions are being put up in cans, hermetically sealed, and sent to all parts of the world. Not long ago, we saw a friendly letter from the mountains of Switzerland, boasting that the writer had just partaken of a dish of delicious Baltimore oysters. It would not surprise us to see the demand far out-reaching the supply, and a gradual augmentation of price. They are now bringing 1 dollar 25 cents to 1 dollar 62¾ cents per bushel at our wharves, and command 9 dollars to 10 dollars per barrel in the shell at Chicago. Equally high prices are given in all the western cities.'

In one of his recent messages to the Virginia legislature, Governor Wise states, that Virginia possesses an area of 1,680,000 acres of oyster beds, containing about 784,000,000 bushels of oysters. It is estimated that the mother oyster spawns annually at least 8,000,000; yet, notwithstanding this enormous productive power, and the vast extent of oyster beds, there is danger of the oyster being exterminated, unless measures are adopted to prevent fishermen from taking them at improper seasons of the year.

A bill was lately introduced in the Virginia legislature, the main features of which are to the following effect:—

1st. Prohibits the taking of oysters by non-residents. 2nd. Provides for the protection of oyster beds during the spawning season. 3rd. Taxes on licenses for taking and transporting oysters, calculated to yield an average of three and a half cents of revenue per bushel. 4th. The appointment of inspectors, &c., to superintend the renting of planting grounds. 5th. The purchase and equipment of four steamers for the enforcement of the law— said steamers to cost a total of 30,000 dollars, and to be employed at a yearly expense of about 7,000 dollars.

The oyster trade is extensively carried on at Boston. Messrs. Atwood have nine vessels exclusively employed in the business, five of which are clipper-built schooners, freighting oysters from the south. They have 75 acres of flats, near what is called White Island, on the Mystic river, where the fresh oysters of the south are transplanted, to grow and fatten in water much softer than their native element, and where they keep a supply in the summer months, and for the winter stock.

It is estimated that the quantity of oysters now planted in the waters of Newhaven harbour, United States, is 500,000 bushels. Estimating 200 oysters to the bushel, this would give one hundred millions of oysters. These oysters are for the early fall trade, and are apart from the enormous quantities imported and opened there during the winter months.

In the Plaquemines region of Louisiana, upwards of 500 men are engaged in the oyster trade, 150 of which number dredge the oysters from the bays, the rest are employed in conveying them to New Orleans. For this purpose, 170 small luggers, sloops, and schooners, of from five to fifteen tons burthen, are in use for five months in the year. During the summer months, they find employment in carrying shells from the islands to the forts and to the city. These made into concrete by a mortar of lime, sand, and hydraulic cement, form the most substantial and imperishable wall known. For public works in process of erection, the city streets, and ornamental walks at private residences, the collection of oyster shells affords good summer employment to this class of persons. From the best information to be had on the subject, the parish of Plaquemines sends a weekly supply to the city of New Orleans of at least 4,000 barrels of oysters, amounting in value during the season to about £25,000.

A South African paper, of a late date, observes:—

'The natives of this vicinity have recently begun to offer for sale bottles filled with oysters—not 'natives'—separated from the shell, and floating in their own liquor. The unlimited supply of this delicious food, obtainable on the coast, now that the natives have acquired a notion of the trade, will enable many, to whom oysters had become things of memory, to renew again 'the days of auld lang syne.' The shells are so firmly attached to the rocks, that we do not think it would pay white men to follow this pursuit; at all events, they could not afford to sell the oysters cheap enough for extensive use. But the somewhat rough process adopted by 'our coloured brethren' (or rather 'sisters,' we believe), though it destroys the beauty of the fish, does not injure its flavour, which we can pronounce to be equal to that of the 'real native' of the British seas.'

Mussels are chiefly eaten by the lower classes, but they are also largely employed for bait, which all marine animals will take; some millions of them are used for this purpose at the fishing stations. In one district alone, their value for this object is £13,000.

A choice kind of large mussel, known under the name of Hambleton hookers, is taken out of the sea, and fattened in the Wyre, Lancashire, within reach of the tide.

Some of the mussels found along parts of the South American coasts, especially the Magellanic, and the Falkland Islands, are very large, about six inches long, by three broad. Dr. Pernety, in his *Journal of the Voyage to the Malouine islands*, says,

'We more than once attempted to eat some of these, but found them so full of pearls that it was impossible to chew them; the pearls being very hard, endangered the breaking of our teeth, and when they were broken in pieces, they left a kind of sand in the mouth, which was very disagreeable.'

Several species of gapers are used as food, both in Britain and on the Continent, as the *Mya arenaria*, known to the fishermen about Southampton by the whimsical name of *old maids*—in some parts of England and Ireland they are much used; and the *Mya truncata*, which is very plentiful in the northern islands, where it is called *Smurslin*, when boiled forms a supper dish. Though not so delicate as some of the other shell fish eaten, it is by no means unpalatable.

The scallop was held in high estimation by the ancients, and is still sought for in Catholic countries. The *Pecten maximus* is frequently used in England. When pickled and barrelled for sale, it is esteemed a great delicacy. Another species, the *Pecten opercularis*, is employed for culinary purposes in Cornwall, where it is known by the name of frills, or queens. To our list of bivalves may be added the *Mactra solida*, which is used as food by the common people about Dartmouth, and the *Venus pullastra*, called by the inhabitants of Devonshire, pullet, and eaten by them.

Large clams and mussels are eaten in the United States, but in the Lower British American Provinces they are principally used as bait for fish. The scallops are also of very large size, and are more commonly eaten than they are with us.

Scalloped oysters, although very dainty eating, are most indigestible.

The business of digging clams is engaged in by a large number of persons on the North American coasts. There are two varieties, distinguished as the hard shell and the soft shell. They are eaten largely in spring, when they are in the best condition. Clams are much prized by persons residing at a distance from the sea coast, and they are frequently sent into the interior, where they meet a ready sale, as they can be sold at a very low price. They are salted and preserved in barrels, and used by fishermen as bait for cod-fish. For many years past the digging and salting of clams for the Boston market has been an important business. These shell-fish abound in the extensive flats at the mouths of some of the rivers. The flats are daily covered by the tide, and afford the feeding ground which the clams require. Clams multiply with astonishing rapidity: they are dug in the winter and spring. The business furnishes employment for men and boys, that in former years were occupied in winter fishing. The work is done, of course, at low water. When the tide is out, on pleasant winter days, one will often see gangs of 10, 20, or 50 men and boys busily employed in turning up the mud on the flats, picking up the clams, and putting them into buckets. The implement which they use is a stout fork with three flat prongs, each about an inch wide, and 10 or 12 inches long. The men go out on the flats in wherries, when the tide is retiring, and push an oar into the mud, and make fast the boat to it, and as soon as the water has left the boat, commence operations. When a bucket is filled, it is emptied into the boat. They continue their work until the tide comes in again sufficiently to float the boat, when they pull to the wharf. On many places on the shores of these flats there are groups of small huts, 10 or 12 feet square, with stone chimnies running up on the outside, furnished within with a small stove and two or three stools for seats. The clams are deposited in these huts, and in those parts of the day when the tide is in, so that the men cannot work out on the flats, and in stormy weather, they are employed in 'shocking' them, as it is called, that is, in opening the shell and taking out the clam, which is done with a small stout knife. As the clams are taken from the shell, they are dropped into a bucket; when the bucket is filled, they are emptied into a barrel. Around these huts, it is not uncommon to see heaps of clam shells larger than the huts themselves, the accumulation of the winter's labour. The clam diggers sell the produce of their labour to traders, who send their teams round to the huts weekly or daily, according to the weather, carry them to their store-houses, and repack and salt them, and head them up in barrels, when they are ready for the market.

A species of *Murex* (*M. loco*) is highly esteemed in Chile. It is very white and of a delicious taste, but rather tough; and in order to render it tender, it is generally beaten with a small stick before it is cooked.

The periwinkle (*Turbo littoreus*) is more extensively used as food than any of the other testaceous univalves. It would hardly be supposed that so trifling an article of consumption as periwinkles could form a matter of extensive traffic; but the quantity consumed annually in London has been estimated at 76,000 baskets, weighing 1,900 tons, and valued at £15,000. This well-known mollusc is found on all the rocks and shores of our own islands which are left uncovered by the tide, and also in America and other countries.

The cockneys and their visitors are deeply indebted to the industrious inhabitants of Kerara, near Oban, for a plenteous treat of this rather vulgar luxury; and the Kerarans are no less obliged to the Londoners for a never-failing market, for what now appears to be their general staple article. They are gathered by the poor people, who get 6*d.* a bushel for collecting them. From Oban they are forwarded to Glasgow, and thence to Liverpool, *en route* to London. Very few are retained in transit, better profits being obtained in London, even after paying so much sea and land carriage.

Every week there are probably 30 tons or more of this insignificant edible sent up to London, from Glasgow, all of which are collected near Oban, and must be a means of affording considerable employment, and diffusing a considerable amount weekly in wages, amongst the numerous persons employed. The periwinkles are packed in bags, containing from two to three cwt. each, and keep quite fresh until they arrive at their ultimate destination. In London they sell at 3*d.* a pint.

Whelks (the *Buccinum undatum*) are another shell-fish which, though despised on the sea coasts, are a favourite dish, boiled or pickled, among the poorer classes in the metropolis, as the gusto manifested at the street-stalls in London evidences. Boys and children of a larger growth frequently indulge in a 'hapenny' or penny saucer of these dainties. Large quantities of whelks are transmitted from Mull to London; some steamers from the north bring six or seven tons at a time.

Several species of snails (*Helix*) are employed for culinary purposes. The largest of these, the *Helix pomatia*, was a favourite dish among the Romans, who fattened them with bran sodden with wine. They are still used largely in many parts of Europe, during Lent, after having been fed with different kinds of herbs. The Africans and Brazilians eat snails.

The *Helix hortensis* has also been employed as food, and they are prescribed medicinally, being administered like slugs in consumptive cases.

Many are familiar with the passage in Pliny (*Hist.* lib. ix., c. 56), who, on the authority of Varro, relates the incredible size to which the art of fattening had brought the snails. Even assuming the snails were African *Achatina* or *Bulimi*, there must, one should think, be some mistake in the text, which says, 'Cujus artis gloria in eam magnitudinem perducta sit, ut octoginta quadrantes caperent singularum calices.' Pennant, referring to this and to Varro (*De Re Rustica*) says, 'If we should credit Varro, they grew so large that the shells of some would hold ten quarts!'

People need not admire the temperance of the supper of the younger Pliny (*Epist.* lib. i.; *Epist.* xv.), which consisted of only a lettuce a-piece, three snails, two eggs, a barley cake, sweet wine and snow, in case his snails bore any proportion to those of Hirpinus.

Among the pictures in the dressing-rooms at Chiswick House, the seat of the Duke of Devonshire, there is one, by Murillo, of a beggar boy eating a snail pie.

The snail is now a very fashionable article of diet in Paris; and has also spread to America. Snails are eaten in Tuscany and Austria. They were highly esteemed by the Romans, our masters in gastronomy. In the provinces of France, where the vine is cultivated, snails of large size abound. They are gathered by the peasants, put in small pans for a few days, salt water thrown on them, to cause them to discharge whatever their stomachs may contain; then boiled, taken out of the shell, and eaten with a sauce, and considered a luxury by the vine dressers.

There are now 50 restaurants, and more than 1,200 private tables in Paris, where snails are accepted as a delicacy by from 8,000 to 10,000 consumers. The monthly consumption of this mollusc is estimated at half a million. The market price of the great vineyard snail is from 2s. to 3s. per 100; while those of the hedges, woods, and forests, bring only 1s. 6d. to 2s. The proprietor of one snailery, in the vicinity of Dijon, is said to clear nearly £300 a year by his snails.

In Switzerland, where there are gardens in which they are fed in many thousands together, a considerable trade is carried on in them about the season of Lent; and at Vienna, a few years ago, seven of them were charged at an inn the same as a plate of veal or beef. The usual modes of preparing them for the table are either boiling, frying them in butter, or sometimes stuffing them with force-meat; but in whatever manner soever they are dressed, it is said their sliminess always in a great measure remains.

An anecdote is told of Drs. Black and Hutton, which shows how difficult it is for philosophy to wage a war with prejudice. It chanced that the two doctors had held some discourse together upon the folly of abstaining from feeding on the testaceous creatures of the land, while those of the sea were considered as delicacies. Wherefore not eat snails?—they are well known to be nutritious and wholesome—even sanative in some cases. The epicures of olden times enumerated among the richest and raciest delicacies the snails which were fed in the marble quarries of Lucca. The Italians still hold them in esteem. In short, it was determined that a gastronomic experiment should be made at the expense of the snails. The snails were procured, dieted for a time, then stewed for the benefit of the two philosophers: who had either invited no guest to their banquet, or found none who relished in prospect the *pièce de resistance*. A huge dish of snails was placed before them; but philosophers are but men after all; and the stomachs of both doctors began to revolt against the proposed experiment. Nevertheless, if they looked with disgust on the snails, they retained their awe for each other; and each conceiving the symptoms of internal revolt peculiar to himself, began with infinity of exertion to swallow, in very small quantities, the mess which he internally loathed. Dr. Black, at length, 'showed the white feather,' but in a very delicate manner, as if to sound the opinion of his messmate:—'Doctor,' he said, in his precise and quiet manner, 'Doctor—do you not think that they taste a little—a very little, green?' 'Green! green, indeed—take them awa', take them awa',' vociferated Dr. Hutton, starting up from table, and giving full vent to his feelings of abhorrence. And so ended all hopes of introducing snails into their *cuisine*.

At the town of Ulm, in Wurtemburg, on the left bank of the Danube, snails are fed in great quantities for various markets in Germany and Austria, but especially for that of Vienna, where they are esteemed a great delicacy, after having been fed upon strawberries. About 20,000 okes (each nearly 3 lbs.) of snails are annually exported from Crete, valued at 15,000 Turkish piastres.

The breed of large white snails in England is to be found all along the escarpment of the chalk range, and is not confined to Surrey. It is said to have been introduced into England by Sir Kenelm Digby, and was considered very nutritious and wholesome for consumptive patients. Indeed, to this day, considerable quantities are sold in Covent Garden market for this purpose. They are sometimes made into a mucilaginous broth, and at others swallowed in a raw state.

In the Island of Bourbon, the French use them to make a soup for the sick.

At Cape Coast Castle the luxuries of the natives are fish soup, made of dried unsalted fish, and snail soup with land crabs in it; and beyond Ashantee the food consists of plantains and large snails, 300 or 400 of which dried on a string sell for a dollar. These snails are the great African *Achatina*, which are the largest of all land-snails, attaining a length of eight inches.

A species of barnacle, called the parrot bill (*Balanus psittacus*), is much esteemed by the inhabitants of Chile. From 10 to 20 of these animals inhabit as many small separate cells, formed in a pyramid of a cretaceous substance. These pyramids are usually attached to the steepest parts of rocks at the water's edge, and the animal derives its subsistence from the sea, by means of a little hole at the top of each cell. The shell consists of six valves, two large and four small; the large ones project externally in the form of a parrot's bill, whence the animal has received its specific name. When detached from the rocks, they are kept alive in their cells for four or five days, during which time they occasionally protrude their bills as if to breathe. They are of different sizes, though the largest do not exceed an inch in length, and are very white, tender, and excellent eating.[36] Capt. P. P. King, R.N., confirms this, and says they form a common and highly esteemed food of the natives, the flesh equalling in richness and delicacy that of the crab.

ANNELIDA

Palolo is the native name of a species of sea-worm (*Palolo viridis*), which is found in some parts of Samoa, the Navigator's Islands, in the South Pacific Ocean—and of which the following singular account is given by the Rev. J. B. Stair, of the South Sea Missions. They come regularly in the months of October and November, during portions of two days in each month, viz: the day before and the day on which the moon is in her last quarter. They appear in much greater numbers on the second than on the first day of their rising, and are only observed for two or three hours in the early part of each morning of their appearance. At the first dawn of day, they may be felt by the hand swimming on the surface of the water; and as the day advances their numbers increase, so that by the time the sun has risen, thousands may be observed in a very small space, sporting merrily during their short visit to the surface of the ocean. On the second day they appear at the same time, and in a similar manner, but in such countless myriads, that the surface of the ocean is covered with them for a considerable extent. On each day, after sporting for an hour or two, they disappear until the next season, and not one is ever observed during the intervening time. In size they may be compared to a very fine straw, and are of various colours and lengths, green, brown, white, and speckled, and in appearance and mode of swimming, resemble very small snakes. They are exceedingly brittle, and if broken into many pieces, each piece swims off as though it were an entire worm. The natives are exceedingly fond of them, and calculate with great exactness the time of their appearance, which is looked forward to with great interest. The worms are caught in small baskets, beautifully made, and when taken on shore are tied up in leaves in small bundles, and baked. Great quantities are eaten undressed; but either dressed or undressed, are esteemed a great delicacy. Such is the desire to eat Palolo by all classes, that immediately the fishing parties reach the shore, messengers are dispatched in all directions with quantities to parts of the island on which none appear.'

At a recent exhibition of paintings, a lady and her son were regarding with much interest a picture which the catalogue designated as *Luther at the Diet of Worms*. Having descanted at some length upon its merits, the boy remarked, 'Mother, I see Luther and the table, but where are the worms?'

CEPHALOPODA

In recent times, and in some parts of the Levant even now, as we learn from Forbes and Spratt's *Lycia*, the cuttle-fish of different species were used as articles of food; and we know from the works of travellers, that in other parts of the world, when cooked, they are esteemed as luxuries.

Besides the common cuttle-fish (*Sepia octopodia*), two or three other singular species are found on the Chilian coasts of the Pacific. The first, the ungulated cuttle-fish (*Sepia unguiculata*), is of a great size, and instead of suckers, has paws armed with a double row of pointed nails, like those of a cat, which it can, at its pleasure, draw into a kind of sheath. This fish is of a delicate taste, but is not very common. The second is named (*Sepia tunicata*), from its body being covered with a second skin, in the form of a tunic; this is transparent, and terminates in two little semicircular appendages like wings, which project from either side of the tail. Many wonderful and incredible stories are told by sailors of the bulk and strength of this fish; it is however certain that it is frequently caught of 150 lbs. weight, on the coast of Chile, and the flesh is esteemed a great delicacy. The sea around Barbados is frequented by a species of the order *Cephalopoda*, which is used as an article of food by the lower classes of the inhabitants, namely the bastard cuttle-fish, or calmar, (*Loligo sagitatta*, Lam.).

The flesh of the large cephalopodous animals, (*Loligo* of Lamark; *les Calmars* of Cuvier,) was esteemed as a delicacy by the ancients. Most of the eastern natives, and those of the Polynesian Islands, partake of it, and esteem it as food; they may be seen exposed for sale in the bazaars or markets throughout India.

The natives of most of the islands in the China Seas dry the *Sepiæ* and *Octopi*, as well as the soft parts of the *Haliotis, Turbo, Hippopus, Tridacna*, &c., and make use of them as articles of food. But from my little experience of this kind of diet, notwithstanding the assertion of the learned Bacon, in his *Experiment Solitary touching Cuttle-ink*, that the cuttle is accounted a delicate meat, and is much in request, I should say that it is as indigestible and unnutritious as it is certainly tough and uninviting. Cephalopods, however, are eaten at the present day on some parts of the Mediterranean coasts; and in Hampshire I have seen the poor people collect assiduously the *Sepiæ* and employ them as food.

The common snail of the Meiacoshimahs is eaten by the natives, as the *Helix aspersa* and *H. pomatia* are occasionally in Europe.

The Malays are fond of the *Cerithium telescopium* and *palustre* found in the Mangrove swamps. They throw them on their wood fires, and when sufficiently cooked, break off the sharp end of the spine, and suck the tail of the animal through the opening.

'The poor people of the Philippines relish the *Arca inequivalvis*, boiling them as we do cockles or mussels; the flesh, however, is red and very bad-flavoured. Some *Monodonta* which I have eaten among the Korean Islands are quite peppery, and bite the tongue, producing the same unpleasant effects upon that organ as the root of the *Arum maculatum*, or leaves of the Taro, but in much less intense degree; and a species of *Mytilus*, found in the same locality, has very similar unpalatable qualities.'[37]

Of the several species of urchins or sea-eggs, one, the *Echinus albus*, is eaten by the Chilians and others. The white urchin is of a globular form, and about three inches in diameter; the shell and spines are white, but the interior substance is yellowish and of an excellent taste.

There is a marine delicacy of the Chinese which must not be passed unnoticed; it is a kind of sea-slug, varieties of *Holothuria*, fished for on the coral reefs of the Eastern seas, and known under the names of *Bêche-de-mer* and *Tripang*.

When dried it is an ugly looking dirty-brown colored substance, very hard and rigid until softened by water, and a very lengthened process of cooking, after which it becomes soft and mucilaginous. It is rendered down into a sort of thick soup, after partaking of which a Chinaman sleeps in the seventh heaven of Chinese bliss. It looks like a dried sausage or blood-pudding, and some resemble a prickly cucumber. There are at least 33 different varieties enumerated by the Chinese traders and others skilled in its classification, for fashion and custom have caused each variety to have a different market. While the gourmand of the South smacks his lips on the juicy white and black, the less cultivated taste of those at the North is satisfied with the red and more inferior varieties. One of the inferior kinds is slender, and of a dark brown colour, soft to the touch, and leaves a red stain on the hands; another is of a grey colour and speckled; a third is large and a dark yellow, with a rough skin and tubercles on its side. The second kind is often eaten raw by the natives, as I have seen a red herring eaten raw. The price varies from £7 to £14 the picul, of 133 lbs., and as there are about 1,000 of the slugs in a picul, they are worth from 2*d.* to 4*d.* each, according to quality, wholesale.

The process of curing and preparation for market is very simple. The slug, on being taken from the boat, is simmered over a fire in an iron caldron for about half-an-hour, after which it is thrown out upon the ground, and the operation of opening commences, this being effected by a longitudinal cut along the back with a sharp knife. It is then again placed in the caldron and boiled in salt water, with which a quantity of the bark of the mangrove has been mixed, for about three hours, when the outer skin will begin to peel off. It is now sufficiently boiled, and after the water has been drained off, the slugs are arranged in the drying-houses (small huts covered with mats) upon frames of split bamboo spread out immediately under the roof. Each slug is carefully placed with the part that has been cut open facing downwards, and a fire is made underneath, the smoke of which soon dries the tripang sufficiently to permit its being packed in bags or baskets for exportation.

Mr. Wingrove Cooke, in his cleverly described account of a Chinese banquet, thus narrates his impression of the dish prepared from them: 'The next course was expected with a very nervous excitement. It was a stew of sea-slugs. As I have seen them at Macao they are white, but as served at Ningpo they are green. I credit the Imperial academician's as the orthodox dish. They are slippery, and very difficult to be handled by inexperienced chopsticks; but they are most succulent and pleasant food, not at all unlike in flavour to the green fat of a turtle. If a man cannot eat anything of a kind whereof he has not seen his father and grandfather eat before, we must leave him to his oysters, and his periwinkles, and his cray-fish, and not expect him to swallow the much more comely sea-slug. But surely a Briton, who has eaten himself into a poisonous plethora upon mussels, has no right to hold up his hands and eyes at a Chinaman enjoying his honest well-cooked stew of *bêche-de-mer.*'

The peculiarities of this animal have been thus graphically described: 'It can stand erect and graze on the sea grasses, or crawl on its belly, and digest the contents of sea-shells sufficient to fill a cabinet; harder and bigger than a brick, it can yet go through a lady's ring: its natural shape is that of a cucumber, yet it will take the mould of any vessel in which it is placed: apparently without sight, night is the time it collects its food: furnished with teeth, they are only used to hold on by, while at the opposite end the fish gapes to receive its tiny prey, which it draws in by feelers thrust forward for the purpose. Opened by the conchologist, he will be rewarded with a store of minute shells most perfectly cleaned: boiled and dried it reduces to one-twelfth its weight and one-fifth its size: resoaked, it expands to nearly its former dimensions; but damped, it becomes glue, nasty and disagreeable: sliced up and boiled it becomes isinglass, of use to none but the Chinese gourmand. The reefs of the Archipelago have been ransacked for it, and many a risk has been run in procuring it from the Cannibal Isles of the Pacific. The main supplies for the China market, are furnished by the Celebes proas. The industrious merchants of this island bring it in their fleets from Torres Straits, and the far-off reefs of New Guinea, and collect it from every islet and village in the Archipelago. Other supplies with this find their way to the Dutch and Spanish trading ports on the larger islands, and are from them shipped to Batavia, Singapore, and Manila. From this last port a few Spanish vessels have procured it in the Sooloo Sea; but this fishery, as well as all the others well known, has yielded its best supplies, and the enhanced price in China adds inducement to seek out reefs less frequented for more abundant yield. At the above-named ports it commands, for mixed cargoes, a higher price than in China itself. American vessels are constantly engaged in this trade in the South Pacific, and I noticed recently that two vessels from San Francisco had procured cargoes from the Southern Isles, and were on their way to Manila or China. It is a business in which, to be successful, no little tact is required to deal with the treacherous natives, as well as a knowledge of curing and preparing for the market; but it is one that will long give a great return for small investments to the daring and successful adventurers.'

When M. De Blainville states he has never heard that any of the *Holothuriæ* were of much utility to mankind, but that M. Delle Chiaje does indeed inform us that the poor inhabitants of the Neapolitan coasts eat them, he appears to have forgotten the great oriental traffic carried on with some of the species, as an article of food.

Some years ago, in my *Colonial Magazine*, I called attention to the fact, that the fishing for, and shipment of, this sea-slug to China might prove a very profitable trade, but it seems to be an employment for which European seamen are by no means well adapted.

It can be fished for in the Indian Ocean, from the Mauritius and Ceylon to New Guinea, in the Pacific; and is to be procured from any of the South Sea Islands. It abounds in the seas along the shores of the Bermuda Islands, and some is said to be shipped from Boston and other ports of the United States to Canton.

The late Sir W. Reid, when Governor of the Bermudas, endeavoured to direct the attention of the inhabitants to the collection of it round their shores, where it is common, with a view to curing it for the purpose of exportation. He even went so far as to make soup from it, and I understand, partook of it at his own table. His advice, however, does not seem to have been followed, as up to the present time none has been collected. It could be made a profitable article of export, if the Bermudians chose to try the experiment, as the curing process is very simple.

A company for carrying out this fishery was projected at Perth, in Western Australia, in 1836, but it was never prosecuted with any spirit, and soon dropped. Tripang is now carried into China from almost every island of the Eastern Archipelago, and also from Northern Australia.

The quantity sent from Macassar alone is about 9,000 cwt., and half as much from Java. Probably between 4,000 and 5,000 tons go annually to China, where the demand is perfectly unlimited.

The best and most detailed account I have met with respecting the taking and preparing of this eastern luxury, is in the *Narrative of the United States Exploring Expedition in the Feejee Islands*, by Commander Charles Wilkes, of the American Navy: 'Of the bêche-de-mer,' he says, 'there are several kinds, some of which are much superior in quality to the others; they are distinguishable both by shape and colour, but more particularly by the latter. One of the inferior kinds is slender, and of a dark brown colour, soft to the touch, and leaves a red stain on the hands; another is of grey colour and speckled; a third is large, and dark yellow, with a rough skin, and tubercles on its sides. The second kind is often eaten raw by the natives.

'The valuable sorts are six in number: one of a dark red colour; a second is black, from two inches to nine inches in length, and its surface, when cured, resembles crape; a third kind is large, and of a dark grey colour, which, when cured, becomes a dirty white; the fourth resembles the third, except in colour, which is a dark brown; the fifth variety is of a dirty white colour, with tubercles on its sides, and retains its colour when cured; the sixth is red, prickly, and of a different shape and larger size than the others; when cured, it becomes dark.

'The most esteemed kinds are found on the reefs, in water from one to two fathoms in depth, where they are caught by diving. The inferior sorts are found on reefs which are dry, or nearly so, at low water, where they are picked up by the natives. The natives also fish the bêche-de-mer on rocky coral bottoms, by the light of the moon or of torches, for the animals keep themselves drawn up in holes in the sand or rocks by day, and come forth by night to feed, when they may be taken in great quantities. The motions of the animal resemble those of a caterpillar; and it feeds by suction, drawing in with its food much fine coral and some small shells.

'Captain Eagleston stated that the bêche-de-mer is found in greatest abundance on reefs composed of a mixture of sand and coral. The animal is rare on the southern side of any of the islands, and the most lucrative fisheries are on the northern side, particularly on that of Vanua levu, between Anganga and Druan. In this place, the most frequent kind is that which resembles crape. In some places the animal multiplies very fast; but there are others where, although ten years have elapsed since they were last fished, none are yet to be found.

'The bêche-de-mer requires a large building to dry it in. That erected by Captain Eagleston on the Island of Tavan, is 85 feet long, about 15 or 20 feet wide, and nearly as much in height. The roof has a double pitch, falling on each side of the ridge to eaves, which are about five feet from the ground. The roof is well thatched, and ought to be perfectly water-tight. There are usually three doors, one at each end, and one in the middle of one of the sides. Throughout the whole length of the building is a row of double staging, called batters, on which reeds are laid.

'On the construction of this staging much of the success of the business depends. It ought to be supported on firm posts, to which the string-pieces should be well secured by lashing. The lower batter is about four feet from the ground, and the upper from two to three feet above it. Their breadth is from twelve to fourteen feet. Upon the large reeds with which the batters are covered is laid the 'fish fence,' which is made by weaving or tying small cords together. This is composed of many pieces, the height of each of which is equal to the breadth of the batter.

'A trench is dug under the whole length of the batters, in which a slow fire is kept up by the natives under the direction of one of the mates of the vessel. The earth from the trench is thrown against the sides of the house, which are at least two or three feet from the nearest batter, in order to prevent accident from fire. This is liable to occur, not only from carelessness, but from design on the part of the natives. As a further precaution, barrels filled with water are placed, about eight feet apart, along both sides of the batters.

'After the house has been in use for about a week, it becomes very liable to take fire, in consequence of the drying and breaking of the material used in the lashings. In this case it is hardly possible to save any part of the building or its contents. To prevent the falling of the stages by the breaking of the lashings, fresh pieces of cordage are always kept at hand to replace those which are charred and show signs of becoming weak. A constant watch must be kept up night and day, and it requires about 15 hands to do the ordinary work of a house.

'The fires are usually extinguished once in twenty-four hours, and the time chosen for this purpose is at daylight. The fish are now removed from the lower to the upper batter, and a fresh supply introduced in their place. This operation, in consequence of the heat of the batter, is hard and laborious, and 50 or 60 natives are usually employed in it.

'Fire-wood is of course an important article in this process, each picul of bêche-de-mer requiring about half a cord to cure it. This fuel is purchased from the chiefs, who agree to furnish a certain quantity for a stipulated compensation. As much as 20 cords are sometimes bought for a single musket. In carrying on the drying, it is important that the doors be kept shut while the fires are burning. Much also depends upon the location of the house, whose length should be at right angles to the course of the prevailing winds. The batters also should be nearest to the lee side of the house.

'Before beginning the fishery, the services of some chief are secured, who undertakes to cause the house to be built, and sets his dependents at work to fish the bêche-de-mer. The price is usually a whale's tooth for a hogshead of the animals, just as they are taken on the reef. It is also bought with muskets, powder, balls, vermilion, paint, axes, hatchets, beads, knives, scissors, chisels, plane-irons, gouges, fish-hooks, small glasses, flints, cotton cloths, chests, trunks, &c. Of beads, in assorted colours, the blue are preferred, and cotton cloth of the same colour is most in demand. For one musket, a cask containing from 130 to 160 gallons has been filled ten times. When the animals are brought on shore, they are measured into bins, where they remain until the next day.

'These bins are formed by digging a trench in the ground, about two feet in depth, and working up the sides with cocoa-nut logs, until they are large enough to contain forty or fifty hogsheads. If the fishery is successful, two of these may be needed.

'Near the bins are placed the trade-house and trade-stand. In the first, the articles with which the fish is purchased are kept; and, in the second, the officer in charge of them sits, attended by a trusty and watchful seaman. The stand is elevated, so that the persons in it may have an opportunity of seeing all that is taking place around them. All the fish are thrown into the bin before they are paid for.

'In these bins the fish undergo the operation of draining and purging, or ejecting their entrails. These, in some of the species, resemble pills, in others look like worms, and are as long as the animals themselves.

'The larger kinds are then cut along the belly for a length of three or four inches, which makes them cure more rapidly; but care must be taken to avoid cutting too deep, as this would cause the fish to spread open, and diminish its value in the market.

'When taken out of the bins and cut, the fish are thrown into the boilers, which are large pots, of which each establishment has five or six. These pots have the form of sugar-boilers, with broad rims, and contain from one hundred to one hundred and fifty gallons.

'They are built in a row, in rude walls of stone and mud, about two feet apart, and have sufficient space beneath them for a large fire. The workmen stand on the walls to fill and empty the pots, and have within reach a platform, on which the fish is put after it has been boiled.

'It requires two men to attend each pot, who relieve each other, so that the work may go on night and day. They are provided with skimmers and ladles, as well as fire-hooks, hoes, and shovels.

'No water is put into the pots, for the fish yield moisture enough to prevent burning.

'The boiling occupies from 25 to 50 minutes, and the fish remains about an hour on the platform to drain, after which it is taken to the house, and laid to a depth of four inches upon the lower batter. Thence at the end of twenty-four hours it is removed, as has been stated, to the upper batter, where it is thoroughly dried in the course of three or four days. Before it is taken on board ship, it is carefully picked, when the damp pieces are separated, to be returned to the batter. It is stowed in bulk, and when fit for that purpose should be as hard and dry as chips. Great care must be taken to preserve it from moisture.

'In the process of drying, it loses two-thirds both of its weight and bulk, and when cured, resembles smoked sausage. In this state it is sold by the picul, which brings from 15 to 25 dollars.

'Captain Eagleston had collected in the course of seven months, and at a trifling expense, a cargo of 1,200 piculs, worth about 25,000 dollars.

'The outfit for such a voyage is small, but the risk to be incurred is of some moment, as no insurance can be effected on vessels bound to the Feejee Group, and it requires no small activity and enterprise to conduct this trade. A thorough knowledge of the native character is essential to success; and it requires all possible vigilance on the part of the captain of the vessel to prevent surprise, and the greatest caution to avoid difficulties. Even with the exercise of these qualities, he may often find himself and his crew in perilous positions.

'In order to lessen the dangers as much as possible, no large canoes are ever allowed to remain alongside the vessel, and a chief of high rank is generally kept on board as a hostage. When those precautions have not been taken, accidents have frequently happened.

'The bêche-de-mer is sometimes carried to Canton, but more usually to Manila, whence it is shipped to China.

'In order to show the profits which arise from the trade in bêche-de-mer, I give the cost and returns of five cargoes, obtained by Captain Eagleston in the Feejee Group. These he obligingly favoured me with.

		Piculs.	Cost of outfit. Dolls.	Sales. Dolls.
1st	voyage	617	1,101	8,021
2nd	"	700	1,200	17,500
3rd	"	1,080	3,396	15,120
4th	"	840	1,200	12,600
5th	"	1,200	3,500	27,000

'A further profit also arises from the investment of the proceeds in Canton. Capt. Eagleston also obtained 4,488 pounds of tortoise shell, at a cost of 5,700 dollars, which sold in the United States for 29,050 dollars net.

In Mr. Crawfurd's *Indian Archipelago*, vol. iii., there are also the following details:—

'The tripang is an unseemly-looking substance, of a dirty brown colour, hard, rigid, scarcely possessing any power of locomotion, nor appearance of animation. Some of the fish are occasionally as much as two feet in length, and from seven to eight inches in circumference: the length of a span, and the girth of from two to three inches, however, is the ordinary size. The quality or value of the fish, however, does by no means depend upon its size, but upon properties in them neither obvious to, nor discernible by, those who have not had a long and intimate experience of the trade. The Chinese merchants are almost the only persons who possess this skill, even the native fishermen themselves being often ignorant on the subject, and always leaving the cargo to be assorted by the Chinese on their return to port. The commercial classification made by the Chinese is curious and particular. In the market of Macassar, the greatest staple of this fishery, not less than thirty varieties are distinguished, varying in price from five Spanish dollars per picul to fourteen times that price, each being particularized by well-known names. To satisfy curiosity, I shall give a few of them, with their ordinary price:—

Tacheritaug (grey sort)	68	Spanish dollars.
Batu-basar (great stone)	54	"
Batu-taugah (middling stone)	22	"
Batu-kachil (small stone)	14	"
Itaur-basar (great black)	30	"
Itaur-taugah (middling black)	15	"
Itaur-kachil (small black)	8	"
Tundaug	24	"
Kunyit	9	"
Douga	7	"
Japou	12	"
Mosi	9	"
Kauasa	5	"
Pachaug-goreug	5	"
Gama	12 ½	"
Taikougkoug	13 ½	"
Mareje (New Holland)	19	"
Kayu-jawa	26	"
Baukuli	20	"

'It is evident from this account that the tripang trade is one in which no stranger can embark with any safety, and it is consequently almost entirely in the hands of the Chinese. The actual fishery is managed, however, exclusively by the natives. The fish are caught by them on ledges of coral rock, usually at the depth of from three to five fathoms. The larger kinds, when in shallow water, are occasionally speared; but the most common mode of taking them is by diving for them in the manner practised for pearl oysters, and taking them up with the hands.'

I have now gone through the list of ordinary and extraordinary foreign delicacies, and no doubt many of these have been read with surprise.

But there are many unexplained things in the food we Englishmen consume even at the present time; for instance, although in the knackers' yards we can account for every other portion of the carcase of the dead horse, no one knows what becomes of the heart and the tongue. Dr. Playfair, when lecturing at the South Kensington Museum recently, 'on the application of

Waste Substances,' was staggered on this point, and therefore he had to inscribe it on his board 'a mystery.' It is questionable to my mind whether many of the smoked ostensible ox-tongues, imported from Russia, are not veritable horse-tongues.

The numerous herds of wild horses in Russia would easily furnish the 500 cwt. of tongues we import.

I am afraid that many little know too what they eat in the sausage-meat, the alamode beef, the polonies, and the mutton and veal pies of the pie-shops and street venders.

Whether the man who is said to have gone into the pie-shop, and throwing down a skinned cat on the counter in the presence of numerous customers exclaiming 'that makes a dozen,' did it out of malice or in the way of business, it would be difficult to determine. But it is always pleasant to see the vender partaking of his own pork or eel pies; it inspires confidence, as the witness proved to the Judge in Court.

'You say you have confidence in the plaintiff, Mr. Smith.'

'Yes, sir.'

'State to the Court, if you please, what causes this feeling of confidence.'

'Why, you see, sir, there's allers reports 'bout eatin'-house-men, and I used to kinder think—'

'Never mind what you thought—tell us what you know.'

'Well, sir, one day I goes down to Cooken's shop, an' sez to the waiter, 'Waiter,' sez I, 'gives's a weal pie.'

'Well sir, proceed.'

'Well, just then Mr. Cooken comes up, and sez he, how du Smith, what be going to hav?

'Weal pie, sez I.'

'Good,' sez he, 'I'll take one tu;' so he sets down and eats one of his own weal pies right afore me.'

'Did that cause your confidence in him?'

'Yes, it did, sir; when an eatin'-house-keeper sets down afore his customers an' deliberately eats one of his own weal pies, no man can refuse to feel confidence—it shows him to be an honest man.'

On the jamb of the door of an eating-house on the North Wall, Dublin, the curious might recently read the following announcement printed, conveying alarming intelligence to the gallant tars who frequent that port— 'Sailors' vitals cooked here.'

Probably none of the foreign epicures, whose numerous dainties I have been placing before you, would eat hare and currant jelly, goose and apple-sauce, fish pies or parsley pasty like the Cornishman, or the squab pie of the Devonshire fisherman.

Now, while we are prone to ridicule others for their choice of food delicacies, we should look at home. Our epicures are extremely fond of woodcocks cooked un-gutted, and the standard dishes of Scotland, the haggis, sheep's-head, tripe, and black puddings, are not palatable to every one.

We have seen, however, from our deliberate survey that whatever enriches the earth and proclaims the bounty of the Creator, illustrates His indulgent regard for Man as chief of the Animal orders. Rich provision has been made for his wants and for his tastes, making glad the fields, the meadows, the vineyards, the orchards, the waters, and the air, peopled as they are with things made to be quartered, and cooked, and eaten. Every creature of God is good, and nothing to be refused if it be received with thanksgiving—'Let no man judge you in meat or in drink.' The Creator granted to the use of Man animal food as well as every green herb. Whatsoever is sold in the shambles and is set before you eat, therefore, asking no questions for conscience sake.

In the course of our investigation, we have seen how difficult it is to determine what is *food* and what really are *food delicacies*; for thereupon the proverb rises before us—'What's one man's meat, is another man's poison.'

Some people eat arsenic in considerable quantities, and if not exactly food, they find it conducive to an enjoying state of existence. Certain tribes of Africans and South American Indians eat an unctuous kind of earth, which, if introduced into our workhouses as food, would raise an outcry far and wide. In some countries sea-weed is food, in others it is manure for land. While we ruthlessly destroy snails and frogs, our continental brethren fatten and feed upon them.

Thus do the food delicacies differ in different parts of the globe, the nature of the alimentary substances varying exceedingly, and the 'daily bread' assuming most diversified forms.

I have confined myself here to the Animal Food, because to have gone into the Vegetable Substances would have carried me too much into detail. As it is, I have only been able to skim over the surface, to make a brief enumeration of some of the more prominent delicacies.

A talented friend has well remarked—'It is a probable thing, that many new varieties of food will ultimately be produced artificially, but it would be difficult to persuade people to eat them knowingly. Handy Andy, in Lover's tale, thought stewed leather breeches very fine tripe till he lighted on a button, which suddenly convinced him it was unwholesome food; and Sir Joseph Banks—so says Peter Pindar—did not think fleas equal to lobsters, though of the same genus.

'The Berlin philosophers have been for many years trying to persuade the community that horse-flesh is good beef, unsatisfactorily; and, amongst civilized communities, it appears to be chiefly in France that people voluntarily eat cats, both as a relish and a vengeance, if we may trust the reports of the Tribunal of Correctional Police, though scandal has long accused inn-keepers, both in France and Spain, of thus feeding their guests, as a substitute for rabbits.

'The French are chemists as well as cooks, and if fetid potato oil can be converted into a delicious scent akin to attar of roses, we may very well imagine that the partridge or venison bouquet may be obtained from other kinds of flesh.

'Glue and scraps of gloves, boiled with garlic, are eaten in Spain, and there is, as I have already stated, an hiatus in the parchment specifications at the Patent Office, caused by an unlucky boy, who changed them away for tarts, in order that they might be stewed down, and converted into calves'-foot jelly. The mechanical problems written and graven on them were doubtless not precipitated on the delicate palates of the ladies or gentlemen consuming them at Almack's, or elsewhere. It was but carbon gathered by the sheep in the shape of grass from the earth's surface—kid gloves in another form. Possibly Chemistry will ultimately enable us to make kid gloves and parchment without troubling goats or sheep for them, and artificial gelatine will become a substitute for calves'-feet. It is probable, that even now we occasionally eat old wool and hair in our gravy soups, as well as make it into what is facetiously called 'felt cloth'—the fibres being glued instead of felted together; and in process of time we may prepare gelatinous tubes, analogous to wool and hair, from carbon, converted into gelatine. It certainly seems odd that a man's coat should be convertible into his dinner; but 'Imperial Cæsar,' according to Hamlet, underwent as strange changes. [38]'

During the time of the Great Exhibition, in 1851, buffalo hides, and sheep and calf skins, advanced cent. per cent. in price. This was caused by the great demand for jellies in the refreshment rooms. Visitors then consumed jellies who never tasted jellies before; and as the usual material was not available, buffalo hides were purchased in tons in Liverpool, for the purpose of making these delicacies. Size and glue were used at first, but the hides were found to be cheapest. No one knows now what he eats in English confectionery. The natives of Java use the fresh hides of cattle as food,—nay even esteem them a dainty beyond any other part of the animal. The first pair of buckskin breeches seen in the South Sea Islands were so little understood, that the natives stuffed them with sea-weed, and had them boiled for dinner.

After the enumeration I have given you of Food Delicacies, who shall venture to determine what is good eating? Some Europeans chew tobacco, the Hindoo takes to betel-nut and lime, while the Patagonian finds contentment in a bit of guano, and the Styrians grow fat and ruddy on arsenic. English children delight in sweetmeats and sugar-candy, while those of Africa prefer rock salt. A Frenchman likes frogs and snails, and we eat eels, oysters, and whelks. To the Esquimaux, train oil is your only delicacy. The Russian luxuriates upon his hide or tallow; the Chinese upon rats, puppy dogs, and sharks' fins; the Kafir upon elephant's foot and trunk, or lion steaks; while the Pacific Islander places cold missionary above every other edible. Why then should we be surprised at men's feeding upon rattle-snakes and monkeys, and pronouncing them capital eating?

I do not know if any of the delicacies I have described may occasion what Charles Lamb calls 'premonitory moistening of the nether lip,' but I trust I may not have spoiled the reader's appetite for dinner or supper. There is a saying of great truth, 'that one half the world does not know how the other half lives.' These pages will, I think, serve to verify the adage.

FOOTNOTES:

[1] Stevenson's *Twenty Years' Residence in South America.*

[2] Hooper's *Medical Dictionary.*

[3] Kohl's *Russia,* and McGregor's *Continental Tariffs.*

[4] Johnston's *Travels in Southern Abyssinia,* vol. 2, p. 226.

[5] McMicking's *Manila and the Philippines.*

[6] Ruschenberger's *Voyage Round the World,* vol. 2. p. 337.

[7] A Paper on Swine, read before the Worcester (Massachusetts) Agricultural Society.

[8] Putnam's *Monthly Magazine.*

[9] *Lettres sur les Substances Alimentaires, et particulièrement sur la Viande de Cheval.* Par M. Isidore Geoffroy St. Hilaire. Paris, 1856.

[10] *Germantown Emporium.*

[11] *Journal of the Society of Arts,* vol. 2., p. 105.

[12] Berncastle's *Voyage to China.*

[13] Bonnycastle's *South America.*

[14] Strong vinegar, veignia, or possibly catsup.

[15] Query.—The dusky petrel.

[16] *Nautical Magazine,* vol. 15, p. 5.

[17] Part II. *Buff. Hist.* ch. 1. sec. 5.

[18] Dr. Truman *On Food and its Influence, &c.*

[19] MacMicking's *Manila, &c.*

[20] *History of the Fishmongers' Company.*

[21] Dr. Truman *On Food and its Influence.*

[22] Symonds's *Observations on the Fisheries of the West Coast of Ireland.*

[23] *The Fish Fancier's Own Book.*

[24] McCulloch's *Statistics of the British Empire.*

[25] Kane, in *Canadian Journal,* March 14th, 1858.

[26] *Natural History of Fishes*, by Dr. Bushnan.

[27] Schomburgk's *History of Barbados*.

[28] Miss Bunbury's *Summer in Northern Europe*.

[29] Wallace's *Travels on the Amazon*.

[30] *Natural History of Insects*.

[31] Wallace's *Travels on the Rio Negro*.

[32] *Journal de Pharmacie*.

[33] *Annals of Natural History*.

[34] Kirby and Spence.

[35] Symond's *Observations on the Fisheries of the West Coast of Ireland*.

[36] Molina's *Natural History of Chile*.

[37] Adam's *Natural History*.

[38] W. B. Adams, in *Society of Arts' Journal*.